# *Africa's* VANISHING WILDLIFE

### CHRIS & TILDE STUART

Smithsonian Institution Press
Washington, D.C.

Published in the United States of America by Smithsonian Institution Press

ISBN 1-56098-678-6

Library of Congress Catalog Number is available

First edition, first impression 1996
First edition, second impression 1998

**First published in South Africa by**
Southern Book Publishers (Pty) Ltd, PO Box 3103, Halfway House 1685

| | |
|---|---|
| **Cover design by:** | Alix Gracie |
| **Cover photograph by:** | Anthony Bannister, ABPL |
| **Maps by:** | Alix Gracie C.C., t/a Design Dynamix, Cape Town |
| **Designed by:** | Alix Gracie C.C., t/a Design Dynamix, Cape Town |
| **Set in:** | Adobe Garamond 9.7/12 |
| **Reproduction:** | Hirt & Carter Repro, Cape Town |
| **Printed and bound by:** | Kyodo Printers, Singapore |

00 99 98 5 4 3 2

**Half title:** *The slaty egret* (Egretta vinaceigula)
*has the most restricted distributional range of any
African mainland heron.* Photo: Clem Haagner, ABPL.

**Title pages:** *The wild dog* (Lycaon pictus) *is the second
rarest canid on the African continent and is heavily
persecuted despite this.* Photo: Beverly Joubert, ABPL.

**Facing page:** *Hamadryas baboon*
(Papio hamadryas) *populations have been
affected by severe drought.*

**Below:** *The bearded vulture* (Gypaetus barbatus)
*occupies high montane country, mainly in the Drakensberg,
Ethiopian Highlands and Atlas Mountains.*

**Contents:** *The Table Mountain ghost frog* (Heleophryne rosei)
*is restricted to a few locations on the mountain that
dominates Cape Town.* Photo: Atherton de Villiers.

# CONTENTS

## 6.
## ANTELOPES: 84
*Grace on the run*

## 7.
## OTHER MAMMALS: 120
*All creatures great and small*

## 8.
## BIRDS: 140
### *As dead as a dodo*

## 9.
## REPTILES, AMPHIBIANS
## AND FISH: 170
### *Uncharted waters*

## 10.
## THE FUTURE: 184
### *And now where?*

## USEFUL READING 190

## INDEX 191

# · ACKNOWLEDGEMENTS ·

*Many people have helped in numerous different ways to make this book possible. The following list of friends, colleagues and contacts may not be complete but we are sure that those we have unwittingly omitted will forgive us. All share our belief in the conservation of Africa's bountiful biodiversity, but we take full responsibility for any omissions, errors or views that may offend in this book. This great continent, despite its huge legacy of problems, is still worth fighting for (in the pacifist sense).*

*The following people have assisted us, in some cases in ways they may not be fully aware of: P.K. Anderson; C. Andrews; George Archibald of the International Crane Foundation; Phil Berry of Luangwa; P.M. Brooks of the Natal Parks Board; John Carlyon; J.B. Carroll; Koen de Smet; Atherton de Villiers; James M. Dolan of the San Diego Zoological Society; Iain Douglas-Hamilton; Charles Doumerge; Andrew Duthie; Keith Eltringham of Cambridge University; Pat J. Frere; Wolfgang Frey; Anthony Hall-Martin of the South African National Parks Board; Tamsin Humphreys of the IUCN/SSC; Les Kaufman; Torben B. Larsen; Sandro Lovari; Helene Marsh; M.G.L. Mills of the South African National Parks Board; Bruno Nebe; Bernhard Nievergelt of Zürich University; James Perran; G. Rathbun; Reinhold Rau; Gordon McGregor Reid; Peter J.H. Reijnder; Rijksmuseum van Natuurlijke Historie, Leiden; Klaus Rudloff; Anne Scott; Roland Seitre; Claudio Sillero-Zubiri; Chris Smaart; Simon N. Stuart; I.R. Swingland; Mark. E. Taylor; Roland van Bocxstaele; Harry van Rompaey; Alan Weaving and Roland Wirth.*

*Last but not least, a special thank you to Louise Grantham of Southern for trying to ensure that we don't have to spend much time in the concrete jungle.*

**Left**: *Mountain zebras have seen massive declines and the Cape subspecies* (Equus zebra zebra) *is still highly vulnerable.*

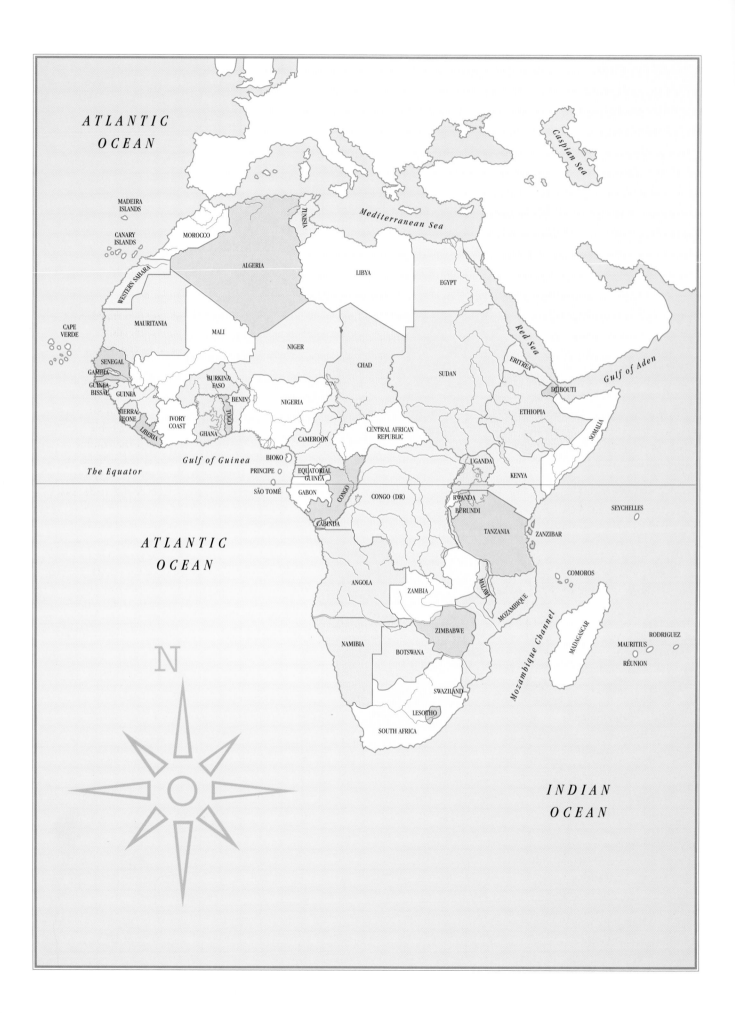

# CHAPTER 1

# INTRODUCTION

## *How did we come to this?*

The relationship between modern man and the planet ...
has been that not of symbiotic partners, but of the tapeworm
and the dog, of the fungus and the blighted potato.

Aldous Huxley – *Ape and essence*

Whatever human beings have in common with other living things, there is one characteristic that is our exclusive genius: we are seemingly the only species working deliberately towards our own destruction.

In compiling this book on Africa's vanishing wildlife we had to look beyond the creatures themselves in order to understand what has been taking place on this fascinating, depressing, diverse and damaged continent. In the first place we need to dispel the myth that when the first Europeans arrived in Africa they found a pristine, unspoiled landmass with the Africans living in perfect harmony with nature. Certainly Africa was in far better shape than it is today, but humans have been around for thousands of years, albeit in much smaller numbers, with settlements and farms, armies and dictatorships, cattle, goats, asses and camels.

The Pharaonic Egyptian civilisation extended its influence far up the course of the Nile River, and to appease their numerous gods and for totems the Egyptians slaughtered and mummified huge numbers of such species as the Nile crocodile and sacred ibis. The Romans and Greeks farmed and exploited the north African Mediterranean coastal plain, cutting trees and planting crops to feed their empires. They caught wild animals, from lions to elephants, to supply the bloody circuses and the private menageries of the nobility. Animals were also hunted for their skins, teeth and meat.

Muslim Arab invaders entered Egypt in AD 639 and less than 100 years later they had overrun the whole of Africa north of the Sahara Desert, using it as a launchpad to invade Europe. In view of our current problems of human overpopulation, it is of interest to note that these early invasions largely resulted from the lands of origin having too many people for available resources. It was only after the collapse of the Nubian Christian kingdom of Dongola in the 14th century that the Arabs started to penetrate to the south of the Sahara. Their influence began, over time, to penetrate deeply into west and east Africa. The Arabs and with them the power of Islam dominated much of the continent, with the exception of southern and central Africa.

They spread the word of Muhammad and penetrated every corner in search of slaves, ivory and precious metals.

There is now evidence that Alexandrian traders were penetrating deep into the east African interior in search of ivory and other goods by the 4th century AD. Ancient writings show that traders and merchants from China, Persia, Arabia and Indonesia were active in African trade during the 7th and 8th centuries, and it was probably at that time that such valuable crops as bananas and coconuts were imported into the continent. Although slaves were an important trade commodity, there was almost certainly much movement of such goods as ivory. Between the 8th and 12th centuries much of this trade was

**Below**: *The extinct quagga* (Equus quagga) *is now known to have been a subspecies of the plains zebra* (Equus burchellii).
PHOTO: *Reinhold Rau. The blue buck* (Hippotragus leucophaeus) *was driven to extinction in 1799. This antelope now exists only in four moth-eaten museum specimens.* PHOTO: *Rijksmuseum van Natuurlijke Historie, Leiden.*

probably dominated by the Hindu kingdom of Sri Vijaya in Sumatra. Then the Muslim traders took control of trade.

The Portuguese occupied the Zanzibar coast but their impact was minimal, although elsewhere they were significant in the commerce of the day. They had established bases at Sofala, Kilwa, Ormuz and Socotra, and coastal settlements in the countries we know today as Mozambique and Angola.

The next major upheavals to affect Africa came from the great European trading companies. The Dutch and British had trading posts and way stations on the routes to their Asian holdings at several locations along the African coast.

The 18th century saw the re-emergence of the Swahili city-states under the rule of Arab dynasties that owed allegiance to the Ya'rubi Imams of Oman. During this time the first determined penetrations of the east African hinterland took place. Serious European exploration of non-coastal Africa began at the end of the 18th and continued through the 19th century. The explorers' motivations were as diverse as their nationalities: missionaries wished to convert the heathen and Islamic masses; some explorers were financed and backed by commercial interests, others had their government's backing; a few were true adventurers and explored for exploration's sake.

What has become known as the "European scramble for Africa" was precipitated by King Leopold II of Belgium who laid claim to the vast drainage basin of the Congo River. Then the Germans laid claim to huge tracts of land in what was South West Africa, Tanganyika, the Cameroons and Togoland. As soon as the other European powers realised what was happening the "scramble" was on, and Africa was divided among them. The drawing of African national boundaries by these European political makers and shakers was to have lasting and devastating consequences for the African tribes, the environment and wildlife. The partition of Africa was in essence a projection of the international politics of Europe onto the African continent.

As the African states received their independence from their European colonisers, mostly in the early 1960s, they became the "footballs" of the conflicting ideologies of capitalism and communism. As a consequence the main proponent of each (the United States of America and the then USSR) armed their favoured group, dictator, general or warlord, with the sole purpose of ensuring the supremacy of their "pet" and their ideology. With the collapse of communism came a more inward-looking United States, and Africa has since been largely left to its own devices.

Africa's woes, and let us not deny that they are numerous, can be partly laid at the doors of foreign colonisers of yesteryear, industrial and commercial giants and such organisations as the World Bank and USAid, European Union and other aid charities. However, Africans themselves are also to blame for many of their problems.

Why, you may well ask, so much emphasis on the history of humans in Africa in a book dealing with the vanishing wildlife of the continent? With a few exceptions it is the people – African and non-African – who are destroying the vegetation and wildlife. Demand for hardwood timbers comes mostly from North America, Europe and Asia, but most of the African trees that fall each year to the axe and the saw are to provide fuel for Africans. The seemingly insatiable demand for natural resources, whether for export or local consumption, is constantly growing.

What the European and North American environmental groups tend to forget is that they are living in radically altered environments in their own countries, and that degradation and destruction are continuing on their doorstep. One has to wonder about priorities when there is outrage about rainforest destruction in the Third World, but little is said about the clear-cutting of the great old forests of North America.

It is the fate of every form of life eventually to enter the tunnel of extinction. In the past, extinct forms were replaced by newly evolving species and races more fitted to survival as conditions changed. Many, many species and subspecies of animal and plant have become extinct during the course of our planet's existence. In prehistoric times there were natural mass extinctions that are still not fully understood, the best known being the rapid demise (in the geological sense) of the dinosaurs. Various explanations have been put forward. These include the theory that a large extra-terrestrial object, such as an asteroid, struck the planet some 66 million years before present and wreaked cataclysmic environmental havoc. Apparent evidence is high levels of the metal iridium, which is extremely rare on earth but common in meteorites, found in clay layers dating from the time that the dinosaurs died out. Then there is the theory that massive volcanic activity blocked out sunlight, creating a greenhouse effect and adversely affecting animal and plant species. Several scientists believe that the iridium layer in fact resulted from this volcanic activity and not from some space-object collision. We believe that mass extinctions in the past resulted from a combination of factors. Some extinctions have been ascribed to global sea-level changes caused by such phenomena as glaciation and plate tectonic activities. Such changes have disastrous effects on animals and plants reliant on the sensitive environments of estuaries and shallow coastal waters.

Later extinctions, such as those of the woolly rhinoceros, the cave bear, mammoth, and Europe's only wild horse, the tarpan, were precipitated by the hunting activities of humans, up to about 10 000 years before present. Declines were also due to climatic and habitat changes. Once humans crossed the land-bridge from Eurasia to North America, several species were rushed into extinction. We know of similar extinctions that took place within the Afro-tropical Realm, and there are probably others that we do not know about.

The massive extinctions that took place during the Pleistocene era are ascribed by some authorities to *Homo sapiens,* with his weapons, fire and carefully planned hunting techniques such as pitfall traps. These had a dreadful impact, particularly on large mammals and ground-nesting birds. Sadly, it is possible to trace the range of expansion of early humans into Africa, Asia, Australia and the Americas by the associated reductions in a number of Pleistocene species. On the mega-island of Madagascar we know that at least 12 species of giant lemur (one was the gorilla-sized *Megaladapis*) were rapidly hunted to extinction when humans first arrived some 1 500 years ago.

With the Madagascan human population now exceeding 12 million, massive habitat destruction and modification have taken place in the last few decades. Despite this something amazing has happened: several species of lemur thought to have slid into extinction have been rediscovered, and new species have been found! We can only wonder how many species had been lost before we knew of their existence. This serves to emphasise the vulnerability of island-dwelling species. Island dwellers that have become extinct include all but one Indian Ocean island giant tortoise, the elephant birds of Madagascar and the dodo and solitaire of the Mascarenes.

changing all the known rules of evolution. Because it is happening so fast and so unnaturally, there is no time for new species or subspecies to evolve. What is more, the fittest do not necessarily survive, which holds serious consequences for entire sequences of evolutionary development.

Over the past two million years there have been seven so-called Ice Ages or glacial periods, which have been interrupted by warmer interglacial periods. These fluctuations have resulted in numerous extinctions. However, when our ancestors entered the scene between one and four million years ago the loss of species accelerated dramatically. Primitive Stone Age hunters caused extinctions of large mammals. Humans continually developed more sophisticated hunting techniques, ensuring ever greater levels of extinction. But now, in the 20th

**Above:** *Many of the isolated western Indian Ocean islands had populations of giant land tortoises when the first Europeans arrived in the area. There were at least eight species; the total is cause for considerable debate among taxonomists. Today only one species remains, but in relatively high numbers.* PHOTO: *John Carlyon.*

Mass extinctions have taken place about every 26 million years, so it would be another 12 million years before the next one, if human intervention were not included in the equation. However, modern *Homo sapiens* is more deadly than any comet or dramatic natural earthly event. Humans destroy at whim, both themselves and all other creatures and plants; they snuff out habitats with impunity and pollute with toxins and other substances. Scientists warn that modern humans are at present creating one of the largest mass extinctions of all time, even outdoing the demise of the dinosaurs. The present crisis is

century, the wave of extinction is reaching levels quite unprecedented in the history of our planet. One great mass extinction observed in recent times has been the loss of the bulk of the amazing cichlid fish diversity in Africa's Lake Victoria, which resulted directly from interference by humans. The most troubling cause of extinction is the combination of factors that result from the activities of people, primarily overpopulation and habitat destruction.

In many instances the rate of habitat destruction and degradation has reached the point where the damage and losses are probably irreversible, even if blocks – greatly diminished – of natural habitat remain. Particularly worrisome is whether declared conservation areas are in fact viable in the long term, given that they are, or certainly will be, marooned in oceans of degradation and agricultural land, and have to resist an inexhaustible demand for natural resources. Will they be able to maintain their original diversity in the long run?

The theory of island biota diversity holds that the number of species capable of surviving on an island is dependent on the island's size, its distance from other islands and from mainland masses, and on other factors such as the availability of water and altitude. This theory can be directly applied to the situation of national parks and other blocks of conservation land on the African mainland. For example, the Parc des Volcans in Rwanda, with its population of mountain gorillas, has lost a number of species after a reduction in its size, despite the fact that apparently suitable habitat is still available. It would seem that the remaining area is now too small to accommodate all the species that previously occurred there.

In this book we take a look at as broad a spectrum of Africa's mammals, birds, reptiles, amphibians and fish as possible. It had been our initial plan to include the invertebrates and plants as well, but with a few notable exceptions, virtually nothing is available on their biology and status. While researching these groups we did encounter some positive notes, specifically on the butterflies of Africa. Torben B. Larsen says in a letter, "Although it is early days [in his research], I do believe that the present network of protected areas will have conserved practically all of the 3 700 or so butterflies in Africa." But he goes on to express concern for species in the montane and coastal forests of east Africa. Nevertheless, his letter was a breath of fresh air after months of reading depressing correspondence and literature, and conducting gloomy personal interviews.

We have tried to reflect conventional thinking on those species considered to be endangered, vulnerable or rare, but we have followed our personal preferences where we feel this is justified. With such a vast array of species we have had to be selective. We know that some readers may not be entirely happy with our choice, because certain species have been omitted, some have been included which may not be formally considered to be under threat, and so on. We must emphasise that the title of the book, *Africa's vanishing wildlife,* allows us to look beyond just the IUCN Red Data books, the CITES compilations and national threatened species lists where they are available. In this book we hope to impress upon the reader that we should not wait until a species becomes endangered or vulnerable before we react. We must always remember what happened to the countless millions of North American passenger pigeons, believed to be so numerous they could never be hunted to extinction. But they were hunted to extinction and are lost forever. Africa's vanishing wildlife should not only be seen as those species teetering on the brink of extinction, but also as those that have seen dramatic population declines although they still survive in seemingly substantial numbers. The reason is that the causes of the declines are, in the majority of cases, still in place.

Over the years several methods of categorising wildlife under threat have been used, the latest in general acceptance being that of Mace and Lande. Their classification forms the basis of the categories used in this book. **Extinct**, the first category, is self-explanatory: it is the point of no return. **Endangered (E)**

implies a 20% probability of extinction within 20 years, or at the 10th generation, whichever is longer. **Vulnerable (V)** implies a 10% probability of extinction within 100 years. We have also included the categories **Declining (D)** and **Rare (R)**; population sizes and factors justifying these labels are given in the text. Although most species in Africa are generally declining, we have used the code **(D)** to draw attention to those particularly hard hit.

The main emphasis in conserving African wildlife has been on the "big or cuddly", usually with solid justification and with some success. However, every species plays some role in the ecosystem, whether it be frog or fly, mongoose or mosquito. Trying to conserve individual species without conserving habitats and biodiversity will in the long run be futile, because all life forms are interdependent. But what is biodiversity? It simply means the total variety of all organisms that are alive on earth today. All species must therefore be drawn into the conservation equation. Every person needs to take a measure of responsibility for conserving biodiversity, because this is of direct benefit to humans. Many medicines, disease-free plant strains and other benefits may be lost to humankind in species that become extinct before they could be fully studied and wisely utilised. Ultimately the survival of biodiversity is in the hands of people. The crucial problem is that the increase in the *Homo sapiens* population is outstripping the earth's natural resources. This causes whole ecosystems to be wiped out, with a huge resultant loss of biodiversity. In Africa the situation has reached critical proportions.

There is a trap threatening those involved in conservation work: we must not become bogged down in endless committee meetings which have little to show in the way of meaningful results. We must avoid research projects that hold little benefit for the conservation of a species, group of species or ecosystem. Consider the following quote:

*Futile, bickering men remind one of the all-too-familiar committees which nowadays meet leisurely to formulate long-term plans for saving some starving tribe but in this process become so occupied with agendas and sub-committees that the tribe becomes extinct before a satisfactory plan is reached.*

Noel Barber – *The black hole of Calcutta: a reconstruction*

The final word in this introduction must go to John Rock, who developed the birth-control pill. Given the problem of human overpopulation, he puts into perspective most of Africa's, and the rest of the world's, conservation problems in just 14 words:

*If we don't solve this problem* [of overpopulation]*, none of our other problems make any difference.*

**Right:** *Game hunters of the 19th and early 20th centuries devastated huge numbers of Africa's wild animals for sport.*
PHOTO: *Barnett/Argus/ABPL.*

A GOOD DAYS SPORT
BARNETT 223

# CHAPTER 2

# ELEPHANTS

## *The super keystone species*

Nature's great masterpiece, an elephant
The only harmless great thing.

John Donne – *The progress of the soul*

### Description and taxonomy

The elephant is the largest land mammal in the world. Adult savanna elephant bulls have a mass of some 5 500 kg and cows some 3 000 kg. The largest animal on record, the so-called Fenykoevi bull, is believed to have been shot in Angola in 1955. It is said to have had a mass of 10 000 kg and a shoulder height of 4 m. The forest elephant is considerably smaller, with bulls having a mass of some 3 000 kg and cows 2 000 kg. However, some individuals reach greater sizes. The elephant is characterised by the long, versatile trunk, the large ears that act as blood-cooling agents, and in most populations the tusks that jut from the upper jaw. The ears of the savanna subspecies are noticeably larger than those of the forest dweller. This reflects the more open and less sheltered nature of their habitat.

An elephant's massive body is supported on great tree-trunk-like legs, with the rounded and cushioned soles of the feet spreading the animal's huge bulk. Elephants walk at speeds of 2 km to 6 km per hour but they can attain 40 km per hour when fleeing danger or attacking something perceived as a threat. Anyone who has experienced an elephant charge will have been amazed, if not terrified, by the incredible turn of speed that can be achieved by these massive animals.

In some populations, such as that in the Addo Elephant National Park (South Africa), many of the cows are tuskless. The heaviest pair of tusks recorded, at 102,3 kg and 97 kg, came from Kenya. Elephant tusks continue to grow throughout life but wear and breakages prevent them from ever reach-

| | SAVANNA ELEPHANT | FOREST ELEPHANT |
|---|---|---|
| | *Loxodonta africana africana* | *L.a. cyclotis* |
| **Shoulder height** | ♂ 3,2-4 m | average 2,35 m |
| | ♀ 2,5-3,4 m | average 2,1 m |
| **Mass** | ♂ 5 000-6 300 kg | 2 800-3 200 kg |
| | ♀ 2 800-3 500 kg | 1 800-2 500 kg |
| **Gestation** | 22 months | |
| **Birth mass** | 100-120 kg | |
| **Life span** | up to 60 years | |
| **Daily water intake** | 100-220 *l* | |
| **Daily food intake** | average 150 kg (up to 300 kg) | |
| **Number surviving** | | |
| 1930: | 5-10 million | |
| 1979: | about 1,3 million | |
| 1992: | about 600 000 | |

**Above:** *Feeding among flowers in Addo Elephant National Park.*
**Right:** *Elephant at sunset, Etosha National Park.*
**Below:** *Although elephants can go without water for two to three days, access to it is essential for their survival.*

ing their full potential length. The tusks are used for stripping bark from trees, digging for roots, excavating for minerals, defence and also as a part of the display complex. It is these ivory tusks, a blend of dentine, cartilaginous substances and calcium salts that have contributed to the decline of these magnificent beasts.

Only two species of elephant have survived to the present day: the African elephant *(Loxodonta africana)* and the Asian elephant *(Elephas maximus)*. These pachyderms can trace their lineage back some 55 million years to the time when the ancestral proboscideans evolved in Africa and south-western Asia. From these areas they were to migrate to every continent except Antarctica and Australia.

The pig-sized *Moeritherium*, with two short tusks in each jaw, roamed north Africa approximately 50 million years ago; *Deinotherium* is said to have had its origins in Africa; the four-tusked *Palaeomastodon* evolved in north Africa. Possibly the first really elephant-like beast to dwell on the continent was *Mammut*, with its prominent tusks and long trunk that enabled it to exploit the food provided by trees and taller bushes.

Other species also appeared and disappeared over time, with the reasons for their demise not fully understood. During the Pleistocene, changes in climate over vast areas resulted in changes to the vegetation to which many animals could not adapt rapidly enough. Certainly in some areas hunting by humans, in relatively recent times, helped speed a number of mammals into extinction. One of the best known examples is the demise of the once widespread hairy mammoth *(Mammuthus)*, of which the last animals were hunted out as little as

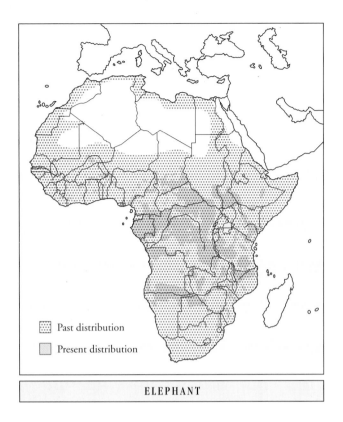

|     | Past distribution |
|-----|-------------------|
|     | Present distribution |

**ELEPHANT**

ble for modifying the vegetation by their feeding habits. Both elephants and humans may have contributed to the desertification of land. This process continues, as people and their livestock turn what used to be dry savanna into uninhabitable wasteland.

There are still a few small populations of desert elephants, such as those that roam north-western Namibia and an isolated herd in the Gourma region of Mali. This is the northernmost viable population remaining in Africa. Until recently the Tuareg people and the elephants lived together in relative harmony but the droughts that have struck the Sahel over the past few decades have resulted in an influx of more people with their stock. Increasing conflicts over limited water sources and

10 000 years ago in North America and Eurasia.

Several *Elephas* species (but not *Elephas maximus*) ranged across Africa, dominating the open country, but with their demise *Loxodonta africana,* which had been a forest dweller, was able to emerge from the forests and occupy the plains. The demise of *Elephas* in Africa was probably in part due to an increase in the areas covered by forest. The human population was small and conflicts between humans and elephants were probably limited.

### Distribution and habitat

The African elephant was once lord of its domain, following its pathways over virtually all of the continent's 30 million sq km. Few areas did not feel the tread of those great cushioned feet, as the grey giants sought out food, water and shade. The paths they followed were used by many generations of elephant and their selection of routes proved to be a boon for early road-builders. Many sections of man-made roads in Africa were laid over these elephant paths, in much the same way that stretches of road built by the Romans in parts of Europe are overlaid by modern thoroughfares.

Elephants occupied tropical forest to desert, coastline to high mountains, grassland to woodland. They traversed much of the area we know as the Sahara Desert, probably at times of unusually high rainfall. Rock paintings and petroglyphs of elephants dated between 11 000 and 5 000 years old are located at numerous sites throughout the Sahara. The drying up of rivers that once flowed through the Sahara no doubt played a critical role in the disappearance of the northern desert elephants. It is surmised that these animals were partly responsi-

pasture have resulted in disruption of this peaceful co-existence. Foreign aid donors have encouraged the local people to cultivate crops and their nomadic way of life is disappearing, resulting in ever more conflicts with the grey giants. Apart from being the most northerly population, these elephants also claim the distinction of annually following the longest elephant migration route on record.

How do Africa's elephant populations stand at present? Estimates vary considerably but the generally accepted figure is that there were between 549 000 and 652 000 individuals in 1997. Some researchers believe these figures are too low, whereas others think they are too high. The present area occupied or traversed by elephants is less than 5,2 million sq km, of which approximately 50% is in central Africa, 21% in eastern Africa, 25% in southern Africa and a meagre 4% in west Africa. However, many of these populations are highly fragmented and there is no contact between them. Of greatest concern is that an estimated 76% of all elephants live outside the boundaries of conservation areas and that controls over many of the parks and reserves are considered to be inadequate.

Despite their massive size, elephants can be very difficult to count. Counting accuracy depends on such factors as the density of vegetation, wet or dry season, topography, and method and frequency of counting. The most accurate population fig-

**Below:** *Social interactions can be easily observed at water.*

ures available are for small populations, such as that in Amboseli National Park (Kenya), which have been monitored by researchers for many years and whose animals are individually known.

Aerial surveying is the preferred method for counting elephants in savanna areas. In most cases the best results are achieved during the dry season when screening foliage is at its lowest density. In the Selous Game Reserve (Tanzania) a wet season aerial survey in 1976 came up with an estimated 85 000 elephants. When the survey was repeated in the dry season about 110 000 elephants were found to be present. In certain large parks, such as the Kruger National Park in South Africa (over 20 000 sq km), aerial counts cover the entire area. Other, even larger elephant ranges are only partly surveyed and estimates are made for the remainder. Accuracy is difficult to establish in the latter case.

It was during aerial surveys in the 1970s and 1980s in east Africa that people such as Iain Douglas-Hamilton, the doyen of elephant research, started encountering increasing numbers of elephant carcasses. This should have been a warning bell to the world that all was not well with elephants. Sadly, many people chose to ignore the evidence, or question its truth. It has been estimated that if 2% to 8% of a population count is represented by carcasses, this is indicative of growth or stability. When the number of carcasses exceeds 9% the population is declining.

The difficulties of counting savanna elephants pale into insignificance against those of counting forest-dwelling animals. Forest elephants are very difficult to approach, particularly in areas where they are disturbed. Therefore direct counts are not usually possible. A valuable technique used in dense forest is to count dung deposits, taking into account such things as quantities produced and the rate of decay. Certainly this is not an ideal method and counts may be far from accurate, but until someone comes up with an alternative, droppings will no doubt continue to determine our estimates of forest elephant numbers.

**West Africa**, with a total elephant range of 229 000 sq km in 1991 (a decrease of 17% since 1989), has the most seriously fragmented elephant population in Africa. Isolated sub-populations are present in 13 countries. An estimated total of between 10 136 and 16 825 elephants survive. Populations in some countries are so low that they are unlikely to survive for much longer. For example, only 20 to 50 individuals are believed to remain in Guinea Bissau, where in 1989 some 560 elephants were known to live. Probably the single largest protected population, some 1 000 animals, dwells in the Tai National Park in Ivory Coast. Like the rest of sub-Saharan Africa, west Africa faces massive human population

*Elephant bulls carrying heavy ivory are rarely seen today.*

growth, which results in continued destruction of elephant habitat and hunting of elephants for their meat.

**East Africa** has a total elephant range of slightly over 1,1 million sq km, with between 102 000 and 122 000 elephants. Estimates for areas plagued by civil war, such as southern Sudan, Somalia and until recently Ethiopia, are nothing better than a thumb-suck. From a possible low of perhaps 16 000 elephants in Kenya in 1989, the latest estimates indicate an increase to 22 000. However, elephant populations in the forests of Mount Kenya, the Aberdares and Mount Elgon may have been undercounted in the past. The Tsavo National Park complex in Kenya holds about one third of the national herd. Nevertheless, when one remembers that in 1973 Kenya was home to perhaps 130 000 elephants there is hardly room for complacency. Estimates for Tanzania indicate that approximately 60 000 elephants remain, but elephants in their principal stronghold, the Selous Game Reserve, and the surrounding area are believed to have been undercounted.

**Central Africa** is estimated to have almost 270 000 elephants in an area exceeding 2,5 million sq km. Until recently much of this population was believed to form a contiguous block but it is now known to be fragmented into several separate populations. Elephants have disappeared from vast areas of Congo (DR). Despite its extensive forests one estimate puts only 63 000 elephants in that troubled country. During the 1980s – the height of the ivory boom – the elephant population of central Africa was probably halved. It is also believed that estimates for swamp forests, such as those in Congo and western Congo (DR), have been too high in the past.

**Southern Africa** has a total elephant range of some 1,3 million sq km in seven countries, with an estimated 130 000 animals. The elephants move across international borders. Poaching south of the Zambezi was minimal during the 1970s and 1980s when the slaughter further north was at its height. This can be ascribed mainly to better controls, policing and motivation of field staff. The present situation in war-torn Angola and ravaged Mozambique is largely unknown. However, it is known that both governments and the rebel movements were using ivory to pay for arms and ammunition for their wars. Certainly their elephant populations are greatly depleted. In Namibia, Botswana and Zimbabwe populations are stable and in some cases growing. In South Africa the principal population, in the Kruger National Park, was maintained at slightly more than 7 000 animals by culling. As far as is known Botswana has the largest remaining contiguous population in Africa. Hwange National Park (Zimbabwe) and Chobe

National Park (Botswana) have the region's largest elephant populations but totals vary according to the season. Zambia suffered dramatic losses during the dark days of the past two decades but the population in the South Luangwa National Park has started to build up again. There are an estimated 6 000 animals in the area.

## Behaviour

The African elephant has attracted considerable attention from researchers and a great deal is known about some populations. As the savanna-dwelling animals *(Loxodonta africana africana)* occupy more open habitats than the smaller forest elephants *(Loxodonta africana cyclotis)* they have been more closely studied. Gathering information on any tropical forest mammals is difficult and frustrating, and unsurprisingly most researchers prefer to work from a vehicle on the plains, rather than be drenched, muddied, bitten and stung by hordes of insects. The few scientists who have ventured to study the forest dwellers deserve considerable praise.

Much of what is known about African elephant biology has resulted from work undertaken in conservation areas such as the Kruger National Park (South Africa), Amboseli and Tsavo National Parks (Kenya), Chobe National Park (Botswana) and Lake Manyara National Park (Tanzania).

The size of the home range and the distances elephants traverse depend on the abundance and nutritional value of food, the availability of water and, in the case of savanna-dwelling animals, shade. Home ranges in arid areas are considerably larger than those in well-watered country. Where conditions are ideal the home range of matriarchal herds may be from 15 sq km to more than 50 sq km. That of bulls is considerably larger (up to 1 500 sq km), as they move around seeking cows that are receptive to their advances. In East Tsavo National Park in Kenya, where low rainfall and arid conditions prevail, home ranges of up to 3 120 sq km have been measured. Ranges of *Loxodonta africana cyclotis*, the forest elephant, are usually considerably smaller than those of savanna-dwelling animals, primarily because of the abundance of food and the ready availability of water.

Elephants have a complex social system. We discuss this briefly in order to explain the disruptions caused by hunting and the fragmenting of populations. Elephants are highly social animals, living in small family groups led by an older cow who is frequently referred to as the matriarch. Each group consists of the matriarch and her offspring, with larger groups also including other related cows and their young of different ages. At certain times, for example at water, several of these family groups may gather and may number in the hundreds but each family unit retains its identity. These large gatherings are usually temporary and they hold no reproductive or social benefits for the elephants.

Young female elephants remain with the group into maturity, but as the unit grows a subgroup of young adult cows will separate to form their own family unit. Young bulls, however, leave the group on reaching puberty. If they are reluctant to do

so the matriarch may show aggression towards them. The bull elephants live apart from the matriarchal groups, either alone or in small, unstable groups that are constantly changing in numbers and composition. Adult bulls are highly mobile and circulate among the different family units within their home range, checking for cows that are sexually receptive.

Breeding rarely takes place before the age of 15 to 20 years, particularly as young bulls are unable to compete with larger and more experienced animals for mating rights. Mature cows give birth to a calf every three to four years. The interval depends to a large extent on conditions: a severe drought, for example, will lengthen the intervals between births but a prolonged period of food abundance will shorten them. In areas with relatively harsh conditions, or where animals are under constant stress, females may only conceive for the first time at 18 years and birth intervals can be as long as eight years.

Although mature bulls compete with each other for receptive cows, fights resulting in death or serious injury are rare. A cow may be covered by one bull or several in succession. The breeding cycle is to a large extent dictated by the seasonal availability of food and water but births can occur at any time of the year. Savanna cows cease to ovulate during the dry season when food is not as abundant, nor of such high nutritional value, ensuring that the single calf is dropped in the wet season. The gestation period is 22 months. In the case of forest elephants where food abundance and quality are less variable, breeding seasons are not as clearly defined.

In the case of the savanna elephant the calf has an average mass of 120 kg at birth. Sexual maturity is reached at about 10 years of age but this can vary considerably according to conditions prevailing during the development period. Growth is fairly rapid up to the time the animal reaches maturity but growth continues, at a decreased tempo, throughout life.

About half of all elephants die before they reach 15 years but some survive into old age at some 60 years. Apart from premature death caused by humans, disease, predation or injury, the life span of an elephant is dictated by the length of time the molars (cheek-teeth) last. An elephant has a succession of 24 molars, six on each side of each jaw, if it lives its full life span. However, there are only two molars in each jaw at any one time. As each tooth wears down it moves forward in the jaw and the tooth segments (laminae) fall off until the tooth growing behind it from the back of the jaw replaces it. Once the last four molars have worn away and fragmented the elephant is unable to chew its food and it will die.

Elephants communicate with each other by means of visual signals and touch, but they are also very vocal animals. It has long been known that elephants are able to communicate when not within sight of each other, over distances that sounds audible to humans would not carry. Small family groups scattered over several square kilometres may suddenly stop, turn in the same direction or flee. Although we can hear some elephant calls, such as the trumpeting and the larynx rumble, recent research has shown that elephants also use infrasound that is not audible to the human ear. This is what causes a herd quietly feeding suddenly to become alert and take flight for no apparent reason. These low frequency sounds (14 to 35 cycles per second) have remarkable properties. Dense forest and woodland apparently do not greatly distort the calls. Researchers have found that these sounds travel for several kilometres; the exact limits have not yet been established. Oestrus cows are able to attract bulls by giving off specific infrasound calls. The discovery of infrasound communication has explained certain actions of elephants that previously were a mystery.

After humans, elephants have had the greatest impact in shaping the habitats and vegetation of Africa. To maintain their great bulk they require considerable quantities of food. Estimates of consumption vary around 150 kg per day for adult animals, but the quality of food has a significant impact on the quantity consumed: the more nutritious the food, the less is required.

Forest-dwelling elephants create mazes of tunnels in the undergrowth and in this way make pathways for other forest residents, including humans. As they feed their way through their bowered home they occasionally tug down lianas that are tangled in the canopies of the forest trees. Sometimes they dislodge mighty branches, allowing the sun's rays to reach the forest floor. This stimulates the growth of herbaceous plants (monocots) that are rich in protein and starches and are the favoured food of the elephants and many other species. In this way the elephants are unwittingly creating gardens of abundance and contributing to the maintenance and diversity of the forest environment.

Forest elephants also feed on a wide variety of tree fruits, many of which produce succulent coatings that attract these forest inhabitants. In this way the trees have evolved a sure means of having their seeds scattered over a wide area in the dung of the elephants. Many seeds are shaped in such a way that they pass smoothly down the gut and when they emerge they are already set up for germination in a wonderfully rich growth medium. Another method that has evolved in some of the forest trees is to produce flowers and therefore fruits growing directly on the lower parts of the trunk which are readily accessible to the elephants.

Elephants living outside the tropical forests have had a massive impact on their habitats, and are regarded by some as far more destructive than the forest dwellers. They feed on a wide variety of plants, ranging from grass to trees. Elephants use their tusks to strip the bark off trees and they push over whole trees to gain access to leaves, buds, twigs and flowers. The fruits of certain trees, such as the marula (Sclerocarya birrea), attract elephants when they ripen and fall to the ground. In the wet season grass forms an important part of their diet and they will travel considerable distances to areas where rain showers have stimulated new growth. Grass may be pulled directly out of the ground with the trunk, or held by the trunk and the roots loosened by scuffing and kicking of the front feet. Elephants will wade into swamps, lakes and river shallows to feed on succulent reeds and other water-associated plants. In high montane areas, such as those of Mounts Kenya and Kilimanjaro, they feed on tussock grasses and heath.

Elephants transform savanna woodland into grassland. Under natural circumstances this would benefit many grazing species, but now that elephant herds are largely confined to conservation areas and unable to move freely, these areas do not get the chance to recover. In the past, when elephants could move freely away from heavily utilised areas and give these areas a chance to recover, the natural cycle ensured that no area or species suffered unduly. Today, elephants are forced to continue utilising the same areas, and with no chance of recovery all species suffer.

Not only do savanna elephants modify the vegetation structure by their feeding, but like their forest cousins they disperse the seeds of many plants, particularly trees (for example the acacias). Elephant dung, produced in large quantities, is a perfect medium for seed germination. It provides nutrients for existing vegetation and is a food source for many insects, such as termites and dung beetles. A wide variety of bird species, including hornbills, plovers, starlings and rollers, and several mammals such as civet, feed on the seeds in elephant dung and on the insects attracted to the dung.

During dry periods elephants excavate holes in dry river beds with their tusks, trunks and feet to gain access to underground water. When the elephants are not in attendance many other species make use of this otherwise inaccessible supply. Existing waterholes are enlarged when elephants wallow and splash mud on their thick (up to 4 cm) but sensitive skins, thus increasing the capacity of the holes and ensuring that water is retained longer.

Many salt and other mineral deposits are opened up and utilised by elephants and in turn by many other species. The most impressive excavations are those on the slopes of Mount Elgon (Kenya-Uganda border) where the elephants must penetrate several hundred metres to reach the deposits. Elephants have been moulding and modifying the African landscape for many thousands of years.

## Conservation

Elephants occur or have occurred in every African country. It is difficult, if not impossible, to estimate early elephant numbers, but according to different sources there were possibly between five and ten million elephants roaming Africa's forest, savanna and semi-desert in 1930. By 1979 the number of elephants had fallen to about 1,3 million, and by 1989 to possibly slightly more than 600 000. No one can escape the fact that this was a drop of catastrophic proportions. To understand the reasons we have to look at the two major causative factors: the demand for ivory and the rapid growth in human populations throughout the range of the elephant.

The regular diamond pattern seen in a cross section of elephant tusk is not present in the ivory of any other species, such as the hippopotamus, walrus or sperm whale. It is this patterning that gives elephant ivory its special qualities.

Ivory has played an important role in the life of humans for many thousands of years. In times past it was important in personal adornment and as payment to many royal houses. In some tribes only the king or chiefs were allowed to own ivory; in others one tusk was forfeit to the tribal head from every elephant killed in his territory.

The Egyptians, Romans and Greeks, as well as other peoples, valued ivory. It was no doubt this demand that forced into extinction the elephants that once wandered the plains and hinterland of the Mediterranean shores of north Africa. The Carthaginian warrior Hannibal fought his wars against the Romans with the help of elephants that had been captured in Africa and trained. The Romans introduced elephants into their infamous circuses. However, all of these activities together probably had little impact on elephant numbers in sub-Saharan Africa.

Arab slave traders used their human captives to carry ivory and other goods to the coast to be shipped out in dhows. This trade continued for many hundreds of years but it is unlikely that the impact on the elephant population as a whole was significant, except perhaps on a very local scale. In 1800 Africa's main exports were slaves and modest quantities of such goods as ivory, gold, timber and animal skins. Zubair Pasha and other powerful merchants dominated the trade in slaves and ivory in north-eastern Africa, using the White Nile and the Bahr al-Ghazal to gain access to the unexploited area to the south.

During the course of the 19th century the export of ivory

played a critical role in the economy of all the new states in equatorial Africa. In fact the Cokwe people, who occupied the south-western sector of the Congo Basin, rose to prominence during the last half of the 19th century because of their skill at hunting elephants. By 1855 they had exterminated all the elephants in the forested Quiboco region and started to foray further afield in search of the white gold. The Lunda chiefs welcomed the Cokwe and allowed them to hunt in the areas under Lunda control in return for half of all tusks taken. By the 1880s elephant stocks had been greatly depleted in the Mwata Yamvo kingdom of the Lunda people. From the middle of the 1800s to almost the end of the century the most important trade items passing through Zanzibar were cloves, ivory and rubber. The slave trade had been outlawed and was therefore not reflected in the official trade figures, although it continued illegally.

In all of Africa's European-controlled territories ivory was an important trade product, the demand created by the tastes of the European bourgeoisie. Tusks were turned into keys for pianos, ornaments, jewellery boxes, billiard balls and many other items. The "great white hunters" became legends in their own lifetime: Jacobus Coetse, Petrus Jacobs, William Cotton Oswell, Frederick Selous, William Finaughty, Henry Hartley and Karamojo Bell. The unprecedented elephant slaughter had begun in earnest between 1900 and 1910. There was little legal control. Of course the group that suffered most was the big tuskers, for the bigger the tusks the greater the profits. One

**Below:** *An elephant cow feeding in a dry-season swamp in Amboseli National Park, Kenya.*

region, southern Africa, had lost virtually all its elephants by the early 1900s. Only remnant and isolated populations were left.

Despite the intensity of hunting, it was estimated that between five million and ten million elephants still roamed Africa. However, with European settlement came Western agricultural practices which called for fencing. Elephants simply walked through the fences as they did through thorn-scrub thickets; they ate and trampled the crops and frightened the settlers' stock. Unlike the indigenous inhabitants of Africa, the settlers had modern and efficient firearms and these were used to great effect on the foraging herds. Soon tribespeople called on the colonisers to shoot animals destroying their crops. So elephants disappeared from intensively cultivated areas, but there was still plenty of space into which they could disperse.

But much has happened since the 1930s: human population growth has spun out of control, great tracts of forest and woodland have fallen to the axe, and plantations and cropland have replaced the natural vegetation. Armed with guns, chain saws, tractors, bulldozers and medicines for livestock and humans, we've "developed" the land, forcing earth's largest terrestrial mammal into ever smaller and more isolated pockets of sub-Saharan Africa.

The 1970s and 1980s saw a massive upsurge in the illegal slaughter of elephants for their tusks. Numerous regional conflicts fuelled a breakdown in law and order in many countries, while modern armaments poured into the continent from Western and Eastern powers. Corrupt officials, freely available weapons, poorly paid and under-equipped conservation staff and an increased demand for ivory in the Far East, Europe and the United States of America contributed to an assault on the elephant population at a level never before experienced. Tusks became underground currency. Collection and sales were organised by ivory barons in a network that spread like a cancerous growth over much of the continent. During the 1970s the price of ivory climbed to heights never previously seen. For poor peasants the benefits of shooting elephants now far outweighed the risks, even though their payment was a minute fraction of what the ivory barons made. It is said that poachers operating in Kenya in 1990 were only receiving between US $2 and $3 per kilogram for ivory, while dealers received about $300. Yet to the African peasant, this is a fortune.

Soon the large tuskers and the bulls that carried heavy ivory were decimated and the poachers turned their firepower (even RPG rocket launchers were used) on cows, subadults and even juveniles showing minimal ivory. In 1988 the poachers were having to shoot twice as many elephants to collect the same tonnage of ivory as in 1979. With the slaughter of adult cows the reproductive capacity of populations was being lost. The young's learning of traditional migration routes and dry-season water sources was affected. Herd cohesion suffered as the social structure of family groups and herds was disrupted and leaderless groups of subadults and weaned juveniles wandered aimlessly. Because of the lack of leadership these "mobs" frequently turned to cultivated areas for food and came into conflict with

**Left:** *A young calf with mother at a waterhole.*

farmers who persecuted them for their depredations on crops.

A number of scientists and individuals had started ringing early warning bells about the threat to elephants. Their appeals went unheeded and many were accused of crying wolf.

The price paid for ivory varied according to the size of a tusk, its quality (better prices were paid for the lighter-coloured ivory of the savanna elephant) and the deal struck between seller and buyer. Up to 1970 ivory fetched an average of US $10 per kilogram, but by 1989 the wholesale price had soared to $300 per kilogram. These sums proved an irresistible temptation for many top government officials in various countries, who for huge profits abetted either the poaching of elephants or the trading of ivory.

In just ten years, from 1979 to 1989, the world's elephant population was reduced by half. During the 1980s on average 800 to 1 000 tons of ivory entered the international market every year, for which an estimated 100 000 elephants had to have been killed each year. Surveys revealed ever higher numbers of elephant carcasses with the tusks hacked out. In some cases where teams of poachers were operating, chain saws were used to cut up the skulls. By the middle of the 1980s ivory exports were starting to drop as elephants became more difficult to locate. This caused the price of ivory to rise even further. While the slaughter continued unabated over much of central, eastern and western Africa, in southern Africa (Namibia, Botswana, Zimbabwe and South Africa) elephant populations remained stable and in some cases were growing. This can be largely ascribed to more efficient policing, better equipment and salaries for field

staff and the fact that a large percentage of the herds in this region are confined to conservation areas.

As a result of the huge quantities of ivory entering international trade – up to 1 000 tons a year in the mid-1980s – CITES (the Convention on International Trade in Endangered Species) introduced an ivory control system in 1985. This resulted in the quantities of legally traded ivory dropping considerably, but the illegal trade, if anything, increased. An ivory quota system was implemented but could only record the ivory that "officially" left Africa. The volume of contraband ivory from poached elephants could only be guessed at, but it has been estimated at 80% of all ivory leaving Africa during this time. The CITES initiative had clearly failed to stem the slaughter of these animals.

From 1986 to 1989 CITES issued permits for the export of more than 500 tons of ivory from an estimated 50 000 elephants. Although these figures sound high, if all ivory had been traded in this legal and permitted fashion, this situation could have been allowed to continue if submitted to regular review. However, all of these new regulations did nothing to halt the illegal trade.

Throughout its range the elephant had retreated or disappeared from an estimated 10% of its former range between 1989 and 1992. By the end of the 1980s Kenya's elephant numbers had dropped from some 140 000 individuals in 1970 to about 16 000; Tanzania lost almost 190 000 elephants in the same period, leaving between 50 000 and 30 000, and Uganda was left with no more than 1 600.

On 18 January 1990 the African elephant was removed from the CITES Appendix 2 (trade allowed with controls) to Appendix 1, which allows no commercial trade in any of the animal's products. The decision to ban the sale of all elephant products was a last-ditch attempt to save this keystone species. Many countries promptly signed the moratorium but a number of principal ivory producers and consumers were reluctant to do so. Eventually, however, they bowed to international pressure. With the banning of any commercial ivory trading prices plummeted to pre-1970s levels. Since then limited numbers of permits have been issued to allow sport hunters to transport their trophy tusks to their home countries but commercial trade in the ivory is forbidden.

The world rallied, if belatedly, to save the elephant when scientists and conservationists proved the link between ivory sales and the slaughter of the gentle giants, and warned that only a handful of protected populations could survive the onslaught. However, an unseemly slanging match developed between the guardians of the well-managed southern African elephant populations and the officials of eastern Africa who through a combination of ineptitude, corruption, political turmoil and the easy availability of cheap semi-automatic and automatic weapons were unable, or unwilling, to halt the slaughter. The southern African conservationists who had saved their elephants were portrayed as the evil ones but countries from the north-east which were rapidly losing their elephants were being heaped with praise. The Director (at that time) of Wildlife Conservation International, Dr David Western, succinctly put the conflict into perspective, "Management no more endangers elephants than sentimentality saves them."

Japan had been buying 40% of all ivory, primarily to produce *hanko*, the finger-sized personal signature seals required on official documents. Most ivory traded in the 1970s and 1980s passed through Hong Kong. Traders in that territory also used places such as Singapore as way stations in order to keep one step ahead of international conservation laws. Countries in what was then the European Economic Community absorbed 20% of ivory exports and the USA 15%.

The countries in southern Africa (Namibia, Botswana, Zimbabwe and South Africa) with well-managed and stable elephant populations had objected to being prevented from selling legally harvested ivory (mostly from essential culling operations) because of the inability of countries such as Kenya to control poaching and illegal trading. The National Parks Board of South Africa however decided to adhere to the moratorium on the sale of elephant products in sympathy with the efforts of the Kenyan Wildlife Service to gain control over elephant poaching, until the situation has been stabilised.

Countries such as Kenya, which had been suffering catastrophic elephant losses to poachers, first proposed rescheduling elephants to Appendix 1 and remain strongly opposed to the reopening of the ivory trade. Before the CITES ban went into effect Kenya is believed to have lost between 3 000 and 5 000 elephants every year to poachers; since the ban only 55 illegally killed elephants have been found (18 in 1991). The reasoning is that if the ban can be maintained it will no longer be advantageous for poachers to hunt down the grey giants. Those in favour of retaining the moratorium believe that a premature lifting or easing of the ban would send a message to

**Left**: *Although the burning of the ivory stockpile in Nairobi National Park, Kenya, generated much international publicity for the plight of the elephant, this action has been questioned in many circles.* PHOTO: *Ralph Klumpp.*
**Below**: *Nature's great masterpiece, an elephant. Sadly we could be facing the twilight of the giants.*

the rest of the world that elephant populations were now healthy and ripe once more for exploitation. It is believed that this would once again fuel the illegal exploitation of threatened elephant populations in parts of Africa where controls are limited.

A number of governments hold large stockpiles of tusks that because of the CITES ban they cannot sell. Kenya captured the world's attention on 18 July 1989 by burning its stock of 12 tons of ivory in a well-publicised event in the Nairobi National Park. The latest CITES 1997 directive allows Botswana, Namibia and Zimbabwe to sell their existing ivory stocks, mainly to Japan. Fourteen countries will be allowed a non-commercial (government) disposal of existing stocks.

Although the ivory trading ban was a critical component in controlling elephant poaching, improved policing in Kenya, Tanzania and a few other countries was also important. Poaching levels have fallen drastically in some countries; poaching is continuing at lower levels in others but is said to be increasing in a few regions. As far as is known very little ivory is entering the illegal trade. However, it is rumoured that dealers are stockpiling ivory until they can establish new trade networks.

The large, healthy elephant populations in the Kruger National Park (South Africa) and Hwange National Park (Zimbabwe) have to be maintained at levels of reasonable carrying capacity. Populations have to be kept viable in order to preserve genetic diversity. The vegetation must be protected from being overtaxed to the detriment of the ecosystem as a whole. The only way to achieve all this is through culling.

Culling is a highly emotive issue. No-one likes to see elephants, or any other species for that matter, shot, particularly in conservation areas. However, culling is often essential to prevent overpopulation and destruction of habitats. It becomes ever more necessary to control numbers as more and more parks and reserves are fenced or become ringed by human set-

# Anthrax

Anthrax is a zoonosis caused by the aerobic gram positive spore forming *Bacillus anthracis*. Spores are extremely resistant to environmental conditions and they remain viable in soil for many years. By contaminating grazing the spores may infect a wide range of game species, as well as people. Carcasses of infected animals are scavenged by such species as vultures, spotted hyaena, black-backed jackal and lion, which disperse the spores over wide areas in their droppings. Efforts are made by people to burn or bury infected carcasses but this is not always possible.

Outbreaks of anthrax are not uncommon in such regions as the Kruger National Park (South Africa) and Etosha National Park (Namibia). Efforts have been made to inoculate elephants in Etosha National Park but despite this between 20 and 30 animals die each year. In 1992 the 80 or so elephants that roam the desert of north-western Namibia attracted attention when an anthrax-infected elephant carcass was found in the bed of the Hoanib River. The Namibian authorities feared that as many of the available waterholes were drying up the herd utilising the area around the Hoanib could become dependent on a single anthrax-infected waterhole. As this is one of only two surviving desert-dwelling elephant populations (the other is located in Mali) an operation was undertaken to inoculate these animals against anthrax. Nineteen animals were inoculated, using barbless darts fired by an official from a helicopter. No further cases of anthrax have been recorded.

**Above:** *Elephants being darted.*
PHOTO: *Bruno Nebe.*

tlements, forcing elephants that formerly lived outside the parks into their confined area. The advocates of letting nature take its course have a case in very large, undisturbed areas, but these are now few and far between. Elephants are becoming increasingly stranded in small enclaves from which they cannot escape. As we disrupt migration routes and erect fences, and as domestic livestock numbers climb, it becomes increasingly necessary to manage areas, populations and species.

Because culling is repugnant to many people, Kenya is looking at alternatives to limit elephant population growth in specific areas. Kenyan arguments against culling include ethical considerations, the negative impact that killing elephants in conservation areas would have on the tourist industry and the destabilising effect that culling would have on population dynamics. Alternative methods being examined are abortion, contraceptive vaccines and steroid implants. Whatever solution is found some form of elephant population control will eventually be required in Kenya to prevent conflict with people and overutilisation of vegetation in closed or restricted ele-

phant ranges. The Kenyan authorities have been quick to point out that their country does not have an overpopulation of elephants at present. Their concern is for the near future, as an increasing number of elephant populations will be enclosed by fences. In Zimbabwe culling teams operate on the ground, moving in close to herds and first taking out the matriarch. This causes the surviving animals to mill around and they can be picked off with rifles. In the Kruger National Park (South Africa) herds were shepherded towards a road where the animals are drug-darted from a helicopter with excessive dosages of Scoline; they were then finished off with brain shots and transported to a modern abattoir for processing.

The ban on ivory trading was necessary and will probably have to stay in place for some time. Should even limited trading be allowed in the short term, it is almost certain that ivory will regain its popularity. Poaching and trading would soon reach pre-ban levels, at least for as long as the supply lasted. However, the ivory ban should not be seen as a long-term solution. Elephants will have to pay their way, either as subjects for tourist cameras, by providing trophies for sport hunters, by supplying meat to protein-starved communities or even by producing ivory. For this reason cheap and easy to use methods of source verification will have to be found to prevent illegal ivory entering the market.

Now that the ivory ban is well advanced, it has proved itself in that trade has decreased to a trickle and the price of ivory has plunged to pre-1970s levels. The elephant's slide to extinction has been halted, or has it? Although the ivory trade ban has allowed the elephant breathing space we must not lose sight of the main threat to the long-term survival of these magnificent animals and all other biota: the uncontrolled population growth of *Homo sapiens,* and the habitat destruction that goes along with this.

It will be a sad day when elephants are but a memory. We can only hope that we are not seeing the twilight of the gentle grey giants.

**Below**: *Young bulls sparring.*

# CHAPTER 3

# RHINOS

## *On the horns of a dilemma*

This medicine is carefully prepared from the
best selected Rhinoceros Horn ...

### Description and taxonomy

Of the five living rhino species, two, the white rhinoceros *(Ceratotherium simum)* and the black rhinoceros *(Diceros bicornis)* are found only in Africa. The names "white" and "black" rhino are deceptive. Both species are similar in colour: usually different shades of grey, depending on the dust, soil or mud in the area where they occur.

The authors prefer the name square-lipped or grass rhino for the white rhino, and hook-lipped for the black rhino, because these names refer to the most obvious difference between the two species. However, the use of the names "black" and

"white" rhino is so entrenched that we will follow convention so as not to confuse the reader.

The white rhino is the second-largest land mammal, second only to the elephant, with body mass in adult bulls exceeding two tons and shoulder height almost reaching 2 m. It is larger than the black rhino, and also differs from it in having a large, distinctive hump on the neck. This hump was a favourite delicacy in the days when these animals were much more numerous. The head is long and carried close to the ground. The broad square muzzle, from which it draws its alternative name, is distinctive. The ears are large and pointed. The horns, made up of hair-like tubular filaments, are located one behind the

other on the front of the face. The record front horn length is an amazing 1,58 m.

The black rhino reaches about half the mass of its white cousin. Average shoulder height is 1,6 m. It has no raised hump on the neck and the triangular, prehensile upper lip is distinctive. Despite its markedly smaller size, this rhino can also bear horns of considerable length: the record is 1,2 m.

The two African rhino species have survived in their present form for at least three million years. Ancestors that were distinctly similar to modern rhinos had been around for as much as 40 million years.

At present, two subspecies of white rhino and four subspecies of black rhino are recognised. Although the father of modern taxonomy, Linnaeus, first described the black rhinoceros in 1758, the southern race of the white rhinoceros was only described in 1817 and its northern race as late as 1907. However, the presence of the northern white rhino was already known in the last years of the 19th century.

The two white rhino races are widely separated. The northern form *(Ceratotherium simum cottoni)* is now restricted to Garamba National Park in Congo (DR) on the Sudanese border. The southern form *(C.s. simum)*, apart from numerous introduced and reintroduced populations, survives in northern KwaZulu-Natal province and the Kruger National Park (South Africa), where the single largest population is resident.

Differences between the two subspecies are minimal, with *cottoni* said to be somewhat longer in the leg and shorter in the body. These differences are difficult to detect in the field and may well not be valid, given the small numbers examined. Because the white rhino once occurred over large areas of savanna Africa, even extending into the southern Sahara when it was better watered, and almost certainly formed one contiguous population in the not too distant past, evolutionary differences will be limited. Nevertheless it is of great conservation concern to protect the minute northern population, the last white rhinos occurring naturally above the equator.

In the case of the four recognised black rhinoceros subspecies mitochondrial DNA sequencing suggests only very small sequence divergence between them (less than 0,4%). These differences are so minute that perhaps no subspecies should be recognised. However, they may have some hidden and unknown adaptive specialisations. It is therefore expedient to recognise the subspecies as valid, at least until such time as it is possible to prove, or disprove, their validity.

**Below**: *Black rhinoceros* (Diceros bicornis) *on the lush green plains of the Ngorongoro Crater, Tanzania.* PHOTO: *Gavin Thomson, ABPL.*

| | BLACK RHINOCEROS | WHITE RHINOCEROS |
|---|---|---|
| | *Diceros bicornis* | *Ceratotherium simum* |
| **Total length** | 3,5-4,3 m | 4,5-4,8 m |
| **Tail length** | 70 cm | 1 m |
| **Shoulder height** | 1,6 m | 1,8 m |
| **Mass** | 800-1 100 kg | ♂ 2 000-2 300 kg |
| | | ♀ 1 400-1 600 kg |
| **Home range** | 0,5-500 sq km | 1-20 sq km |
| (The size of the home range of both species depends on conditions such as food availability, shade and water) | | |
| **Social structure** | solitary | groups of 1-5 |
| **Gestation** | 450 days | 480 days |
| **Birth mass** | 40 kg | 40 kg |
| **Diet** | browse | graze |
| **Habitat** | bushed areas | open woodland; short grasses |
| **Number surviving in 1994** | *D.b. bicornis* 741 | *C.s. simum* over 8 441 |
| | *D.b. longipes* 10 | *C.s. cottoni* 25 |
| | *D.b. michaeli* 485 | |
| | *D.b. minor* 1 363 | |
| **TOTAL** | 2 599 | over 8 466 |

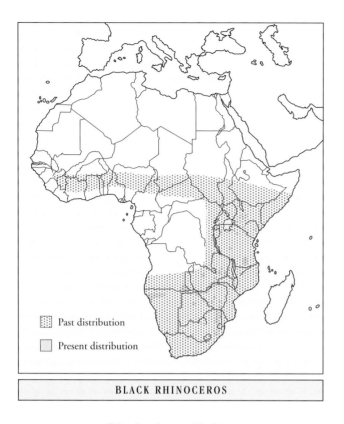

**BLACK RHINOCEROS**

[ ] Past distribution
[ ] Present distribution

## Distribution and habitat

Before we head into the tragic present and future of both of Africa's rhino species, perhaps we should first take a glimpse at their much rosier past. When reading old accounts written by naturalists, hunters and travellers, one starts to realise how abundant rhinos were, in particular black rhinos.

In the historical accounts dealing with rhinos it is unfortunately seldom possible to distinguish between white and black. However, there is sufficient documentation to allow us to draw conclusions on their former range. We know from historical accounts that the black rhino was distributed from Nigeria eastwards to the Horn of Africa, and throughout east, central and southern Africa. When the first Europeans settled in present-day Western Cape (South Africa), black rhinos were wandering the bush country within sight of Table Mountain, the great sandstone ridge that dominates the city of Cape Town.

As far as we are aware the first documented record of the black rhino in the Cape is from one Leendert Janssens, who along with several companions was shipwrecked in Table Bay in 1647. He reports that they shot a rhino and notes that "... the flesh was firm and tasty."

One of Governor Van Riebeeck's earliest reports to mention rhinos was based on an account by one of his men:

*In the evening marched 7 miles. Saw two rhinoceroses which charged us and threatened to destroy us, but God protected us. Jan Verdonck had to abandon his hat and sword ... Took our rest for the night alongside a brook, in God's name ... Had to leave this place when two rhinoceroses advanced upon us.*

All this within a few kilometres of Cape Town! A rather blood-thirsty and gruesome account of an encounter with a black rhino was recorded by one Johan Nieuhof in 1654:

*We heard that a rhinoceros, or nosehorner, was fallen in a marsh and, because of its weight, could not get out. Commander Rietbeek sent some soldiers with muskets, but the bullets rebounded from its hard wrinkled skin. They cut an opening in its withers and fired into this until at last they killed it. The horns are still preserved in the Fort at the Cape and from them at times healths are drunk.*

We find one description of the so-called "Cape" rhinoceros particularly delightful, written by Kolben in 1731:

*His mouth is like that of a Hog, but somewhat more pointed ... He is not fond of Feeding on Grass, chusing rather Shrubs, Broom and Thistles. But the delight of his Tooth is a Shrub ... the Rhinoceros-Bush.*

The description leaves no doubt that these are black rhinos. Similar accounts can be located for most areas throughout their former range.

White rhinos probably did not occur anywhere near Cape Town. Reports of the white rhino are more scanty, primarily because of its more limited distribution. Also, its less aggressive nature is not conducive to tales of daring and bravery.

No accurate estimates of past abundance are available for either white or black rhinos but some authorities have estimated that 60 years ago probably as many as one million black rhinos inhabited the savanna woodlands of central, eastern and

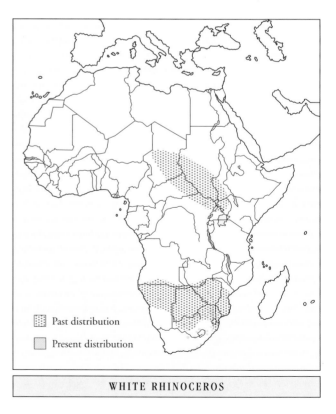

[ ] Past distribution
[ ] Present distribution

**WHITE RHINOCEROS**

**Above**: *White rhino* (Ceratotherium simum) *cow with calf.*

southern Africa. Today a total of 2 599 survive, a frightening 0,2% of the past estimate.

The black rhino once occurred in the following countries: South Africa, Swaziland, Namibia, Botswana, Angola, Zimbabwe, Mozambique, Zambia, Malawi, Tanzania, Kenya, Uganda, limited areas of Congo (DR), Somalia, Ethiopia, Sudan, Central African Republic, Chad, Cameroon, Nigeria and Mali.

There is considerable uncertainty as to how far west the black rhino ever occurred, although it was definitely present at least until 1935 to the north of the Benue River in Nigeria, in the vicinity of the Yong Plateau and along Nigeria's border with Cameroon. Much earlier reports by Arabs and local people who operated in the area between Lake Chad and the upper Niger River frequently mentioned rhino sightings. Sir Harry Johnstone, writing in 1906, mentioned that the tribal group known as the Mandingos in northern Liberia assured him that rhinos once lived in their tribal area. They could identify the animals from pictures. We hold the opinion that there is no reason why black rhinos should not have occupied much of the acacia woodlands of the Sahel belt through west Africa, but hard evidence is lacking.

However, there are definitely no rhinos surviving to the west of Cameroon today. The last remnants of the "western" race of

the black rhino, *Diceros bicornis longipes,* hang on to a precarious existence in northern Cameroon. A mere 10 are all that remain. Over the years there have been persistent rumours of black rhinos occupying areas within forests inland from the greater Gulf of Guinea, in for instance Congo, but as far as we know these have never been verified. Given the types of habitat rhinos occupy today it would seem unlikely that they ever lived in tropical lowland forests, except marginally in association with more favoured habitats.

At the beginning of this century the black rhino was considered to be very common in Zambia but by 1934 the country-wide population was estimated at fewer than 1 500.

Further northwards Tanzania was once home to a large percentage of Africa's rhinos. The following gives some idea of the great numbers occurring in suitable habitat: in 1887, close to Mount Kilimanjaro, John Willoughby shot 66 black rhinos in just four months; the hunter Delegorgue killed 56 rhinos on an expedition lasting eight months. During the First World War, when this was German territory, hunting parties made regular forays in order to hunt rhinos for their meat, which was used to feed the black askaris.

In Kenya, one relatively small area, associated with the Makueni tsetse-fly belt, was designated for human settlement in 1948. This entailed the shooting of many game animals, including an incredible 1 000 or more black rhinos. One hunter operating in Kenya claimed to have personally shot 1 600 black rhinos, mostly in official cropping programmes. Today Kenya's total rhino population is about one third of the number killed by that one man!

It is hard to imagine today, but only a few decades ago visitors to the Kenyan national parks were routinely warned, "Find your rhino before it finds you!" The warning was issued because rhinos, which can be aggressive, were so plentiful. Today the average visitor is lucky to catch even a fleeting glimpse of this prehistoric-looking animal in any Kenyan conservation area. In Tsavo National Park, in south-eastern Kenya, black rhinos were estimated to number between 6 000 and 9 000 in 1969. When the park was first proclaimed in 1948 this total may have been much higher, perhaps double. Daphne Sheldrick has said of the number of black rhinos in Tsavo in the 1960s, "They were so thick on the ground, if you didn't see 40 in an afternoon, you'd had a bad day." It is surmised that the decline of this particular population was associ-

**Above:** *Removing the horns from a white rhino.* Photo: *Bruno Nebe.*

ated with a considerable increase in elephant numbers, to more than 35 000. Elephants tend to outcompete rhinos for similar food plants. The decline in rhino numbers could also be directly linked to the catastrophic drought that hit south-eastern Kenya in 1961.

In 1980 it was estimated that a total of about 20 000 black rhinos survived in Africa, although some reports put the figure as high as 30 000. By 1984 numbers had dropped to fewer than 9 000, and two years later barely 4 000 still roamed the bushlands of Africa. In 1989 a mere 3 000 were left and in 1992 numbers had fallen below 2 600.

These figures are shocking enough, but when one looks at the declines in a few specific countries the true enormity of the disaster hits home. Zambia had a national population of 2 750 black rhinos in 1980; now there are none. Tanzania had an estimated 3 795 rhinos in the same year and today there are fewer than 46 – probably far fewer.

Kenya lost 98% of its rhino population between 1970 and

1985 but today it is one of only two countries that have stable and growing populations. Since 1985 the Kenyan rhino population has expanded by 5% per year under intensive protection. There are about 560 rhinos in Kenya now. Although this is good news, we should not lose sight of the fact that there may have been 18 000 rhinos in that east African country in 1969.

Zimbabwe's black rhino population, until recently the largest of any country, has gone from perhaps 1 400 in 1980 to no more than 340 today. This population is still under severe pressure, despite vast sums of money pumped into poaching control. An illustration: in August 1994 an intensive capture operation was carried out in a 6 000 sq km block in the Zambezi Valley which was believed to hold a fair number of rhino. Only one cow and a large calf were found!

By far the most seriously threatened black rhino subspecies is *Diceros bicornis longipes,* now found only in tiny fragmented populations in a very limited area of Cameroon, with a mere 35 surviving at the time of writing. By the time you read this the total is almost certainly lower.

There are now no naturally occurring black rhinos outside the KwaZulu-Natal province in South Africa, although satellite populations have been introduced or reintroduced to a number of conservation areas, including Augrabies Falls, Vaalbos, Kruger and Addo national parks and a limited number of provincial and privately owned sanctuaries. The population in Addo is of the east African subspecies *michaeli.*

White rhinos, once abundant north of the Victoria Nile, were estimated to number only some 335 individuals there in 1957. In 1928 an estimated 130 or so white rhinos managed to cling to survival in Uganda, but by 1950 this population had grown to about 500. However, from that time there was a steady decline. In 1963 it was known that only 71 animals remained – the price of rhino horn was rising! In an attempt to save the northern white rhino, 15 animals were darted and removed to the apparent safety of Uganda's Murchison Falls National Park. The Ajai sanctuary was set aside specifically to conserve a remnant population. In 1972 about 120 white rhinos lived in Ajai but by 1978 they had been reduced to 80. In the same year only 25 were known to live in Murchison. The fate of the Ugandan rhinos was sealed when the Tanzanian army invaded in order to overthrow the dictator Idi Amin. By 1980 white rhinos were but a memory in Uganda.

In 1958 more than 1 000 northern white rhinos were estimated to roam Garamba National Park in Congo (DR), and in the early 1950s perhaps slightly more than 1 000 still occurred in southern Sudan. How times and circumstances have changed, with probably fewer than 30 animals in both countries combined today!

The picture for the white rhino is somewhat brighter in South Africa, which has about 8 000 individuals. However, the figure has suffered a "paper reduction" of perhaps 800 rhinos following apparent counting overestimates in the Hluhluwe-Umfolozi-Corridor Game Reserve complex controlled by the Natal Parks Board. So at the stroke of a pen perhaps 15% of South Africa's white rhino population was "lost" and we are left with about 8 000 animals.

## WHITE RHINOCEROS

### Ceratotherium simum

| Subspecies | Country | Estimated number | Trend | Comment |
|---|---|---|---|---|
| C.s. cottoni | Congo (DR) | 25 | falling | |
| C.s. simum | Botswana | 23 | falling | from SA |
| | Kenya | 137 | rising | from SA |
| | Namibia | 141 | rising | from SA |
| | South Africa | 7 913 | rising | |
| | Swaziland | 50 | rising | from SA |
| | Zimbabwe | 167 | falling | from SA |

## BLACK RHINOCEROS

### Diceros bicornis

| Subspecies | Country | Estimated number | Trend | Comment |
|---|---|---|---|---|
| D.b. longipes | Cameroon | 10 | falling | |
| D.b. michaeli | Kenya | 424 | rising | |
| | Rwanda | 4 | falling | |
| | South Africa | 33 | rising | from Kenya |
| | Tanzania | 24 | falling | |
| D.b. bicornis | Namibia | 707 | rising | |
| | South Africa | 34 | rising | from Namibia |
| D.b. minor | Mozambique | 13 | falling | |
| | South Africa | 976 | rising | |
| | Swaziland | 10 | rising | from SA |
| | Tanzania | 22 | falling | |
| | Zimbabwe | 339 | falling | |

The white rhino (both subspecies) has become extinct in recent years in the following countries (note that this includes reintroduced populations in three countries): Angola (RI), Central African Republic, Sudan, Mozambique (RI), Uganda and Zambia (RI). The distribution of this species was much more extensive in the distant past. The black rhino has become extinct in Central African Republic, Ethiopia, Malawi, Nigeria, Angola, Bostwana, Zambia, Somalia, Sudan and Uganda. Although there is a slender chance that tiny numbers of rhino may still cling to life in these countries, they are extinct as breeding populations, with little or no chance of recovery.

The accompanying table is based on information compiled by the IUCN/SSC African Rhino Specialist Group in 1998, although we have updated totals for sev-eral countries where declines in populations have continued.

Although for some countries the population estimates are fairly accurate, for others it is highly likely that the true totals are much lower. These countries include Angola, Mozambique and Rwanda, where warfare and banditry have curtailed the activities of researchers and conservation workers.

The predominantly falling trend in rhino numbers is likely to continue despite attempts at stopping illegal trading. Although South Africa has secure and growing rhino populations at the time of writing, we are of the opinion that they will come under severe pressure in the near future.

## Behaviour

Rhinos lie up in the shade during the hot midday hours. Despite their cumbersome appearance they can reach a speed of 40 km/h when under stress. Both African rhino species have acute senses of smell and hearing but their eyesight is very poor. Although the white rhino is generally more docile than its smaller cousin, this should never be taken for granted as charges resulting in fatalities are not unusual.

Bulls only start competing for oestrus cows from about the age of 12 years, when they can first establish territories. Cows start breeding from about their fourth year. Although calfs may be dropped at any time of the year, in KwaZulu-Natal there are calving peaks in March and July. The single calf, with an aver-age mass of 40 kg, is dropped after a gestation period of about 480 days for the white rhino and 450 days for the black. The calf is able to walk and suckle within three hours of birth. The calf of the white rhino runs in front of the mother, this being in contrast to the calf of the black rhino which runs behind, or at the side of, the cow.

The white rhino is the more social of Africa's two rhino species. A typical grouping consists of a territorial bull, subor-dinate bulls, cows and their accompanying young. The territo-rial bulls usually only move out of their area if they do not have direct access to water, leaving every three or four days to drink and wallow. These are usually linear movements with little detouring between the bulls' territory and the water source. In nearly all cases the same pathways, or routes, are followed.

Territory-holding white rhino bulls are in general tolerant of male intruders if they show subordinate behaviour and make no threatening gestures. This tolerance decreases when an oestrus cow is in the vicinity. The size of bulls' territories is quite small, with one study in KwaZulu-Natal (South Africa) revealing an average of 3 sq km. Size is, however, dictated by the quality and abundance of food. Cows occupy home ranges of between 6 sq km and 20 sq km that may overlap the terri-tories of several bulls. Although fights over territories are usually avoided, severe conflicts do on occasion occur, particularly when a bull is in the company of a receptive cow. Bulls mark their territories by depositing large dung middens around the area's perimeter and within it. The hind feet are frequently used to scuff freshly deposited dung, and the ground after urination. Urine spraying is also used in the marking of territories.

Most feeding takes place during the cooler daylight hours, as well as at night. White rhinos are strictly grazers, the large lips cropping off the grass, as the animals lack incisors. They are very selective feeders, with only a few grass species making up the bulk of their food.

Unlike its larger cousin, the black rhino is a solitary animal, although on occasion several may gather at waterholes or at sites with mineral-rich soils. Bulls and cows only consort briefly to mate and the single calf may accompany the mother for between two and four years. The accompanying calf is driven off during the cow's next pregnancy, or at the birth of the next offspring.

Black rhinos live in an established home range but they are not territorial in the sense that they defend their areas against other rhinos. Home ranges of both bulls and cows may overlap with those of others in a population. Adult bull black rhinos do, however, establish a dominance hierarchy, particularly in areas of fairly high density. Fighting takes place between established bulls to determine dominance and in competition for cows in oestrus.

Home range sizes vary according to the abundance and quality of food, as well as access to water. Generally, the more arid the region in which the animal lives, the larger the home range. Home ranges vary from 0,5 sq km to over 500 sq km. This latter range was recorded in the desert lands of north-western Namibia.

Despite black rhinos' mainly solitary nature they can live at very high densities. In the Lerai Forest in Tanzania, 23 black rhinos were known to live in a 2,6 sq km stand of mainly yellow-barked acacias in the Ngorongoro Crater, prior to the massive declines resulting from poaching.

Black rhinos feed during the cooler daylight hours and at night. In arid areas black rhinos may be forced to move considerable distances between their home range and surface water. These movements are nearly always linear in nature and rarely include detours.

The dung may be deposited at midden sites, or at random throughout the home range. Several individuals may defecate at the same midden. Bulls kick the freshly deposited dung vigorously with the hind feet at the midden sites, leaving distinct grooves in the ground. It is probable that this serves some marking function that is as yet not properly understood. It is easy to distinguish the dung-balls of the two rhino species by examining their content. Those of the white rhino are made up of relatively fine plant fibres, whereas those of the black rhino contain more coarse, woody material.

The black rhino's prehensile, pointed upper lip is used to grasp leaves and twigs which are then either snapped off or cut through by the cheek-teeth. Plant parts out of reach of the mouth may be broken off by "horn-thrashing", and on rare occasions black rhinos may raise their front feet off the ground, giving them additional reach. Browse, meaning plant parts taken from trees and bushes, forms most of their diet and they are selective feeders. Acacia trees supply a large percentage of their food, with euphorbias being important in some areas. In certain regions they are said to eat the large fruits of the sausage tree *(Kigelia)*, one of the few herbivores to do so. Green grass is usually taken in small quantities but in some locations, such as on the floor of the Ngorongoro Crater in Tanzania, grass forms an important component of their diet.

Although lions and spotted hyaenas will on occasion take young rhinos of both species, and rarely adults, their principal enemy is without doubt humans.

## Conservation

Probably no large wild mammal has declined so rapidly and dramatically as the rhino, as a direct result of hunting.

The conservation of both rhino species has become a matter of critical importance: they are hovering on the edge of extinction. Originally hunted mainly as a "problem animal" and as a trophy, in recent years they have been slaughtered on a massive scale for their horns. The horns are used as an ingredient in Asian traditional medicine. Highly prized dagger handles were also made from them in Yemen. We should point out that contrary to media reports, powdered rhino horn is not in general demand as an aphrodisiac. Only in India, particularly in Gujerat and Bengal, is rhino horn reputed to be used for this purpose.

A vast array of traditional medicines are produced from various rhino parts, not only from the horns. Sliced or powdered rhino horn is most commonly used as a traditional remedy for high fever, but also as a cardiotonic, antipyretic, antitoxin for snake bite, and headache treatment. In Asia many traditional healers believe that the horns of Asian rhinos are best for this purpose. For this reason they fetch higher prices than African rhino horn.

A company operating from Johor Baharu in Malaysia produces a medicine called Three Legs Brand Rhinoceros Horn Anti-fever Water. It carries the following notification label:

> *This medicine is carefully prepared from the best selected Rhinoceros Horn and Anti-Fever Drugs, and under the direct supervision of Experts. This wonderful medicine acts like a charm in giving immediate relief to those suffering from: Malaria, High Temperature, Fever affecting the Heart and Four Limbs, Against Climate Giddiness, Insanity, Toothache, etc.*

With such a wonderful health billing, who could resist? However, it has to be said that no scientific trials have supported the claims made for the healing properties of rhino horn.

Strangely, rhino horn is extremely rare in use in African traditional medicine. Before the explosion in demand outside Africa rhinos were therefore generally left unmolested.

Although rhino products have been part of the Asian medicinal armoury for many centuries massive pressure on buying countries, such as China, Taiwan, Singapore and Hong Kong, in recent years seems to have slowed but not stopped the flow of rhino horn. This is of course not just as a result of more effective law enforcement. There are simply very few rhinos left to supply the market.

Alternatives to rhino horn, such as saiga horn, are coming increasingly into use but none of these is deemed to be as effective as rhino horn. Some traditional healers even specify that the best horns come from recently killed rhino bulls and that the tip of the horn is the most effective portion.

A prized symbol of Yemeni manhood is the traditional curved dagger, the *jambia,* the handle of which preferably should be carved from rhino horn. Yemeni men flocked to the worker-hungry Saudi Arabia and the Gulf States after the 1969 Yemeni civil war. All workers in these wealthy countries were extremely well paid. This meant that the Yemeni workers were able to take large sums of money home to what was then one of the poorest nations in the world. It is estimated that one sixth of the Yemeni population was working in neighbouring countries in 1978. Their sudden wealth generated an unprecedented demand for the daggers with their carved rhino horn handles. Between 1969 and 1977 it is estimated that the horns of 8 000 rhinos were imported into North Yemen. Because demand was leaping ahead of supply, rhino horn prices continued to rise. This market is now greatly reduced.

Poachers usually only remove a rhino's horns, as speed is of the essence, but there is also a market for its skin, viscera, penis and toenails. When trade was allowed in rhino products a number of game farmers in South Africa could offer surplus white rhino bulls to sport hunters for the horn trophies, and the farmers then marketed the skin for considerable sums in the Far East.

There is a misconception about who profits most from the trade in rhino horn. Poachers receive a miniscule proportion of the sums made by the retailer. Remember that the end user buys only a few grams of rhino horn at a time, but is prepared to pay an exorbitant price for it.

The quoted price of rhino horn obviously does not reflect the final retail price. Nevertheless a comparison of the quoted price over the years is illuminating. Between 1909 and 1914 the London wholesale price of rhino horn went as high as US $9,30 per kilogram and in 1929 it reached $22,68, but in the 1930s the price dropped to an average of $6,93. By the early 1950s it again cleared the $20 mark, with a slight increase in the 1960s. By 1976 the trouble really started, and the price began to climb at an unprecedented rate, helped along by the entry of the Yemeni market for rhino horn. By 1978 the wholesale price had reached $300. This was a meteoric rise, but the retail price charged for the small amounts of horn in traditional remedies rose much more sharply still. Today the retail price of rhino horn may top many thousands of dollars (we have been given a figure of about $17 000 per kilogram).

The estimated amount of rhino horn entering the world market between 1972 and 1979 implied the loss of about 22 000 rhinos each year. The combination of diminishing numbers of rhino and increasing sums of money for their products caused all five species of rhino to disappear from much of their ranges.

Conservation of the two African rhino species took on an air of absolute desperation, particularly in the past five years. The first attempts to conserve rhinos had involved both the northern and southern white rhino, but the black rhino was still relatively abundant and believed to be safe. Attempts to secure the white rhino in Uganda ended in catastrophe and extinction. The white rhinos in Garamba National Park in northeastern Congo (DR) were under severe pressure but they have survived, although there are now 25 individuals.

The saga of the southern white rhino has had a much happier ending, thanks to Operation Rhino. A remnant population had clung to survival in the triangle of land between the Black and White Umfolozi rivers in South Africa. There is no accurate figure as to how many animals survived here but it was certainly no more than a few score. One estimate puts the figure as low as 30 but this has been questioned in some circles. The status of this area as a game reserve had been confirmed by the then Natal Provincial Council in 1939. Over the

**Above:** *A dehorned black rhino.* Photo: *Bruno Nebe.*

next 20 years, with increased protection, there was what can best be described as a rhino population explosion. It was feared that the animals would have a negative impact on the vegetation. In 1960 it was decided that some animals would have to be moved, both to prevent overgrazing and to create satellite populations so that a major catastrophe would not destroy the entire population.

With the advent of the drug M99 in 1963, the immobilisation and transport of rhinos became feasible. Operation Rhino was launched. Up to 1969, 627 white rhinos were translocated to various reserves, zoos and animal parks (one Natal Parks Board report puts the figure at 616). In 1963-64, in Operation Kruger Park, 97 white rhinos were translocated to that South

African sanctuary. Further translocations to it followed and today the world's largest white rhino population is found in the Kruger National Park.

Sadly, translocations to other national parks such as Hwange in Zimbabwe and Chobe in Botswana are now viewed as failures. Although they were initially very successful, the authorities were unable to cope with the subsequent massive increase in poaching. Several thousand white rhinos had been captured and moved to areas within their former range, but the new populations outside South Africa have been heavily poached.

Over the past three decades several thousand southern white rhinos have been distributed from the KwaZulu-Natal reserves to many other parts of South Africa, to southern and east African countries and to numerous zoos and animal parks throughout the world. Although most reintroduced populations in South Africa have thrived, other African translocations have had a generally sad record.

Let us take the example of Botswana: the loss of the reintroduced white rhinos in that country can be largely ascribed to the indifference of the Department of Wildlife and National Parks. During the 1970s over 70 white rhinos were translocated from KwaZulu-Natal (South Africa) to Botswana. It is estimated that natural growth probably doubled this initial population to 150 individuals by the mid-1980s. However, in the latter part of 1992, during the course of an intensive survey, only seven white rhinos were counted. Even taking into account animals that may have been overlooked, the total could not have exceeded 12 rhinos.

A short time later a capture operation was launched to save these animals from the poachers' guns. Only four rhinos could be traced. They were translocated to the Khama Sanctuary. Of these four, two rhinos turned out to be individuals originally translocated from KwaZulu-Natal. A glare of publicity surrounded this exercise and much credit was given to Botswana's Department of Wildlife and National Parks.

However, one cannot help but wonder what these conservation officials were doing while the poachers were decimating the rhino population. Rather than being given credit, officials should have been heavily censured and "high heads" should have rolled!

In July 1984 the Department of National Parks and Wildlife Management of Zimbabwe put into action Operation Stronghold, an attempt to arrest the drastic increase in poaching. Despite the best efforts of some staff members the entire exercise proved to be an unmitigated failure, and the Zimbabwean rhino population has been brought to the brink of extinction. From the middle of 1984 to the end of 1991 at least 954 rhinos were killed for their horns; 145 poachers were shot and four conservation officials lost their lives. The majority of rhinos died in the Zambezi Valley but those elsewhere were not spared the poachers' bullets. Particularly hard hit were the white and black rhinos in the Matabeleland national park, Hwange. The only small populations that have remained largely untouched are those that were introduced to privately owned ranches towards the centre of the country. However, small, until now secure populations on privately owned con-

servancies are now threatened by government land confiscations for the resettlement of rural peasants.

There are now three options for the conservation of rhinos, particularly black rhinos: horn removal, translocation to small and highly protected sanctuaries within the rhino's natural distribution area, and translocation to ranch areas in other countries with a suitable climate and food plants similar to those utilised by rhinos.

Horn removal is a controversial last-ditch attempt to prevent the extinction of the black rhino in some areas. It has been undertaken in the Damaraland-Kaokoveld area of northwestern Namibia and in the Zambezi Valley and elsewhere in Zimbabwe. Some conservation authorities view de-horning with a large degree of apprehension, for the following reasons: it is an acknowledgement that control has been lost over the particular rhino population, and in certain areas it has not proved to be as successful as was originally expected.

The largest populations of both species of rhino, now in South Africa, have not been de-horned but this may have to be done in the future, particularly in the more vulnerable reserves. The de-horning of black rhinos in north-western Namibia,

**Above:** *White rhino bull wallowing, Mkuzi Game Reserve.*

known as Operation Bicornis, was necessitated by a sudden upsurge in poaching. The massive depletion of rhinos to the north had caused the middlemen to move their attentions to the relatively large rhino populations to the south of the Cunene-Zambezi river line. The Namibian authorities had to act, or lose their rhino populations. It was decided to de-horn the black rhinos of Damaraland. These lived in relatively open terrain and, as they had been studied for a decade, the individuals and their home ranges were known. Animals were located, darted and de-horned. Then they were monitored.

One aspect that has worried wildlife managers is the impact that horn removal may have on the behaviour of rhinos. In Damaraland the rhinos rarely, if ever, used their horns when feeding, for example to break high branches. However, animals living in the dense bush of the Zambezi Valley may well do so, and de-horning could have a detrimental effect on them.

Horn removal may also affect the ability of rhinos, particularly cows with small calves, to defend themselves against large predators such as lions and spotted hyaenas. It is unclear what impact, if any, de-horning could have on general interactions between individuals, for instance between a horned and a de-horned rhino.

In May 1992 the government of Zimbabwe, in an act of desperation, embarked on the logistically nightmarish operation to de-horn all of the country's wild rhinos. It was viewed as essential to the survival of these animals in the country that until recently had held Africa's largest national herd of black rhinos. This move followed the experimental de-horning of the Hwange National Park population of white rhinos towards the end of 1991. In the initial capture of 71 animals, five individuals died but in later captures no losses were suffered. Techniques had been refined.

When de-horning a rhino the horns are cut off either with a handsaw or a small chain saw. Then the edges are filed down and the remaining stump covered with Stockholm tar. Unfortunately this is not a permanent solution: the horns, like fingernails, regrow and the entire exercise has to be repeated. The rate of regrowth varies, but the front horn is estimated to regrow at 6,7 cm per year, and the back horn at half this rate. What has to be remembered is that even a small length of horn is saleable. All rhinos should therefore ideally be recaptured and de-horned at least once a year, but the costs would be beyond the means of most countries. In the open country of north-western Namibia, would-be poachers in theory can clearly see whether a rhino is carrying horns, or is de-horned, but in the dense bush of such locations as the Zambezi Valley poachers find it much more difficult to make this determination. A number of de-horned animals have died as a result.

It is certainly preferable to see a live, de-horned rhino in the wild than a bloated and maggot-filled carcass with a bloody, hacked skull; nevertheless it is a sad indictment against humans that these magnificent mammals have to undergo these indignities to save them from people who covet their horns for carved dagger handles as proof of manhood or for medicines of dubious benefit.

The concept of closed sanctuaries, initiated in Kenya, holds out considerable hope for the protection of small populations of rhinos under intensively protected conditions. In Kenya highly protected populations are located on privately owned ranches such as Solio, which lies in the wooded plains between the Aberdares and Mount Kenya, and in small sanctuaries such as Nakuru National Park. Such sanctuaries have the advantage that limited finances can be concentrated and specifically targeted, rather than spread over large parks without any visible benefit. Other advantages are that one can concentrate a greater number of better-equipped guards in a smaller area, and that installing such devices as electric fencing is more economical. For the rhinos an advantage is that they are in closer proximity to each other, which increases their chances of locating each other and mating. In many areas where poaching has

greatly reduced rhino numbers, individuals are now widely scattered, which limits their chances of encountering each other.

The trend towards closed sanctuaries is being followed in Zimbabwe, where small numbers of rhinos are being moved to smaller and more easily controlled areas, away from troublesome national boundaries.

Except for a few populations in South Africa, and possibly in Namibia in the short term, closed sanctuaries offer the only hope for rhinos, particularly the black, to survive in the wild.

The only other option that remains is to establish viable numbers of rhinos, again particularly the black, on other continents. The long-term goal is to be able to reintroduce populations within their former range if demand for rhino horn disappears and conditions once again become favourable. The most suitable countries are determined on the basis of their climate, habitat, food plants and the ability to offer adequate protection. Rhinos have already been sent to the south-western United States of America and to Australia, and the programme will no doubt be expanded in the future.

Existing African populations of the black rhino that are considered to be crucial for survival are those in Cameroon; Damaraland and Etosha in Namibia; the Hluhluwe-Umfolozi-Corridor, Itala, Mkuzi and Kruger in South Africa; Nairobi and Solio in Kenya; Selous in Tanzania; and Hwange and the Midlands Conservancy in Zimbabwe. Key populations of the white rhino are in Garamba in Congo (DR) (the only site remaining for the northern race); the Hluhluwe-Umfolozi-Corridor, Itala, Kruger, Loskop, Manyaleti, Mkuzi, Ndumo, Pilanesberg and Sabi Sand in South Africa and Solio in Kenya (the only viable population of the southern race outside South Africa).

What a sad testimony to the greed of humans that the total African rhino population has been reduced to about 11 000, and is decreasing still.

**Below:** *White rhino cow "growling" at approaching bull.*

# CHAPTER 4

# CARNIVORES

## *Threatened hunters*

Julius Caesar celebrated the consecration of his forum with the
slaughter of 400 lions, one giraffe and 40 elephants ...

C. Guggisberg – *Simba*

Africa has a vast array of carnivore species. They belong to five families. There are at least 73 recognised species and as it is possible that new members of the family Viverridae could be described in the future this total could well rise. Not included in this figure are a further eight species of viverrid living on the island of Madagascar, which lies off the southeastern coast of Africa, and two exotic species. There are 12 species in the dog family (Canidae), 10 species of mustelids (Mustelidae), four members of the hyaena and aardwolf family (Hyaenidae), 10 cat species (Felidae) and 38 species of mongooses, genets and civets (Viverridae). There is, however, some taxonomic uncertainty within several viverrid groups, particularly the genets.

The term "carnivora" simply means "eaters of flesh" but within this diverse order of mammals are many smaller species that could be more correctly described as omnivores. The earliest fossils of members of the Carnivora, belonging to the family Miacidae, date from the Upper Eocene era. Members of this now extinct family were the ancestors of all the carnivores we know today. All the larger carnivores have decreased in num-

ber as a result of direct persecution, because they pose, or are perceived to pose, a threat to domestic livestock and even people. In the past some species have faced eradication programmes, even within exalted temples of conservation such as the Kruger National Park in South Africa.

Some species, such as the large spotted cats, have been heavily hunted for their attractive pelts. Many carnivores are also hunted as a source of meat. Food hunting is particularly heavy within the Congolean-Guinean forest block.

Scientific opinion now is that carnivores, particularly the larger species, are sensitive indicators of the health of any ecological community. When a carnivore species, or group of species, is eradicated or greatly reduced in numbers this loss has a ripple effect and an entire suite of organisms can be threatened.

Apart from direct persecution of carnivores by humans because they are seen as potential predators of domestic stock, and for trophy, meat and pelt hunting, the principal threats facing African carnivores are the ever-increasing human popula-

*Below: Wild dogs* (Lycaon pictus) *at play in the Savuti River, Botswana.* Photo: *Beverly Joubert, ABPL.* **Right:** *The caracal* (Felis caracal) *is considered to be a pest species in the southern part of its range, but is rare and even endangered in some regions.*

tion and the wholesale habitat destruction that goes hand in hand with this growth. Habitat destruction poses a particularly serious threat to the smaller carnivores that occur within tropical lowland forests. Those species in the large, relatively undisturbed forests of Congo (DR) are as far as is known the least threatened, but of grave concern is the long-term survival of species found only in the Upper Guinea forests of west Africa and the isolated forest pockets in east Africa. Even in species where direct persecution is not the principal cause of population declines, a reduction in available habitats causes the loss of adequate prey or food. This does not only apply to carnivores, of course, but to all animals. Habitat loss fragments populations, and they may be reduced to the point where "island pockets" are no longer viable. Genetic diversity may be lost when small sub-populations are isolated from each other. This makes them less resistant to certain infectious diseases and generally reduces their fitness to survive.

Apart from the five carnivore families now represented in Africa, a sixth, the Ursidae, appears in small numbers in the fossil record, even as far south as South Africa. There are poorly documented historical records of the so-called Crowther's bear *(Ursus arctos crowtheri)* from the Atlas Mountains near Tetuan, Spanish Morocco. The presence of bears in the mountains of north Africa in ancient and historical times crops up in the literature but there is no certainty whether these animals occurred naturally in the area or were introduced from Eurasia by invading nations, such as the Romans, Arabs and Ottoman Turks. All of these invaders and colonisers kept bears for sport and entertainment and it can be presumed that from time to time individuals escaped into the wild. Wild bears *(Ursus arctos syriacus)* were still known to occur in what is now northern Israel (Palestine), near the northern shores of the Sea of Galilee in the 1880s and in parts of Syria at least into the 1950s.

Although there are no documented records of the wolf *(Canis lupus arabs)* ever having occurred on the African continent, for completeness' sake we feel we should mention that

these animals still survive on the Sinai Peninsula, a geographical part of Egypt. The population is highly endangered and it is unlikely that more than 30 individuals remain. Their survival is in doubt as they receive no legal protection and the almost total destruction of their wild prey has forced them to resort to feeding primarily on domestic livestock. Their presence in Sinai makes one wonder whether they did not extend their range into continental Africa, even if only marginally, in the past, as before the construction of the Suez Canal there was no physical barrier to prevent access to continental Africa.

In 1981 Blanford's fox *(Vulpes cana)* was recorded for the first time, from Israel. Subsequent records have shown that it is present in Sinai, a geographical part of Egypt. This small fox is apparently a specialist in occupying cliff habitats in Israel and elsewhere, and it was recently confirmed that it occurs on the rugged, arid and zoologically poorly known Red Sea coast of Egypt.

In the following accounts we briefly discuss each family and its representative species in Africa, and cover in more detail those species that are endangered or threatened.

# CANIDAE

## *Dogs*

Of the 12 species of canid, or members of the dog family, that occur on the African continent, only two, the African wild dog *(Lycaon pictus)* and the Ethiopian wolf *(Canis simensis)* are considered to be seriously endangered.

The three species of jackal *(Canis mesomelas, C. adustus* and *C. aureus)* are still widespread and under no threat at this stage, despite the fact that the first, the black-backed jackal, is heavily persecuted in southern Africa as a predator of small domes-

**Above:** *The Ethiopian wolf* (Canis simensis) *is Africa's rarest canid and is threatened by habitat changes, but more particularly by hybridisation with domestic and feral dogs.* Photo: *Claudio Sillero-Zubiri.*

tic stock. In a few regions this jackal has been greatly reduced in numbers but with current control measures it is unlikely that it will face any major threat in the foreseeable future.

The Cape fox *(Vulpes chama)* is restricted to southern Africa and despite the fact that several thousand are killed each year in predator control operations, their overall distributional range has increased. However, in areas of intensive control such as the South African province of Free State, numbers have apparently declined. Bat-eared foxes *(Otocyon megalotis)* occur in two separate populations, one in southern and the other in eastern Africa, and neither is threatened. Research in both areas of Africa indicate that populations are highly susceptible to diseases such as rabies, which cause considerable fluctuations in numbers. However, populations appear to be able to recover rapidly from such outbreaks. Large numbers are killed in problem animal control programmes in South Africa and southern Namibia despite the fact that they are not killers of lambs or goat kids. Many are hunted in Botswana for their skins. They are also frequently run over on roads. However, all observations indicate that they can sustain heavy losses. The bat-eared fox is another species that has greatly expanded its range in southern Africa.

An additional five species of canid are restricted to northern Africa. Little work has been done on any of these animals but the very nature of their arid habitats indicates that all are probably safe at present although occurring at low densities.

The widespread red fox *(Vulpes vulpes)* occurs in north-western Africa, primarily in the Atlas Mountain belt, and in the east in a broad belt southwards along the Nile through Egypt and Sudan. The tiny (1 kg to 1,5 kg) fennec *(Fennecus zerda),* the pale fox *(Vulpes pallida)* and Rüppell's fox *(Vulpes rueppelli)* occupy some of Africa's driest areas. Of the three, only the pale fox is endemic to Africa. Blanford's fox *(Vulpes cana)* is only, so far, known from a limited area of the African Red Sea Hills.

# Ethiopian wolf
## *Canis simensis* Ⓔ

### Description and taxonomy

The Ethiopian wolf, an extremely handsome animal, is rather long-legged. In build and form it closely resembles the coyote of North America. The overall colour is tawny rufous to reddish-brown with clearly defined white underparts, including the throat and chest. Much of the face, the muzzle and the back of the ears are more distinctly reddish. The bushy tail is mostly white towards the base but black towards the tip. Known variously as the Simien fox, Abyssinian wolf and red

| ETHIOPIAN WOLF | |
|---|---|
| **Total length** | ♂ 1,3 m; ♀ 1,2 m |
| **Tail length** | ♂ 31 cm; ♀ 28 cm |
| **Shoulder height** | ♂ 59 cm; ♀ 54 cm |
| **Mass** | ♂ 14-19 kg; ♀ 11-14 kg |
| **Home range** | 2,4-12 sq km |
| **Social structure** | average group size 7; up to 13 adults and young |
| **Sexual maturity** | ♀ 2 years |
| **Gestation** | 60-62 days |
| **Number of young** | probably 2-6 |
| **Diet** | over 90% rodents |
| **Number surviving** | 340-520 |

Below: *Fennec* (Fennecus zerda). Photo: *Antwerp Zoo.*

jackal, this is one of Africa's rarest mammals, as well as being the world's rarest canid and one of its most handsome carnivores. In the local Oromo language it is known as "jedalla farda", or horse's jackal, because of its habit of foraging, on occasion, in the vicinity of domestic livestock.

Much of what we know about this canid comes from the work of two scientists, Sillero-Zubiri and Gottelli. The correct taxonomic status of this wolf has long been in question but recent phylogenetic analyses have shown it to be more closely related to the grey wolf *(Canis lupus)* and the coyote *(Canis latrans)* than to any African canid. It has been suggested that the Ethiopian wolf may be an evolutionary relict of a shared ancestor with the grey wolf which entered north Africa from Eurasia, possibly in the late Pleistocene.

Two subspecies of the Ethiopian wolf are recognised, *Canis simensis simensis* and *C.s. citernii*, the former occurring north of the Rift Valley and the latter to the south-east of the Rift.

### Distribution and habitat

The northern form, *C.s. simensis,* is estimated to number only between 70 and 150 animals in the Simien Mountains National Park, Mount Guna and north-east Shoa in Ethiopia. It has been suggested that this wolf may survive in the rugged country of western Wollo province but no information is available. The south-eastern population, *C.s. citernii*, survives in the Arssi Mountains and west Bale province but the vast majority are located in the Bale Mountains National Park. It is estimated that 205 to 270 wolves live here, constituting perhaps more than half of the entire population. This population is considered to be the only one that is viable. Within the 2 400 sq km

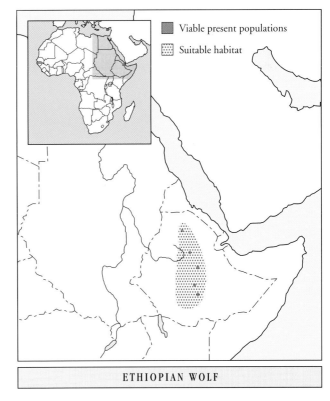

Viable present populations

Suitable habitat

ETHIOPIAN WOLF

of Bale Mountains National Park only the northern areas are occupied by Ethiopian wolves. This wolf is endemic to the Ethiopian Highlands above 3 000 m. It has been recorded at altitudes above 4 000 m. In the past it probably occurred more extensively, as the Afro-alpine moorlands to which it is restricted covered a greater area. During the gradual warming that took place in the late Pleistocene this habitat retreated to higher altitudes, and the wolves were forced into ever smaller, isolated pockets. This forced isolation has been aggravated by increasing human utilisation of the moorlands.

Most favoured habitats are areas of short grass and herbaceous plants where their principal prey, rodents of several species, may reach densities of as much as four tons per square kilometre. Although these wolves have been observed feeding on calves of antelope species, as well as scavenging, rodents form the bulk of their diet. These include the giant molerat (*Tachyoryctes macrocephalus*), which reaches almost 1 kg, and several smaller species which range in mass from 90 g to 120 g.

## Behaviour

Although these wolves are social canids, much of their hunting is done alone. Each group, or pack, defends a territory against intruders but up to 70% of matings observed in one study involved pack females being covered by males from packs in adjacent territories. Mating takes place between August and December. When pups are present in a den both parents as well as subadults feed them by regurgitation.

## Conservation

The Ethiopian wolf has been forced into smaller ranges by long-term climatic changes, but encroachment by people is forcing it to the brink of extinction. Several factors have been implicated in the animal's catastrophic decline. They include loss of habitat as a result of increasing settlement of favoured areas by humans, particularly in the north. People's domestic herds overgraze and trample the land, resulting not only in a loss of habitat for the wolves

*Above: The wild dog* (Lycaon pictus) *is Africa's most threatened large carnivore, mainly because each pack needs vast tracts of savanna in which to roam and hunt.*

| AFRICAN WILD DOG | |
|---|---|
| *Male and female dogs are similar in size. Southern animals are on average slightly larger than those in eastern populations.* | |
| **Total length** | 1,05-1,5 m |
| **Tail length** | 30-40 cm |
| **Shoulder height** | 65-80 cm |
| **Mass** | 20-36 kg (average 25 kg) |
| **Home range** | 450-2 500 sq km (up to 3 800 sq km) |
| **Social structure** | packs, usually 10-15 adults and subadults, but also smaller and larger |
| **Gestation** | 69-73 days |
| **Number of young** | 2-19 (average 7-10) |
| **Weaned** | 10 weeks |
| **Diet** | mainly small and medium-sized antelope |
| **Number surviving** | 3 000-5 500 |

but also in drastic reductions in their principal prey, the rodents. However, of even greater concern are the large populations of domestic dogs that cross-breed with the wolves, resulting in the loss of genetic purity. Dogs also compete for food (rodents) with the wolves and are carriers of diseases that could be transmitted to the wolves and wipe out the remaining isolated populations. As the numbers of wolves decline they become more vulnerable to food competition from such species as golden and black-backed jackals.

The future facing the Ethiopian wolf is one of the bleakest of any of Africa's many threatened species.

# African wild dog
### *Lycaon pictus*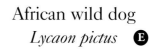

## Description and taxonomy

This is Africa's largest wild canid, with long legs, large rounded ears and a very variable coat pattern. The body is blotched with black, white, yellow and grey and each individual can be identified by its own distinctive colour distribution. The tail is bushy and frequently white-tipped.

Until recently it was generally held that all African wild dog populations were the same but it has now been shown that animals in southern and eastern Africa are genetically distinct from each other. In western Africa no known viable populations survive and it seems likely that the African wild dog will become extinct in that part of the continent in the near future,

**Above:** *The Arabian wolf* (Canis lupus arabs) *has been reduced to perhaps 30 individuals on the Sinai Peninsula.*

without our ever having discovered its genetic relationship with wild dogs in other areas.

## Distribution and habitat

Apart from areas of dense tropical lowland forest and some true desert stretches, the African wild dog was once found throughout sub-Saharan Africa, with populations even extending into the southern Sahara Desert.

This canid is now extinct, or nearly so, in 19 sub-Saharan countries. Populations are small (below 100) and probably non-viable in a further nine countries. It is possible that a remnant population reported from southern Algeria in the late 1980s still survives. Up to the early 1980s potentially viable populations probably still survived widely in west Africa. They are now but a memory except for small numbers surviving in but not entirely confined to Niokolo-Kobo National Park in Senegal, Bouda-Ndiida National Park in Cameroon and the Ouadi Rime-Ouadi Achim Faunal Reserve in Chad.

Potentially viable populations remain in only six countries: Botswana, Kenya, South Africa (Kruger National Park only) Tanzania, Zambia and Zimbabwe. Namibia could also be included in the latter group but most packs occur in the northeast and free movement of animals takes place between this country and neighbouring Botswana.

Wild dogs are able to utilise a wide array of habitat types from desert to relatively high rainfall regions, open savanna, light to moderately bushed country and occasionally forest. They have even been recorded on the snow-capped peak of Mount Kilimanjaro.

The decline in range and numbers of the wild dog has been frighteningly rapid throughout its range, with the pace increasing in more recent times. For example, the wild dog once ranged throughout most of South Africa but the last known

animals south of the Orange River were shot on 16 July 1925 at Gray's Halt, Amabele, in the then Eastern Province. Today the only population in the country is found in the Kruger National Park (1993 estimate: 375 dogs) and in adjacent privately owned game reserves.

## Behaviour

This much maligned, intelligent and highly social animal has had little chance given the bad publicity it has received in the past, and continues to receive in many areas today.

Maugham, writing in his *Wild game in Zambesia* of 1914, says it all about attitudes:

> *Let us consider for a moment that abomination – that blot upon the many interesting wild things – the murderous Wild Dog. It will be an excellent day for African game and its preservation when means can be devised for its complete extermination.*

Active eradication programmes were implemented by the colonial authorities. Although they were aimed at most large carnivores, it would seem that special efforts were made to "rid Africa of this bloodthirsty killer".

And it seems little has changed. An article (The Serengeti: the glory of life) which appeared as recently as 1986 in *National Geographic,* states:

> *in the shade of the tailgate lay one sullen dog, yellow-eyed, mud-colored, thick-footed, head on its forepaws – an eerie embodiment of the hound of hell.*

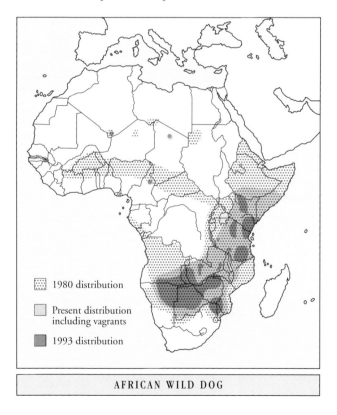

1980 distribution

Present distribution including vagrants

1993 distribution

**AFRICAN WILD DOG**

gitated meat by other members of the group.

Hunting is undertaken by the pack. The dogs move slowly towards the intended prey and gradually increase the tempo as the targeted animal starts to move away. Once the target is selected the pack rarely deviates and will maintain the chase for several kilometres. The wild dog has the highest overall hunting success rate (more than 70%) of all the large carnivores, compared with less than 50% for lion and spotted hyaena. Lower success rates have been recorded and seem to be influenced by the season and type of prey taken.

The wild dog has gained its bad reputation from the manner in which it bites and tears at larger prey until it weakens from loss of blood, or shock, and can be overpowered. Packs only kill for their immediate needs and, contrary to popular belief, do not kill wantonly.

Wild dogs have been recorded as feeding on a wide range of mammals including buffalo, plains zebra, hares and rodents, but by far the bulk of their prey consists of small to medium-sized antelope. The most abundant species are usually taken; for example in the Kruger National Park they hunt mainly impala, in parts of east Africa mainly Thomson's gazelle and in the Serengeti ecosystem mainly blue wildebeest.

African wild dogs are not territorial but roam vast home ranges, except for about two to three months of the year when the pups are too small to keep up with the pack and hunting is limited to a smaller range. Within these home ranges they roam widely and often for long distances, this being particularly important in dispersing young animals as it increases the likelihood of genetic exchange and therefore long-term viability.

## Conservation

Throughout their range wild dogs are under considerable threat, even where they receive legal protection. Take for example the case when, during the course of 1988, a farmer bordering on the Kruger National Park (South Africa) shot 20 African wild dogs that had strayed out of the conservation area.

The fact that packs are becoming increasingly isolated from each other by human influences, decimation of prey species and direct persecution holds serious implications for the viability of this magnificent carnivore. Such isolation has almost certainly resulted in a reduction in genetic exchange between packs. In a healthy situation there is dispersal of non-breeding female and male dogs to join other packs, or to form new packs, thus ensuring genetic interchange. Today, as packs become more isolated, breeding takes place only within the pack, and this inbreeding can be detrimental to the dogs' ability to resist epizootics and parasites. Lack of genetic diversity can also result in infertility, higher juvenile mortality and abnormalities.

Wild dogs share with most other wild creatures the dangers inherent in loss of habitat, but because of their normally low population densities and their utilisation of huge home ranges, they are even more vulnerable to fragmentation. Apart from the loss of habitat and natural prey species, wild dogs still suffer direct persecution by people, as in the past. Between 1956

**Top**: *One of the last Barbary lions in captivity, a fine male in Frankfurt Zoo.* Photo: *Wolfgang Frey.*

**Above**: *A leopard* (Panthera pardus) *shot for killing sheep in Western Cape province, South Africa, where despite protective legislation they are still heavily persecuted.* Photo: *Jaco van Deventer.*

We could fill many pages with such quotations but we feel that the point has been made. In much the same way that the public at large were fed inaccurate accounts of the ferocity of the gorilla, they were regaled with tales of this "vicious, bloodthirsty and wanton killer". The truth is quite different.

The behaviour of the wild dog has been well studied in several major conservation areas in eastern and southern Africa and several long-term studies are in progress at present. The wild dog is a highly social canid, living in packs that vary in size from region to region. Packs consist of a number of related adult males and one or more females from a different pack. Usually only the dominant female in any pack will successfully raise pups. She and her young at the den are fed with regur-

and 1975 at least 3 404 wild dogs were killed in Zimbabwe (then Rhodesia); today fewer than 600 dogs are believed to survive in that country.

A major concern is that wild dog populations appear to be increasingly affected by a number of different diseases. Here again genetic isolation could well be playing a part, as well as increasing contacts with growing populations of domestic and feral dogs. Rabies has had a serious impact on some populations, and killed 20 of a 22-member wild dog pack in the Masai Mara in south-western Kenya in 1989. An anthrax outbreak in 1987 killed many wild dogs in the Luangwa Valley in Zambia. They are also believed to be highly susceptible to canine distemper.

Although the plight of the African wild dog is receiving greater attention today than ever before, its long-term survival outside a handful of very large national parks in southern and east Africa seems highly unlikely. Can wild dogs survive these problems without genetic intervention by humans? Attempts to reintroduce wild dogs into Etosha National Park in northern Namibia have failed, for various reasons. Wild dogs have also been released on a large private nature reserve in Northern Province (South Africa). Early observations indicate some success but it seems doubtful that the dogs can be kept within this area.

**Below**: *The cheetah* (Acinonyx jubatus) *is the most threatened large cat in Africa.* PHOTO: *John Carlyon.*

# FELIDAE

## Cats

The cats are highly specialised carnivores. They are well represented in Africa: 10 species occur here, of which three are endemic to the continent. The remainder occur into Eurasia but generally at much lower population densities than in Africa. For example, the only surviving lion *(Panthera leo)* population occurring outside Africa is located in the Gir Forest in north-western India and numbers fewer than 300. Cheetah *(Acinonyx jubatus)* were once found widely outside Africa, through the Middle East and as far eastwards as central India, but the few remnant populations can now be considered ecologically extinct. Possibly slightly more than 200 individuals survive in Iran, but the vast majority of cheetah occur in Africa. The leopard *(Panthera pardus)* still has a wide African and Asian distribution. Although it has been eradicated or greatly reduced in numbers in some regions, it is still by far Africa's and Asia's most successful big cat. It is the only large cat still to survive close to the southern tip and the north-western tip of Africa, although the population surviving in the Atlas Mountains of Morocco is probably coming close to extinction. Nevertheless, the major populations of these three big cats survive in Africa.

| CHEETAH | |
| --- | --- |
| Total length | 1,8-2,2 m |
| Tail length | 60-80 cm |
| Shoulder height | 80 cm |
| Mass | 30-72 kg (average 40-60 kg); ♂ heavier than ♀ |
| Home range | 40-1 500 sq km |
| Sexual maturity | ♂ 30-36 months; ♀ 21-33 months |
| Gestation | 92 days |
| Number of young | 1-5 (average 3) |
| Birth mass | 250-300 g |
| Diet | medium-sized mammals (about 60 kg); birds |
| Number surviving | 9 000-12 000 |

The caracal *(Felis caracal)* is still widely distributed in Africa, being absent only from tropical forest regions. It is reported to occur even in the central Sahara Desert, although only in association with the principal mountain ranges. Large numbers are killed each year in South Africa and southern Namibia during predator control programmes because of depredations on domestic small stock, but it is in this region that they reach their highest known population densities. They are considered to be endangered, or at best seriously threatened, throughout their Middle Eastern and Asian range.

A cat of similar size, the serval *(F. serval)* has a wide sub-Saharan range but is largely absent from dense forest and desert areas. Although it has become extinct in the south and west of South Africa in recent years and greatly reduced in north-western Africa, overall it is under no serious threat. In some areas it occurs at fairly high densities.

The African wild cat *(F. libyca/silvestris)* is absent only from forest, the coastal Namib Desert and fairly large areas of the Sahara Desert. In some taxonomic circles this cat is believed to be the same species as the Eurasian wild cat. Although it is still abundant and widespread in some regions, for example South Africa, the major threat to its long-term survival is the ease with which it hybridises with the domestic cat. Feral domestic cats are frequently encountered many kilometres from human settlements. Not only is interbreeding a problem, but feral cats also compete with a range of small wild carnivore species for rodent, bird and reptile prey.

A species that is somewhat larger but similar in appearance to the wild cat is the so-called swamp, or jungle, cat *(F. chaus).* It occurs widely in Asia but in Africa is restricted to the Nile Delta and an unknown distance southwards. Given the extremely high human population in this area and the possibility of hybridisation with domestic cats, it could well be endangered within its African range. Although there are some old

records of this species from the mountains of southern Algeria, it seems unlikely that it would have occurred in this habitat.

The sand cat *(F. margarita)* occurs widely in the Sahara Desert and through southern Asia to about Afghanistan. Given the nature of its chosen environment, it is likely to occur at low densities but is probably secure.

The African golden cat *(Profelis aurata)* is restricted to tropical lowland forest areas of central and western Africa. Virtually nothing is known of its ecology. It is probably under pressure as a result of habitat destruction, particularly in the western forests. The small spotted, or black-footed, cat *(Felis nigripes)* is a rare southern African endemic.

No felid occurring in Africa can be considered to be highly endangered, with the possible exception of the swamp cat. It is true that other species are declining, even if only on a regional scale, because of habitat destruction, direct persecution and a whole host of other reasons. However, we believe that only three species deserve coverage here, namely the cheetah, lion and small spotted cat.

# Cheetah
## *Acinonyx jubatus* Ⓥ

### Description and taxonomy

The cheetah derives its name from the Hindi word "chita" which simply means the spotted one.

This is a tall, slender cat, with long legs and tail and a small head. Overall body colour ranges from dirty white to pale fawn

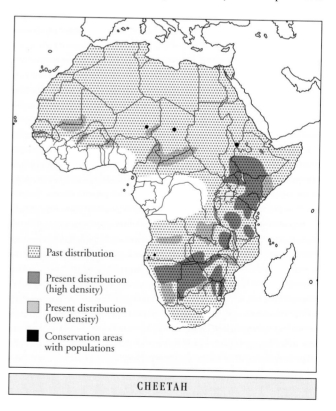

- ░ Past distribution
- ▓ Present distribution (high density)
- ▒ Present distribution (low density)
- █ Conservation areas with populations

**CHEETAH**

with a liberal covering of solid black spots and a black "tear-mark" that runs from the corner of each eye to a corner of the mouth. The cheetah is the only cat that does not have fully retractile claws.

Much has been made of the so-called king cheetah, a genetic mutation that results in animals having a magnificently blotched coat. Until recently all known specimens were recorded from the north-eastern parts of southern Africa, centred on Zimbabwe. There is now, however, a single record of this mutation from wooded savanna in the west African country of Burkina Faso.

Although several cheetah subspecies have been recognised it seems unlikely that many, if any, are valid. Current thinking is that animals occurring in sub-Saharan Africa are probably all *Acinonyx jubatus jubatus*. Asian and Saharan cheetahs are grouped as *A.j. venaticus*. However, it may be that all African cheetahs are better kept under the first subspecies; after all, it was probably only recently that the animals of southern Algeria and northern Niger were cut off from populations to the south. In fact it is possible, given the remote nature of much of this region, that some occasional interchange still occurs between these small and increasingly fragmented populations.

## Distribution and habitat

This elegant "greyhound" cat was once tamed and kept in great numbers by several Asian and Middle Eastern rulers for hunting gazelles and other beasts of the chase, at least as early as 4 000 years ago. Akbar the Great was said to have kept a hunting "stable" of 1 000 cheetahs. Today they have all but disappeared from the great steppes and plains of Asia.

The cheetah once occurred throughout Africa, with the exception of tropical lowland forest. Contrary to popular belief they also make use of various woodland types. They penetrated deep into the Sahara, where remnant populations still survive to this day in southern Algeria (Tassili N'Ajjer and Hoggar) and Air, Tenere and the Termit Massif in northern Niger. These animals probably form one and the same population. Even as late as 1976 cheetahs were recorded in the northern Sahara (Bechar) in Algeria, and around 1960 in southern Tunisia (east of the Eastern Grand Erg). A tiny population is still said to survive in the inhospitable Qattara Depression in northern Egypt. Although it would appear that this population is totally isolated, given the nature of the region, movements to the south and south-west cannot be ruled out completely.

The cheetah's sub-Saharan range has now become seriously fragmented, particularly in west Africa where overall densities are very low. The two principal population blocks are located in eastern and southern Africa. Of interest is that by far the greatest numbers occur outside the large conservation areas. This is probably because other large predators, particularly lions, reach relatively high densities within parks and reserves and the cheetah is unable to compete with these more powerful animals. Cheetahs are frequently robbed of their kills and not infrequently killed themselves in unevenly matched

**Above:** *Cheetahs have their last stronghold in Namibia, but even there they are in serious decline.*

encounters. A number of the smaller and more isolated populations, particularly in west Africa, can be expected to die out within the next decade.

It is estimated that no more than 12 000 cheetahs survive in the wild but the true figure could well be below 9 000, and it is continuing to decline.

Cheetahs are now extinct, or close to it, in at least 10 countries within their former range. They are greatly reduced but possibly viable if adequate conservation programmes were implemented in a further 11, but this is deemed unlikely to happen in most of these countries. The most important populations now survive in Kenya and Tanzania in east Africa (but no recent estimates are available) and in Namibia and Botswana in southern Africa (total estimate between 3 000 and 5 000). The estimate for Namibia is between 2 000 and 3 000, of which as many as 95% occur on privately owned land. It is believed that the Namibian cheetah population has declined by half since 1980. In South Africa the natural cheetah populations are primarily restricted to the Kalahari Gemsbok National Park (over 60 individuals) and the Kruger National Park (about 200). The cheetah is no longer considered to be endangered in South Africa because of high breeding success and substantial numbers in captivity. This is very short-sighted as few areas are suitable, either in size or prey base, for reintroduction of cheetahs. It is akin to saying that as there are several thousand addax in captivity, if only a few hundred in the wild, their protective status can be downgraded.

Cheetahs make use of open as well as woodland savanna and various woodland types previously thought to be unsuitable for these cats. Although the cheetah is frequently portrayed stalking and then sprinting at high speed to catch prey, it is obviously energy-saving if the cheetah can make as close an approach as possible. This is best done where vegetation cover is fairly dense, but not so dense as to hinder movement. We know of an introduced population that specialises in using dense bush cover on hill slopes to hunt helmeted guineafowl. Despite this versatility in habitat usage, cheetah numbers still continue to decline and their range to shrink.

## Behaviour

The cheetah normally occurs singly, in pairs, in related male groups or in small family parties consisting of a female and her cubs. Group sizes are variable but they seem to be on average smaller in east Africa. The reasons for this are not properly understood but could have something to do with the high number of competing predators in east Africa.

Adult males move singly or in bachelor groups but apparently do not always establish territories. Females, at least in some studies, were found to hold territories and defend them against intruding females but not males. Female cheetahs in Serengeti (Tanzania) and on Namibian ranches have been shown to have much larger ranges than males; in Namibia a range averages 1 500 sq km and in Serengeti 800 sq km. Nomadic males in Namibia have been recorded as covering some 800 sq km but one study found that groups of males in Serengeti defend territories of only 40 sq km. Findings in the Kruger National Park (South Africa), where prey species are non-migratory, indicate that both male and female cheetahs occupy small home ranges of similar size, on average 175 sq km.

Cheetahs have a long, drawn-out and complex courtship, leading after seven to 14 days to the female coming into oestrus. The female remains receptive to males for up to 15 days.

Cheetah cub mortality is very high, particularly where there are other large predators. This mortality ranges from a recorded 43% in Nairobi National Park to a whopping 90-98% in Serengeti National Park (Tanzania), where mortality of adult male cheetahs is also as high as 50% as a result of competition for territories.

The main prey consists of medium to small ungulates and the young of larger species such as greater kudu and eland. Cheetahs also take such small animals as hares, guineafowl and any other birds, even ostrich. Diet varies according to area and availability of prey species; for example in the Kruger National Park they show a preference for impala, which is abundant, and for Thomson's gazelle in the Serengeti-Masai Mara system.

## Conservation

Apart from direct persecution of cheetahs by people, which includes shooting and trapping despite their protected status in many areas, there are at least two more factors that threaten their survival: genetic homogeneity and interspecific competition with other predators, particularly in conservation areas. Loss of habitat also poses a serious problem.

Cheetahs show a very high level of genetic homogeneity, which means that there is great similarity and very little diversity in the genetic makeup of different populations. There is considerable discussion on the reasons for this, but no clarity. The consequences of genetic homogeneity might be highly detrimental, but no one is sure exactly what these consequences really are. Some authorities hold that this lack of genetic diversity could make cheetahs increasingly vulnerable to disease and could lower breeding success. However, research to date has not pinpointed any particular problems resulting from genetic homogeneity.

Cheetahs are highly vulnerable to interspecific competition with other large predators, including lion, spotted hyaena, leopard and jackal. This takes the form of direct predation on cheetah cubs, the occasional killing of adult cheetahs, and cheetahs being chased off their kills by other carnivores. This competition is a particular problem in conservation areas where other large carnivores are abundant, whereas in areas where there are few competing carnivores the cheetah reaches comparatively high densities. It seems certain that if we rely on existing conservation areas to preserve the cheetah we will lose the battle for its continued survival in the wild.

# Lion
## *Panthera leo*

## Description

This is the largest of the African big cats. Male lions are considerably larger than lionesses. The adult male usually carries a mane of long hair which extends from the sides of the face onto the neck, shoulders and chest, and varies in colour from

| LION | |
|---|---|
| **Total length** | ♂ 2,5-3,3 m; ♀ 2,3-2,7 m |
| **Tail length** | 1 m |
| **Shoulder height** | ♂ 1,2 m; ♀ 1 m |
| **Mass** | ♂ 150-225 kg; ♀ 110-152 kg |
| **Home range** | 26-220 sq km, even over 2 000 sq km |
| **Social structure** | prides, 3-30 or more |
| **Sexual maturity** | ♂ 26-30 months |
| | ♀ about 40 months (first pregnancy) |
| **Gestation** | 100-114 days |
| **Number of young** | 1-6 (average 2-3) |
| **Birth mass** | 1,5 kg |
| **Diet** | medium to large mammals (mainly ungulates); mice to young elephants |
| **Life span (wild)** | ♂ 12 years; ♀ 15-16 years |

**Above:** *A fine male Kalahari lion* (Panthera leo).

blond to black. The body hair is short and ranges in colour from reddish-grey to pale tawny. The tail is the same colour, but tipped with slightly longer, dark hair. Small cubs are faintly spotted on the sides but this usually disappears with age.

Lions have played a major role in the lives of humans for thousands of years. They have been a symbol of power and majesty, and a source of inspiration for warriors and rulers. They feature prominently in spiritual and magical rituals, folklore and myths. They have featured in the artwork of many peoples and empires ever since the Stone Age.

Numerous races and subspecies of lion have been described from Africa, a number based on zoo specimens. However, variation is great even within any one population. We therefore prefer to regard all lions as belonging to *Panthera leo leo;* this is in line with modern taxonomic thinking.

Two races that were (and still are by some) recognised as having occurred at opposite ends of the continent, the so-called Cape (south) and Barbary (north-west) lions, are now extinct. The Barbary lion persisted until the end of the last century and possibly into the early part of this century. The validity of these separate races, despite publications listing slight differences in measurements and pelage details, is questionable. These populations were once contiguously linked with other populations; isolation has been a relatively recent development resulting from circumstances caused by humans.

## Distribution and habitat

The lion, "king of beasts", once occurred virtually throughout Africa, except for the lowland tropical forest belt and the central Sahara. Lions also occurred widely in Eurasia, throughout North America and at least into the northern areas of South America. They reached their peak distribution about 10 000 years ago, but then their range started to shrink rapidly. In the western hemisphere the arrival of advanced hunter-gatherers near the end of the Pleistocene era probably resulted in competition for prey species.

The lion's decline in Europe is believed to have coincided with the development of dense and extensive forests. It managed to hold its own in south-eastern Europe until about 2 000 years ago, when the last lions were killed in the Balkan Peninsula. Populations in the Middle East were probably close to extinction at the time of the Crusades.

No more than 300 lions now survive in the wild outside Africa, all in the Gir Forest in India, in circumstances that are to a large extent artificial.

Although still widely distributed in sub-Saharan Africa, lion populations are becoming increasingly fragmented and isolated from each other. This is particularly serious in west Africa where this cat and many other species are largely restricted to conservation areas. In South Africa, Zimbabwe, Namibia and increasingly in Botswana, lion populations are also mainly confined to national parks and game reserves. Eastern Africa still has fairly substantial lion numbers outside formal conservation areas but even here they are being squeezed out of areas where they are coming into conflict with people and livestock.

Lion populations of varying levels of viability are known to occur in 70 African conservation areas. Lions are believed to be extinct, or nearly so, in 10 sub-Saharan countries.

There is no accurate estimate of the overall size of the lion population, although we can make some reasonably accurate assessments. Our personal estimate of the present lion population, based on several regional surveys and the available literature, is fewer than 50 000 and falling. We know that populations have declined steeply throughout the lion's range, at a steadily accelerating pace. In the 1950s there were possibly

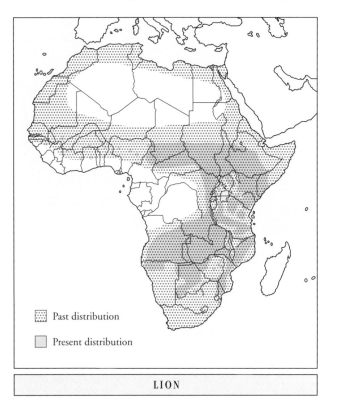

Past distribution

Present distribution

**LION**

as many as 400 000 lions on the continent, but by the mid-1970s the total had probably been more than halved.

Namibia now has no more than 600 lions. The vast majority are confined to conservation areas and wanderers are soon eradicated by farmers. In Zimbabwe there are over 1 000 lions, most being found in the national parks and safari blocks. In South Africa viable lion populations are restricted to the Kruger (over 2 000 individuals in 1993) and Kalahari Gemsbok national parks (over 150 individuals). There are small reintroduced populations in some reserves, most notably the Hluhluwe-Umfolozi-Corridor complex in KwaZulu-Natal province. Lions are able to live in a richly varied range of habitats, from high rainfall to desert. The most favoured habitats are open and lightly wooded savanna with some dense cover, and particularly areas that attract large herds of antelope and other ungulates. However, in some areas lion do, or did, occupy forest fringes and riverine woodland.

## Behaviour

Lion behaviour has been studied in great detail in a handful of national parks, such as Kruger, Etosha, Kalahari Gemsbok, Chobe, Serengeti, Masai Mara and Nairobi, but no attempts have been made to do research on this cat outside proclaimed parks and reserves.

Lions live in complex social groupings known as prides, each consisting of a relatively stable core of related females, their dependent offspring and what is known as a "coalition" of two or more adult males. Solitary males may also hold tenure over a pride under certain circumstances.

On maturing, female cubs may stay with their birth pride or leave in a group to form a new pride, but young males disperse from the birth pride and form coalitions until mature enough to take over a pride themselves. First attempts at takeovers start when males are older than four years. Competition between dominant males and new coalitions for pride tenure is intense. Most males hold tenure for only two to three years; occasionally longer. Larger coalitions are usually able to defend their rights to the pride for longer.

When new males drive away a group of pride males, the new animals usually kill any cubs in the pride. If the new coalition of males is able to hold the pride against potential usurpers, these males have proved themselves suitable sires. The lionesses respond by coming into oestrus some three months after the takeover. During the period of transition the lionesses apparently do not conceive; they only do so once the coalition has established its superiority.

Pride females often conceive at approximately the same time. This has the advantage that cubs can suckle from any lactating lioness, which means the maximum food and maternal care are available to them.

Most hunting is undertaken by lionesses but the males usually take priority when feeding on a kill. Coalitions of males without pride tenure hunt successfully but once such males have taken over a pride much of the work is left to the females.

Prey preferences are varied and differ from region to region. The most common prey are medium to large ungulates, including buffalo and giraffe, many antelope species, plains zebra and warthog. Young elephants, hippos, rhinos and even mice are also eaten, but more rarely. Man-eating is recorded from time to time. The most celebrated case occurred in Kenya during railway construction early in this century (described in *The man-eaters of Tsavo* by J.H. Patterson). Mass movements of refugees in recent years through lion country have resulted in increases in man-eating. Places where this has occurred are the Kruger National Park (South Africa) and on the border between Mozambique and Tanzania.

Prides hunting in the same region may specialise in different killing methods, or prefer different prey; for example, certain lion prides in the Kalahari have become adept at hunting porcupines. Lions will readily expropriate kills made by other predators, and they are not averse to scavenging.

Although lions will drink if surface water is available, they can survive long on fluids from prey and even wild fruits.

## Conservation

Despite the important role these magnificent social cats have played in the life and history of humans, we are slowly but surely pushing them ever closer to the abyss of extinction.

Lions are generally not tolerated outside conservation areas and they are heavily persecuted as a predator of stock or perceived threat to people. Over much of their range and former range, habitats have been greatly modified, domestic stock has replaced their natural prey species, and there are many more people. Lions are shot, trapped, poisoned and harassed. We have encountered several incidents where carcasses of cattle had been laced with glass shards and fragments, which resulted in a number of lion deaths. In one case in eastern Caprivi, Namibia, this method killed a lioness and two large cubs. Many poisons are readily available and are not infrequently used with devastating success.

In some countries, such as Botswana and Zimbabwe, some areas of state land are set aside as hunting blocks and these are rented by hunting safari operators for their clients. Many of these blocks lie adjacent to national parks and game reserves with lion populations. It is believed that excessive shooting of male lions in these hunting areas has resulted in a general depletion of lion populations not only in the blocks themselves but also in the adjacent conservation areas.

Lions are becoming increasingly rare outside conservation areas, as the human population grows and the lions' prey base shrinks. This is almost certain to result in all of Africa's lions being restricted to large national parks and game reserves. This has already occurred over much of west and southern Africa, and is becoming more common elsewhere.

The highly publicised George and Joy Adamson lion-release saga in Kenya did a great deal to increase conservation awareness in the world at large and develop interest in the continent's wildlife, but in many ways damaged the cause of lion conservation. It resulted in the disruption of wild resident lion prides and an increase in the killing of cattle both by dispersing lions and inexperienced reintroduced animals. The local people could naturally not feel the same sympathy as outsiders for lions which were killing their stock. The reintroductions also caused cases of man-eating in areas where this had not previously been recorded, as well as unnecessary and possibly deleterious infusions of genetic material from geographically distant lion populations. Although this aspect is as yet poorly understood, its implications should not be overlooked.

In South Africa several recent releases of lions in small privately owned game reserves have taken place to lure visitors with the Big Five, but at least two tourists have paid with their lives. Reintroductions of lion are fraught with difficulties and generally end in failure. They simply create bad publicity for *Panthera leo* and do nothing to improve the plight of lion populations as a whole.

Under existing conditions there is no future for the lion outside large formal conservation areas. The number and range of lions will continue to decline; this holds the long-term danger of loss of genetic fitness.

# Small spotted cat
## *Felis nigripes* Ⓡ

### Description and taxonomy

With the sand cat of the Sahara Desert, the small spotted cat is Africa's smallest felid. It is a very handsome animal.

Two distinctly marked and coloured subspecies are recognised. *Felis nigripes nigripes* occurs in the northern part of the range and *F.n. thomasi* in the south.

The fur of the northern race is pale tawny to almost white with red-brown spots. The southern race is reddish-fawn with black spotting. The tail is black-ringed and has a black tip. The chest, throat and chin are white with two or three distinct dark bands on the throat.

| SMALL SPOTTED CAT | |
|---|---|
| **Total length** | 50-63 cm |
| **Tail length** | 16 cm |
| **Shoulder height** | 20 cm |
| **Mass** | ♂ 1,6-2,1 kg; ♀ 0,8-1,6 kg |
| **Social structure** | solitary |
| **Gestation** | 63-68 days |
| **Number of young** | 1-3 |
| **Diet** | opportunistic: rodents, hares, birds, insects, carrion |

**Above:** *Restricted to southern Africa, the small spotted cat* (Felis nigripes) *has only recently been studied in the wild.*

## Distribution and habitat

This small cat is endemic to southern Africa and restricted to its drier western and central areas. It occurs at low densities in Namibia, Botswana, South Africa and marginally into Lesotho. Although it has not as yet been recorded in the Kalahari sands of western Zimbabwe, it is likely to occur there. We believe that it may occur more extensively in north-western Namibia, towards the Angolan border. It is present in several conservation areas but at low population levels.

This cat shows a marked preference for open plains with some low vegetation cover. In Western Cape province, South Africa, it occurs right to the coast and in dry hill country.

## Behaviour

Until recently most of our knowledge of this cat was based on museum specimens, road casualties, observations of animals in captivity and the occasional casual observation, but the field work of Alexander Sliwa is starting to reveal a little more about the secretive life of this beautiful felid.

Small spotted cats are primarily nocturnal and solitary hunters, and feed opportunistically on virtually anything they can overpower. They frequently establish dens in hollow termite mounds. This habit has resulted in one of their local names in Eastern Cape province (South Africa): the "anthill tiger". Apart from holes excavated by such species as aardvark and springhares, hollow termite mounds offer them the only shelter on dry, open plains.

Although little is known about this cat, or the sand cat *(Felis margarita)* of the Sahara, their behaviour is probably similar.

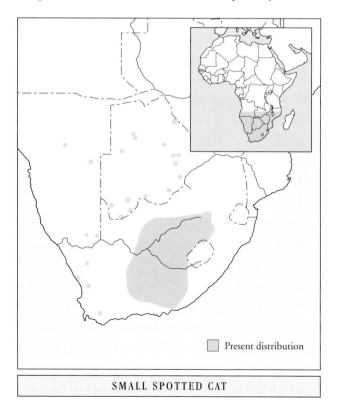

Present distribution

SMALL SPOTTED CAT

**Above:** *The most numerous of Africa's three species of hyaena, the spotted hyaena* (Crocuta crocuta), *has disappeared from many parts of its former range and occurs nowhere in high densities.*

## Conservation

We know so little about this cat that it is difficult to assess its conservation status. It is generally agreed that population densities are low throughout its range, and that this cat could be vulnerable to random, non-selective predator control programmes. The fact that it readily scavenges from carcasses exposes the small spotted cat to poison campaigns to control the black-backed jackal, a canid that occurs throughout the small spotted cat's range. The potential threat faced by the small spotted cat is even higher than that of the sand cat of the Sahara Desert, which also apparently occurs at low densities.

# HYAENIDAE

## *Hyaenas*

Three hyaena species occur on the African continent. The spotted *(Crocuta crocuta)* and brown *(Hyaena brunnea)* hyaenas are endemic to Africa but the striped hyaena *(H. hyaena)* is widely distributed in northern Africa, through the Middle East and eastwards as far as India.

Depending on one's taxonomic point of view there is also a fourth member of this family, the aardwolf *(Proteles cristatus)*. Some authorities place the aardwolf in its own family, the Protelidae. It is widespread in southern Africa, with a separate population far away in north-eastern Africa. Aardwolf occur at fairly low densities. These harmless termite and ant eaters are sometimes wrongly accused of killing sheep and goats and are on occasion deliberately killed. In stock-farming areas they are frequently killed in eradication programmes aimed at such species as the black-backed jackal and caracal. In Namaqualand (South Africa) they are hunted as a delicacy by some people. They have declined in some areas but do not face any major population declines at this stage.

Although all three hyaenas have seen declines both in numbers and range, we will only briefly look at the widespread spotted hyaena and the brown hyaena, a southern African endemic.

# Spotted hyaena
## *Crocuta crocuta* Ⓓ

### Description and taxonomy

Most people are familiar with the appearance of the hyaena, if only from myths and legends that portray it as a messenger of evil and carrier of witches and wizards. The heavily built forequarters, which stand higher than the rump, and the large head with prominent round ears make for easy identification. Body hair colour is variable but a spattering of dark brown spots and blotches gives this animal its common name.

| SPOTTED HYAENA | |
|---|---|
| **Total length** | 1,2-1,8 m |
| | (♀ larger than ♂) |
| **Tail length** | 25 cm |
| **Shoulder height** | 85 cm |
| **Mass** | 60-80 kg |
| **Home range** | 25-2 000 sq km |
| **Social structure** | groups or clans of 3-15 or more (up to 80) |
| **Sexual maturity** | ♂ 2 years; ♀ 3 years |
| **Gestation** | 110 days |
| **Number of young** | 1-2 (rarely 4) |
| **Birth mass** | 1,5 kg |
| **Diet** | they hunt large and medium-sized ungulates, and scavenge |

### Distribution and habitat

Spotted hyaenas have disappeared or been greatly reduced in numbers throughout much of southern Africa, where they are now largely restricted to conservation areas. There have also been considerable declines in east Africa, particularly in Kenya, as well as in west Africa. In areas where their natural prey has been reduced hyaenas readily take domestic livestock and this results in eradication programmes.

In a few locations, such as in parts of Ethiopia, hyaenas are tolerated and even encouraged because they keep villages clear

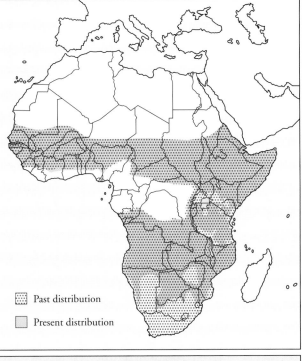

| | |
|---|---|
| ▥ | Past distribution |
| ▩ | Present distribution |

**SPOTTED HYAENA**

of edible rubbish.

The overall number of spotted hyaenas is unknown but it is almost certainly fewer than 100 000 individuals. Southern Africa possibly holds 10% of this total.

Although they are predominantly savanna species, spotted hyaenas are recorded from a range of habitat types, including desert fringes. They are absent from true desert and forest.

### Behaviour

There have been a number of classic studies undertaken on this carnivore. Probably the best known is that of Hans Kruuk in the Ngorongoro Crater of northern Tanzania. All major studies have been undertaken in conservation areas and we have little idea of the situation in other areas.

Female hyaenas form the social nucleus of each clan. Clan size varies from area to area and is influenced by prey abundance and the nature of the habitat. Each clan defends a territory against other clans, marking boundaries with anal gland secretions, droppings and urine.

In our experience spotted hyaenas living outside conservation areas forage as individuals, or in small groups rarely numbering more than three. There is also a tendency for these animals to be less vocal than those in conservation areas. It would be interesting to determine exactly to what extent the behaviour of these animals differs from that of protected populations.

Their reputation as skulking, cowardly scavengers is ill-deserved. Some studies have found well over 60% of their food requirements to come from animals which they hunt and kill for themselves. They do chase other large carnivores from their kills, but so does the lion. They scavenge when there is the opportunity, and this is an extremely valuable and necessary ecological function.

In common with a number of carnivores, they feed on a wide range of food items, from insects to large ungulates. However, their hunting energy is mainly aimed at a wide range of antelope and zebra, particularly in conservation areas. Kruuk once observed a pack of 35 spotted hyaenas completely clear an area of all remains of a plains zebra mare and foal they had killed (total estimated mass of 370 kg) in 36 minutes.

## Conservation

Some readers may query the inclusion of the spotted hyaena in this book. We are aware that it is still widespread in sub-Saharan Africa and even abundant in a number of savanna national parks and game reserves. However, it is becoming increasingly uncommon in unprotected areas. In this book we hope to put across to the reader that we should not wait until a species becomes endangered or vulnerable before we react.

This hyaena, like the African wild dog, suffers under the burden of a false label, as a cowardly, slinking eater of carrion. It has been heavily persecuted in the past and many are still killed today as potential stock killers, usually by means of poisoned carcasses. As human populations and their herds and flocks continue to increase and expand, the spotted hyaena and other large predators will increasingly be shot, trapped and poisoned. It will be a sad day for Africa when the repertoire of yells, giggles, whoops and whines of the spotted hyaena is only heard in some of the larger savanna conservation areas.

# Brown hyaena
## *Hyaena brunnea*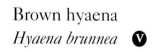

### Description and taxonomy

The brown hyaena has the typical sloping back of the hyaena family. The body is covered with a long, shaggy coat, and there is a well-developed mantle on the shoulders and back. Body colour is variable: usually dark brown but lighter around the neck. The legs are striped with dark and light brown. Ears are large but pointed, not round like those of the spotted hyaena.

### Distribution and habitat

The brown hyaena has the most restricted distribution of the four members of the Hyaenidae. It is found only in southern Africa, primarily in the arid western and central regions. In Afrikaans it is known as the "strandwolf" or "strandjut", a reference to its presence along the entire coastline of the Namib Desert. It also occurs inland.

Although historical records are vague, it is clear that the brown hyaena once occurred virtually throughout southern Africa. Viable populations now occur mainly in the most arid

| BROWN HYAENA | |
|---|---|
| Total length | 1,3-1,6 m |
| Tail length | 17-30 cm |
| Shoulder height | 80 cm |
| Mass | ♂ 47 kg; ♀ 42 kg |
| Home range | 19-480 sq km or more |
| Social structure | clans of 1-9 (average 4) |
| Gestation | 90 days |
| Number of young | 1-4 |
| Weaned | 12-15 months |
| Diet | scavenge: many small vertebrates, insects, wild fruits |

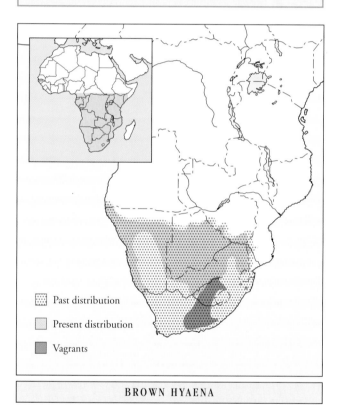

Past distribution

Present distribution

Vagrants

BROWN HYAENA

regions, particularly the Kalahari and Namib deserts and associated areas. This hyaena is also present on ranchland in areas of the North-West and Northern provinces of South Africa, where it is frequently overlooked by ranchers. A small population roams the western sector of the Soutpansberg Mountains in the last-mentioned province, towards the Zimbabwe border.

## Behaviour

The behaviour of the brown hyaena has been studied in detail in the Kalahari Desert. They live in small social groups or clans. The clan defends a shared territory but members forage singly and not as a group. Members of clans are usually related but small numbers of males are nomadic. These animals mate with receptive clan females.

Brown hyaenas are predominantly scavengers, killing only a small percentage of their food. Wild fruits are an important component of their diet, in contrast with the spotted hyaena which rarely takes plant food. Along the Namib Desert coastline brown hyaenas feed mainly on dead animals such as Cape fur seals and birds, but during the pupping season they also kill and eat young fur seals.

We observed one group of hyaenas living at the mouth of the Orange River in extreme south-western Namibia. Scavenging off oryx and donkey carcasses was important but they also hunted dogs and cats in the neighbouring town. They also scavenged from dustbins and the town's rubbish dump.

Of all the large African carnivores this is perhaps the one best suited to coexist with people.

## Conservation

Once thought to be endangered, the brown hyaena is now known to occur in relatively stable populations, particularly in the large conservation areas of the Kalahari and Namib deserts, and at low densities in Kruger, Hwange and Etosha national parks and on a number of cattle ranches and game farms in the northern areas of South Africa.

Even though brown hyaenas are protected animals they are still killed in unknown numbers. They are deliberately and accidentally killed during predator control operations, and are particularly susceptible to poisoning campaigns.

Incidents of brown hyaenas killing stock are known, but these are extremely rare. The presence of brown hyaenas on several ranches with which we are familiar posed no threat to stock. In some cases ranchers were tolerant of the animals, and in two cases the ranchers were ignorant of the presence of hyaenas. On at least one of these properties the hyaenas had obviously been in residence for some time.

This is a species that could well benefit from widespread publicity and education programmes emphasising the useful role that this animal plays in cleaning up carcasses.

# MUSTELIDAE

## *Mustelids*

No African mustelids can be considered to be endangered, or even threatened, throughout their range but a few have certainly declined in their distribution and numbers. Some have a very wide distributional range, such as the honey badger or ratel *(Mellivora capensis)*, which occurs throughout most of Africa except the central Sahara Desert, as well as in the Middle East and into Asia. Although the honey badger is considered to be rare in some areas, such as South Africa and Morocco, it never occurs at high densities and is often overlooked. The fact that it occupies all major habitats, including tropical lowland forest, is a major factor in making it reasonably secure.

Two species occur in extreme northern Africa, the weasel *(Mustela nivalis)* and the European polecat *(M. putorius)*, but little is known of their present conservation status.

The otters are important indicators of the health of wetland systems. Three species occur in Africa: two in sub-Saharan Africa and one, the Eurasian otter *(Lutra lutra)*, in north-western Africa. The two sub-Saharan species, the Cape clawless otter *(Aonyx capensis)* and the spotted-necked otter *(Lutra maculicollis)* are still widespread and not uncommon in some areas. However, the deterioration of water quality and destruction of waterside vegetation has had an impact on populations in some areas. Otters are also prone to drowning in fishing nets. The range of the spotted-necked otter in the Eastern Cape province, South Africa, has been greatly reduced because of siltation of many rivers in which it once occurred. This species relies on hunting its prey by sight, and siltation of rivers hinders this.

Recent taxonomic thinking has placed the Congo clawless otter *(Aonyx congica)* together with the Cape clawless otter. Nothing is known of the ecology of the *congica* form but it apparently replaces *capensis* in the rivers, lakes and streams of the Congolean forest block.

The only otter of conservation concern is the Eurasian species, which in Africa only occurs in limited areas of Morocco, Algeria and Tunisia, where it is under considerable pressure as a result of habitat degradation and unknown levels of direct persecution. Populations are centred on rivers that rise in the Atlas Mountains.

# Eurasian otter
## *Lutra lutra* Ⓥ

### Description and taxonomy

The overall coat colour is dark brown, with light underparts and off-white throat. The feet are well webbed and the toes are clawed.

| EURASIAN OTTER | |
|---|---|
| **Total length** | 1-1,3 m |
| **Tail length** | 35-40 cm |
| **Mass** | about 6 kg (up to 12 kg) |
| **Home range** | not known in Africa |
| **Social structure** | family groups, usually female and young; also males |
| **Gestation** | 59-63 days |
| **Number of young** | 1-5 (average 2-3) |

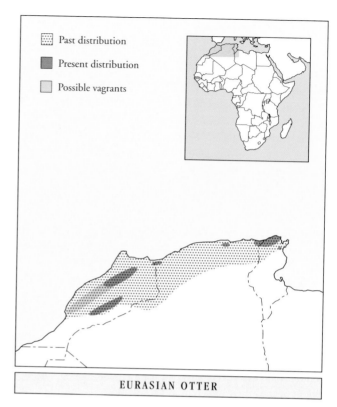

Past distribution
Present distribution
Possible vagrants

**EURASIAN OTTER**

### Distribution and habitat

In Algeria the Eurasian otter is very localised, occurring at low densities in coastal hill ranges. Populations are contiguous with those in Morocco and Tunisia. Morocco's otter population is said to occur at low densities in the foothills of the Moyen Atlas and also in a few streams that drain towards the Sahara Desert. The most important population in Tunisia lies west of Tunis and north of Oued Medjerda, where this otter is said to be widespread and common in parts. Lake Ichkeul and its associated rivers are held to be of particular importance for the future survival of this otter in Tunisia.

### Behaviour

No detailed behavioural study of the Eurasian otter has been undertaken in north Africa.

### Conservation

Major threats facing the north African otter populations are: the construction of dams, the expansion of irrigation schemes which decrease water flow and result in higher levels of agricultural poisons entering freshwater systems, industrial pollution, increased siltation of rivers and streams and the destruction of bankside vegetation, which deprives the otters of cover.

These threats have both direct and indirect effects, the latter including a reduction in the availability of the Eurasian otter's species. It is these and other threats that have placed this otter under extreme pressure in Europe.

**Above:** *Water, or marsh, mongoose* (Atilax paludinosus).

# VIVERRIDAE

## Herpestids and Viverrids

This is the carnivore family with the most species in Africa. It includes the mongooses, genets, civets and linsang.

## MONGOOSES

Several mongoose species are diurnal and communal and have wide distributions, such as the banded mongoose *(Mungos mungo)* and dwarf mongoose *(Helogale parvula* and *H. undulata)*. The yellow mongoose *(Cynictis penicillata)* and the suricate *(Suricata suricatta)* are restricted to the more arid areas of southern Africa. However, the vast majority of African mongoose species are solitary and very poorly known. It is therefore difficult to know which species are in fact rare and threatened, as opposed to secretive and nocturnal.

Some species have wide distributions and are reasonably abundant, such as the large grey mongoose *(Herpestes ichneumon)*, the white-tailed mongoose *(Ichneumia albicaudata)* and the water, or marsh, mongoose *(Atilax paludinosus)*.

A few seemingly rare mongooses are found in savanna and lightly wooded habitats, such as the bushy-tailed mongoose *(Bdeogale crassicauda)*, Meller's mongoose *(Rhynchogale melleri)*, Selous's mongoose *(Paracynictis selousi)* and Pousargues' mongoose *(Dologale dybowskii)*. It is likely that none of these is seriously threatened, but that they occur naturally at low densities and are easily overlooked, given the nature of their favoured habitats and the low levels of field research undertaken in most of the areas where they are known to occur.

## Pousargues' mongoose
### *Dologale dybowskii* Ⓡ

This mongoose is known from 30 museum specimens collected in a narrow belt from south-eastern Central African Republic, across extreme northern Congo (DR) and marginally into Sudan and Uganda. It occurs in the vegetation zone lying between savanna and closed forest. There have been no sightings or specimens collected in more than a decade. It is known to occur in Garamba National Park in Congo (DR).

**Above:** *Dwarf mongooses* (Helogale parvula) *are among the most frequently observed small viverrids.*

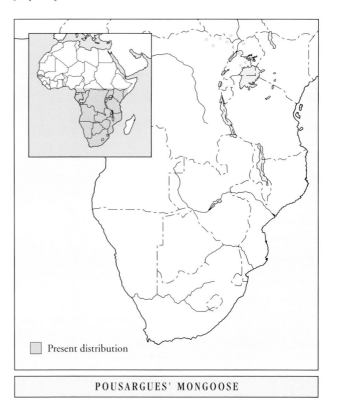

POUSARGUES' MONGOOSE

| POUSARGUES' MONGOOSE | |
|---|---|
| **Total length** | 38-50 cm |
| **Tail length** | 16-22 cm |
| **Shoulder height** | 8 cm |
| **Habitat** | savanna |
| *Nothing else is known* | |

☐ Present distribution

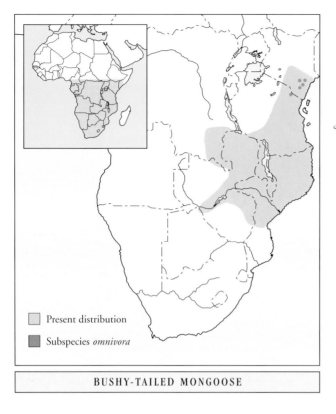

Present distribution

Subspecies *omnivora*

BUSHY-TAILED MONGOOSE

Present distribution

JACKSON'S MONGOOSE

## Bushy-tailed mongoose
### *Bdeogale crassicauda* Ⓥ

Two subspecies of the bushy-tailed mongoose are considered to be vulnerable, if not endangered. The Sokoke bushy-tailed mongoose (*B.c. omnivora*) is only known from the ever-diminishing coastal rainforests of Kenya, and possibly Tanzania, but this has not been confirmed. A recent intensive trapping programme in the Arabuko-Sokoke Forest, near Malindi (Kenya), succeeded in catching one animal, which was later released.

Jackson's mongoose (subspecies *jacksoni*), considered by some authorities to be a full species, is only known from a few forests on some east African mountains, such as the Aberdares and possibly Mounts Elgon and Kenya.

The whole genus *Bdeogale* is in urgent need of study and revision but given numerous other pressing priorities this seems unlikely to happen in the near future.

### BUSHY-TAILED MONGOOSE

| | |
|---|---|
| **Total length** | 60-80 cm |
| **Tail length** | 20-30 cm |
| **Mass** | 0,9-1,6 kg |
| **Habitat** | coastal forest to acacia savanna |

*Nothing else is known*

## Genus *Crossarchus*

It is even more difficult to establish the conservation standing of mongooses that live in the forest belt. One of the most complex and least-known groups is the genus *Crossarchus*, of which four species are recognised at present (*obscurus, platycephalus, ansorgei* and *alexandri*). The status of a number of subspecies is still uncertain.

## The cusimanse group

Here we can only present a brief outline of one of the better-known species, Ansorge's cusimanse (*Crossarchus ansorgei*), as our understanding of even this animal is very limited. We know that it occurs south of the Congo River and west of the Lualaba River in Congo (DR), and south of the Dembos Forest and north of the Cuanza River in Angola. All known specimens have been collected, or observed, in deciduous rainforest. They may be the rainforest equivalent of the savanna-dwelling banded mongoose (*Mungos mungo*). They move in troops of 20 or more individuals. Their diet consists primarily of small vertebrates and insects.

They are hunted by local people for "bush meat", of which they make up an important component. The impact on animals of hunting for "bush meat" crops up in most chapters of this book. It is of particular importance in the tropical lowland forest belt where conditions are unsuitable for keeping domestic livestock and the people do not have a tradition of animal husbandry. In many areas meat from wild animals forms the

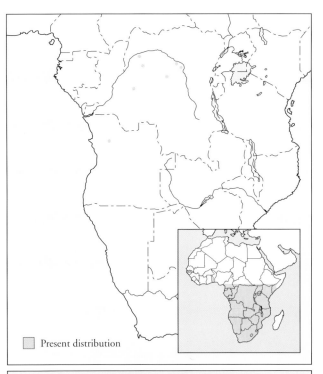

## ANSORGE'S CUSIMANSE

**Above:** *The Liberian mongoose* (Liberiicis kuhni) *is probably Africa's most threatened mongoose species.* PHOTO: *Mark E. Taylor.*
**Right:** *Habitat of the Liberian mongoose.* PHOTO: *Mark E. Taylor.*

bulk of all protein intake. The impact on huntable species is huge. Combined with habitat destruction, it will force animal diversity and abundance to continue declining. This is already happening in the Guinean forest blocks of west Africa.

### THE CUSIMANSE GROUP

| | |
|---|---|
| **Total length** | 45-76 cm |
| **Tail length** | 15-32 cm |
| **Shoulder height** | 18-20 cm |
| **Mass** | 1,5 kg |
| **Gestation** | 70 days |
| **Number of young** | 2-4 |
| **Diet** | predominantly invertebrates but also small vertebrates |
| **Habitat** | lowland tropical forest |

**Above:** *The beautifully marked large-spotted genet* (Genetta tigrina).

## Liberian mongoose
*Liberiictis kuhni* **E**

Probably the most intriguing detective story involving an African animal must be the one resulting in the discovery of this mongoose. In 1957 eight skulls of a small carnivore were collected from villagers in the Nimba County of Liberia. These were so clearly different from anything previously described that they were placed in their own genus. Two additional skulls were obtained in 1960 and 1964. Only in 1974 were the first dead specimens obtained by scientists from local hunters. Now a description of their appearance could be given. They have a mass of about 2 kg; the coat is rich brown in colour with dark and light brown stripes on the neck.

Another 25 museum specimens had since been obtained, but a search began for living animals. In 1988 Mark Taylor, a Canadian zoologist, spent six weeks trying to locate the Liberian mongoose in the Sapo National Park, but without luck. During travels to villages in surrounding areas he did obtain one freshly killed, partially cooked specimen, and was told that "the species was declining in many areas, that it was

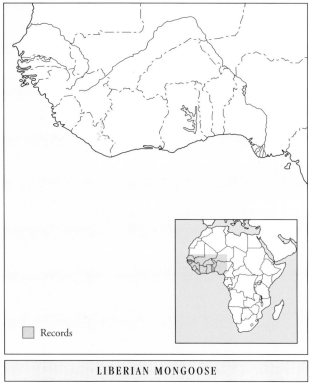

Records

**LIBERIAN MONGOOSE**

difficult to shoot, and ... if caught in a snare it was very fierce."

The search was resumed the following year. The aim was to catch a nucleus stock to start a captive breeding programme. Taylor and his team returned to the Gbi National Forest where the previous year's specimen had been obtained, but caught nothing. All was not lost, however: a villager had managed to catch a male and although slightly injured by the snare, it was transferred to the Metro Toronto Zoo in Canada.

Although it was planned to return to catch further specimens, civil war broke out in Liberia. Now not even the most dedicated scientist will risk taking up the search until hostilities cease.

Not all is bad news, however, as in 1990 this mongoose was observed in the Tai National Park in south-western Ivory Coast. Biologist Mary Gartshore is the only scientist to have observed this animal in the wild. The animal she watched was searching for food in the mud and under stones in a stream by digging holes into which it then stuck its long snout. Although this observation was of a solitary animal, locals report that these mongooses generally move in troops. One troop of 15 has been recorded. The structure of their teeth, the few stomach contents examined and the single observation indicate that they are specialised invertebrate feeders. The single captive male has since died.

# GENETS

Genets *(Genetta spp.)* pose even worse taxonomic and conservation problems than the mongooses.

Some species, such as the small-spotted (or common) genet *(Genetta genetta)* and the large-spotted *(G. tigrina)* are widespread and relatively common, but particularly the latter species presents taxonomic difficulties.

One of the least known species is the Abyssinian genet *(G. abyssinica)*, which has markings distinctive enough for it to have been placed in its own subgenus *(Pseudogenetta)* by some authorities. It is known from only six museum specimens and a number of doubtful sightings, all but one from Ethiopia (including Eritrea). It is not even clear whether it is a forest inhabitant, or of the arid lowlands, or both.

Another species, Johnston's genet *(G. johnstoni)* is known

| GENETS | |
|---|---|
| **Total length** | 0,8-1,5 m |
| **Tail length** | 40-88 cm |
| **Shoulder height** | 15-25 cm |
| **Mass** | 1,3-3,5 kg |
| **Number of young** | 1-5 |
| **Diet** | small vertebrates, invertebrates |

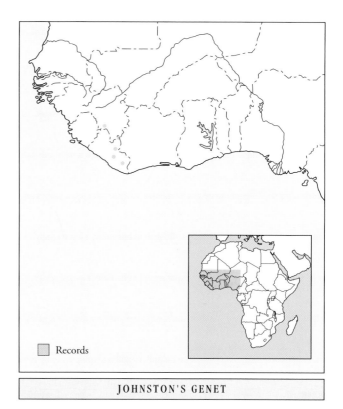

| Records |

**JOHNSTON'S GENET**

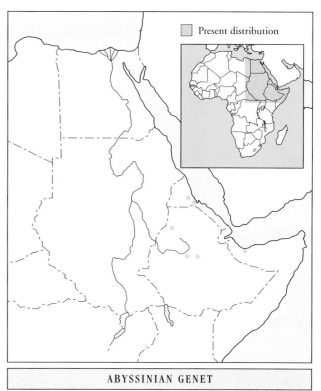

| Present distribution |

**ABYSSINIAN GENET**

from only eight specimens, with no records for over 20 years, and it is apparently restricted to a small area of rainforest in eastern Liberia, Guinea and on Mount Nimba, whose slopes are shared with Ivory Coast. Given the continuing habitat destruction in the area this species could be seriously threatened and vulnerable.

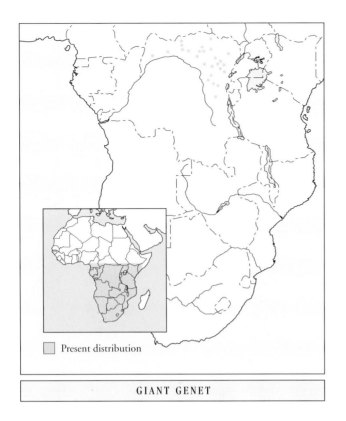

Present distribution

**GIANT GENET**

Present distribution

**AQUATIC GENET**

The largest of all genets, the giant genet *(G. victoriae)*, is restricted to the forests of northern and north-eastern Congo (DR) where it apparently occurs patchily, but the reasons for this are unknown. Its total length exceeds 1 m and its mass 3,5 kg, but these measurements are based on very few specimens. It is longer in the leg than the other genets and almost civet-like.

## Aquatic genet
### *Osbornictis piscivora* Ⓔ

This is another poorly known tropical forest carnivore. It is a very attractive animal (we have only seen museum skins) with long, dense chestnut-red body hair and a black, bushy tail. There is a distinctive elongated white spot over each eye. Total length is about 80 cm and mass 1,5 kg.

This genet is apparently restricted to dense forest at altitudes between 500 m and 1 500 m in north-eastern Congo (DR), and possibly in adjacent areas of Uganda, but this has not been confirmed. The genet occurs between the right bank of the Zaïre/Lualaba River and the western ridge of the Albertine Rift Valley. There is a single record for north-western Congo (DR). The latter could indicate a more extensive distribution but this area is zoologically poorly investigated. Although it is not definitely known to occur in the Maiko National Park, the nature of the habitat is such that it could well be present. There seems to be a strong corrrelation between the known distribution of this genet and large homogenous blocks of *Gilbertiodendron* forest.

The aquatic genet has been called Africa's rarest carnivore and probably with some justification. Only 31 specimens have been lodged in museum collections and much of the available

**Above:** *A mounted specimen of the aquatic genet.* Photo: *Harry van Rompaey.*

information is based on these and observations of local people. The genet is thought to be semi-aquatic as several of the specimens were collected in or near streams, and fish apparently forms an important part of its diet. It is probably solitary and presumably occurs at low densities. The only pregnant female collected was carrying a single foetus.

# LINSANG

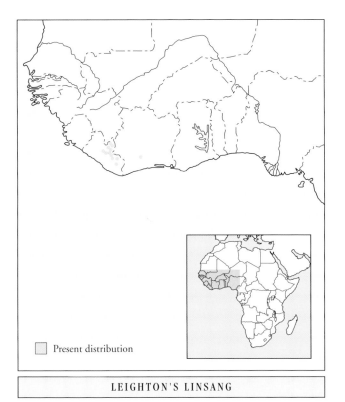

Present distribution

LEIGHTON'S LINSANG

Another poorly known forest viverrid is the genet-like linsang *(Poiana richardsoni)*. Given its wide lowland forest distribution, it is probably secure, although it does occasionally appear in "bush meat" markets. The west African subspecies *liberiensis* is known only from about 12 museum specimens collected mainly in eastern Liberia. Given the overall conservation problems in west Africa it could be highly vulnerable.

With very few exceptions the small carnivores of Africa are poorly known or understood.

**Right**: *A museum skin of the giant genet* (Genetta victoriae). *Because of its forest habitat this species is very seldom seen.*
**Below**: *A last surviving Barbary lion in the wild, photographed at the end of the 19th century near Algiers.*

CHAPTER 5

# PRIMATES
## *Our closest relatives*

Monkeys, who very sensibly refrain from speech,
lest they should be set to earn their livings ...

Kenneth Grahame – *The golden age*

When one thinks of the primate fauna of Africa, images of gorillas and chimpanzees immediately spring to mind, as these species have received considerable attention from scientists and the media, and have been popularised on the silver screen and television. People have been fascinated by these most human of the primates ever since they were first brought to the attention of the non-African world.

However, the continent is home to 58 species of primate, one of the richest assemblages of these fascinating creatures in

the world. If one includes the large island of Madagascar, which is part of the Afro-tropical Realm, with its unique lemur fauna, one would have to add a further 23 species. This total of 81 primate species may in fact be too low, as new species are periodically discovered. There are still several large areas of forest in the Congolian block in central Africa that are zoologically poorly known.

Before we take a more detailed look at the endangered and threatened primates of Africa, it is important to look at the

**Above:** *Hamadryas baboon* (Papio hamadryas) *group.*
**Right:** *Young common chimpanzee* (Pan troglodytes).

overall distribution patterns and other factors affecting all species. This is not a uniform order but its members are diverse both in size and appearance.

The African primates are divided into distinctive groups. The Prosimians, or lower primates, include the lemurs of Madagascar and the bushbabies, potto and angwantibo. The true monkeys and apes, or higher primates, include the baboons, macaque, colobus, guenons, mangabeys and the so-called great apes.

If we look at the number of primate species country by country, we find that Congo (DR) is host to at least 30 (possibly 32) different species. The uncertainty arises because one species has not been observed but is expected to occur; a second species may or may not be merely a subspecies. Running a close second is Cameroon with 29 species, yet it has only about one fifth of the land surface area of Congo (DR). Tiny Rio Muni or Equatorial Guinea (which includes Bioko Island) covers only 28 000 sq km but 21 species of primate live in its forests. Other countries with impressive inventories of primate species are Central African Republic (19 species; possibly 20), Congo (22), Nigeria (between 20 and 24), Tanzania (20) and Uganda (19 species). In general, the further one moves away

from the equator the less diverse is the primate fauna. South Africa at the southern tip of the continent has only five species, and north of the Sahara only one, the Barbary macaque (*Macaca sylvanus*), occurs.

Despite the massive research efforts that have been directed at a few primate species, the vast majority are poorly known and the taxonomic status of several has still to be resolved.

Among the diverse family Cercopithecidae, which has 47 African species and in some cases several subspecies, there are 15 species and subspecies that are considered to be endangered, 13 that are vulnerable and likely to approach extinction in the not too distant future, four that are classed as rare and 21 that appear not to be threatened at the present time. But even among the latter group some species and subspecies are threatened on a regional or local level, although not throughout their range.

There is confusion in the genus *Papio*, particularly among the savanna baboons, but none is under threat except in a few localised cases. The red colobus monkeys have the most subspecies and without doubt generate the most taxonomic confusion. They form the largest segment of the primate population to be allocated endangered status.

There are five distinct species of red colobus. Twelve subspecies are recognised, belonging to three of the species. Of these, seven have been accorded endangered status and a further three are vulnerable or rare. The remainder are so poorly known that they cannot be assigned to any clear category.

Even within the higher primates there is confusion as to the validity of subspecies, but three subspecies of the chimpanzee and three of the gorilla are generally recognised.

In general the primates that inhabit wooded savannas, and those that can utilise secondary forest, are least threatened by humans. The potto *(Perodicticus potto)* and angwantibo *(Arctocebus calabarensis)*, and all but one member of the nine species of bushbaby or galago (subfamily Galaginae) are generally considered to be under no major threat, although most are very poorly known.

By far the majority of primates are restricted to the high-rainfall forested tropics, with a few species inhabiting woodland savannas and montane regions. Most of the endangered and vulnerable species occur in tropical lowland forests. Areas facing the greatest crisis are the Guinean forest block of west Africa and the coastal forests that extend down the eastern shores of the Gulf of Guinea. Recent upheavals caused by civil war and countless refugees in central and eastern

Africa could result in rapid habitat deterioration and an increase in the hunting of primates.

Not only is Africa important for its diversity of primate species, but it is probably from here that the higher primates evolved and dispersed. The continent is considered by many to be the cradle of humankind, where humans are believed to have evolved. From here they dispersed to the other land masses.

The human fascination with our roots has caused scientists to delve into the fossil record and to study the members of the Pongidae family both in captivity and in the wild, in an attempt better to understand the evolution and behaviour of the world's most abundant primate, *Homo sapiens*. Unfortunately for the non-human primates their similarity and close resemblance to us have resulted in their being used extensively for medical and other research.

Although the trade in primates has greatly decreased in recent years, it still continues at both the legal and illegal level. In some areas hunting for food has greatly reduced the numbers of some species. Many species, including the gorilla, chimpanzee and bonobo, end up in the "bush meat" markets of west and central Africa, even though there are taboos against eating primates in a few regions. It is, however, the destruction of forest and woodland habitat that is the greatest threat to the survival of many primates. As the destruction continues unabated, the animals are squeezed into ever-shrinking areas.

As in the other chapters in this book it has been difficult to decide which species should be dealt with in detail and which left out. Human pressures, particularly habitat destruction and direct persecution, affect all primates to some extent.

# PONGIDAE
## *Great apes*

Africa is home to three of the world's four species of great ape, the gorilla, the chimpanzee and the bonobo. The gorilla *(Gorilla gorilla)* is the largest of all, and has three recognised subspecies. The chimpanzee *(Pan troglodytes)* is also separated into three subspecies but the bonobo *(P. paniscus)* has none.

Some authorities believe that these apes are so closely related to humans that all should be placed in the same family, but others oppose this on the grounds that it would offend people. Be that as it may, we cannot get away from the fact that anatomically, mentally and behaviourally we really are "naked apes".

## Gorilla
### *Gorilla gorilla* Ⓥ

### Description and taxonomy

The gorilla is the largest of all primates. The build is massive, with a very powerful muscle structure, large head with a low forehead and noticeably small ears. Adult males stand some

| GORILLA | |
|---|---|
| **Standing height** | ♂ 1,7 m; ♀ 1,5 m |
| **Mass** | ♂ 140-180 kg; ♀ 90 kg |
| **Sexual maturity** | ♂ 9-10 years but first mating rarely before 15-20 years ♀ 7-8 years but first mating usually at about 10 years |
| **Gestation** | 250-270 days |
| **Birth mass** | 1,8-2,5 kg |
| **Weaned** | 2,5-3 years |
| **Birth interval** | about 4 years |
| **Life span (wild)** | estimated at 35 years |
| **Number surviving** | |
| western lowland gorilla: | 35 000-45 000 |
| eastern lowland gorilla: | 3 000-5 000 |
| mountain gorilla: | about 600 |

1,7 m when erect and have a mass of 140 kg to 180 kg. The females are considerably smaller, reaching an average height of 1,5 m and a body mass of about 90 kg. Many of the animals one sees in zoos are unusually heavy and in some cases they are positively obese.

Many different races, or subspecies, have been recognised since the gorilla was first described, but as this primate varies greatly from population to population, only three subspecies are now generally accepted. They are the western lowland *(Gorilla gorilla gorilla)*, the eastern lowland *(G.g. graueri)* and the mountain gorilla *(G.g. berengei)*. Recent work undertaken on genetic fingerprinting suggests that the mountain and eastern lowland subspecies are more closely related to each other than either is to the western animals. The differences are considered to be so great that in some scientific circles raising the western lowland gorilla to full species status is being considered.

A number of other characteristics separate the three subspecies. The western lowland gorilla has relatively short hair which frequently has a brownish tinge, particularly on the top of the head. The adult male's silvery-white saddle extends onto the rump and thighs. This subspecies is said to have the most muscular torso, presumably an adaptation to its active lifestyle, which entails covering larger home ranges and spending more time feeding in the trees than the other subspecies.

The eastern lowland gorilla has a black coat and the adult male's silvery-white saddle is restricted to the back. The jaws and teeth are larger, the face is longer and the chest is broader.

Mountain gorillas are the largest and most impressive of the three. They have longer black hair, especially on the arms, which are shorter than in the other two subspecies. The silver saddle may extend onto the rump and thighs, like that of the western lowland gorilla. The jaws and teeth are the most massive. The chest is the broadest, as is the nasal cavity: presumably additional adaptations to breathing in the thin mountain air.

Although the gorilla has been known outside Africa for many centuries, the original description of the "gorillai" was almost certainly based on sightings and collected skins of the chimpanzee, or possibly Guinea baboon, from the forested foothills of mountains in Sierra Leone. The original "discovery" was made in 470 BC by Hanno, who had left Carthage with 60 fifty-oared galleys transporting settlers and goods. He described hairy man-like creatures who aggressively threw stones at their attackers.

The first accurate description of what was almost certainly the gorilla was provided by one Andrew Battell in 1559. This English adventurer, press-ganged into the Portuguese colonial army, was posted near the Mayombe River in west Africa. He spent several years in the area, which resulted in his writing a book entitled *Purchas his Pilgrimes*. In it he gives the first detailed description of the western lowland gorilla. Because of the rather obscure nature of his book, his discovery went unnoticed.

Over the years there were other descriptions but it was only in 1846 that real proof of the occurrence of gorillas was produced. The missionary, Thomas Savage, was visiting his fellow church worker, Wilson, at his home on the Gabon River when he encountered "a skull represented by the natives to be of a monkey-like [animal], remarkable for its size, ferocity, and habits." Over a period of several months they collected a number of skulls which were sent to the anatomists Richard Owen and Jeffries Wyman.

**Below:** *A silverback male mountain gorilla* (Gorilla gorilla beringei) *controls a small group of females and their young of different ages.* PHOTO: *Tony Ferrall, Kimbla Safaris.*

## Distribution and habitat

The first indication that an eastern population of gorillas existed was recorded by the explorers Speke and Grant as they travelled along the eastern border of what is now Rwanda and Burundi in their quest for the source of the Nile River. In November 1861 they were informed by natives of man-like

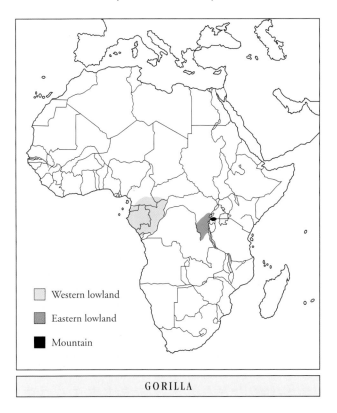

☐ Western lowland

■ Eastern lowland

■ Mountain

GORILLA

monsters "who could not converse with men", living in the mountains to the west, these being the ranges that form the borders between the present-day countries of Congo (DR), Rwanda, Burundi and Uganda.

In 1866 the missionary-explorer Livingstone walked from the Arab slave-trading post of Ujiji on the shore of Lake Tanganyika westwards to Nyangwe on the upper reaches of the Congo River. In his diary he makes mention of gorillas but from the descriptions it seems most likely that he was in fact referring to chimpanzees.

The explorer-journalist Stanley in 1890 was convinced that gorillas were present in the north-east of the then Congo and he was to be proved correct. In 1898 E. Grogan, who was travelling between Cape Town and Cairo on foot, was hunting elephants in the Virunga Volcanoes when he "came on the skeleton of a gigantic ape". But it was left to a German army

**Above:** *Western lowland gorilla* (G.g. gorilla) *male.* Photo: Roland Wirth.

officer, Captain Oscar von Beringe, to collect the first gorilla from the eastern population. He was travelling from Usambara at the northern point of Lake Tanganyika northwards to the then German colony of Ruanda-Urundi. On 17 October 1902 Von Beringe and a Dr England attempted to ascend to the summit of Mount Sabinio, one of the Virunga Volcanoes. They established camp on a narrow ridge at about 2 835 m from where they observed several large apes above them, of which they shot two. They were able to retrieve one body. The skeleton was prepared and sent to the German anatomist

Matschie. He gave it the name *Gorilla gorilla beringei* to honour its collector. This led to a general free-for-all with hunters and collectors descending on the Virunga forests in order to amass carcasses, as was generally done at that time.

It has been estimated that at least 54 gorillas were collected in the Virungas between 1902 and 1925. Prince Wilhelm of Sweden led an expedition to the area in 1921, which accounted for 14 gorillas; the American Burbridge shot and captured nine animals within the space of three years. Many others also took their toll until, on 21 April 1925, the Albert National Park was established and the gorillas in it were given protection. It was enlarged on 9 July 1929 to include the entire chain of the Virunga Volcanoes in order to afford protection to the mountain gorilla.

Although there is no certainty, it is generally believed that the gorilla had its origins in the western lowland tropical forests. Then, during the early Pleistocene, they migrated eastwards as far as the Virunga Volcanoes. There are recognised differences between western and eastern populations but they are relatively minor and indicate that the separation was recent. The populations are separated by just over 1 100 km of the central Congo Basin but there is some evidence that gorillas formed one contiguous population until about one million years ago, when a period of aridity resulted in the central forests and their associated biota, including these large primates, being wiped out. Although the forests eventually grew again when climatic conditions became more favourable, the gorilla populations did not become reunited.

As far as is known no gorillas occur within the great arc made by the Congo River, but there are rumours that small numbers may still be present on the east bank of the Congo River to the south of the Busira River. There are also persistent rumours of gorilla populations in the largely unexplored expanses of forest to the north of the Congo River in Congo (DR). The almost total lack of infrastructure in this area prevents scientists from doing any meaningful surveys of gorillas, or any other species for that matter.

There are great difficulties involved in trying to count secretive forest-dwelling animals. For this reason scientists tend to err on the conservative side and react with joy should populations prove to be more secure than previously thought.

The **western lowland gorilla** is the most numerous subspecies and it has proved to be far more abundant than previously thought. It occurs widely in Gabon where more than 85% of the country is still covered by forest. Over much of the remainder of its range the populations are by and large fragmented. In the small country of Rio Muni (Equatorial Guinea) there are four main areas of distribution ranging in size from 1 000 sq km to 1 800 sq km, with smaller isolated pockets elsewhere. Within Congo gorillas are concentrated mainly within three separate areas, in the extreme north-west adjacent to the Gabon and Cameroon borders, in the extreme south-west to within about 20 km from the coast, and in the west-central area near the headwaters of the Ogooué River close to Zanaga. In Cameroon populations are also concentrated in separate pockets. Most gorillas live in the forests of the south and south-east but remnant populations are still found in the far north-west in the Takamanda Reserve on the Cross River adjacent to Nigeria, and probably in the region of Pangar Djerem slightly to the south. A small population persists in the extreme south-west of Central African Republic. The gorilla was long thought to be extinct in Nigeria, but a survey undertaken in 1987-88 confirmed its continued existence in small forest pockets adjacent to the southern border of Cameroon. Populations persist at altitudes between 500 m and 1 000 m within the Afi River and Boshi-Okwongwo Forest reserves, and at least until 1988 a tiny population survived on the Obudu cattle ranch. This population is probably doomed because of continuing forest clearance. A small population possibly continues to survive in the Angolan enclave of Cabinda.

The **eastern lowland gorilla** is entirely restricted to the forests of eastern Congo (DR) in an area of some 90 000 sq km. However, populations are not found throughout the area but rather in isolated groupings stretching westwards of the southwestern border of Uganda, Rwanda and Burundi to the northern tip of Lake Tanganyika and then to the south-west as far as the Lualaba River. Because of the inaccessibility of the area it is deemed likely that populations may still occur to the north and west. Of particular interest is the finding that gorillas readily utilise primary forest, albeit in low densities. This gives credence to the possibility of gorilla populations surviving in the central forests of the Congo Basin. In 1908 gorillas were recorded close to the centre of the basin, and given that the area is largely unexplored, these primates could well still be present.

The **mountain gorilla** is restricted to a tiny area of the Virunga Volcanoes which border on Congo (DR), Uganda and Rwanda.

Gorillas are forest-associated animals. They show a marked preference for forest margins, secondary forest (for example abandoned slash-and-burn patches, as well as recovering logging areas) and riverine forest. They occur seasonally in bamboo forest and also in primary, or fully developed, forest. Gorilla density in the latter, however, is generally very low, compared to about one animal per square kilometre in favoured habitats. The mountain subspecies lives in high altitude forests in the Virungas. The animals range up to 3 400 m and even higher on occasional foraging forays. The lowland subspecies occur at much lower altitudes and even down to sea level in some places. Contrary to general opinion the gorilla is not afraid of water. Recent studies of the western subspecies have shown that it is quite happy to wade around in swamp forests in search of edible aquatic plants. Gorillas are now known to wade freely through swamps and streams, and members of the Fang tribe in Rio Muni (Equatorial Guinea) say that gorillas have been observed bathing in forest streams.

## Behaviour

The missionary Thomas Savage did the gorilla a great disservice by publishing a description of its habits that portrayed this magnificent primate as ferocious and highly dangerous. This false picture was to endure for more than 100 years. To quote from his description,

*It is said that when the male is first seen he gives a terrific yell that resounds far and wide through the forest, something like kh-ah! kh-ah!, prolonged and shrill. His enormous jaws are widely opened at each expiration, his underlip hangs over the chin and the hair ridge and scalp is contracted upon the brow, presenting an aspect of indescribable ferocity. The female and young at the first cry quickly disappear; he then approaches the enemy in great fury, pouring out his horrid cries in quick succession. The hunter awaits his approach with his gun extended; if his aim is not sure he permits the animal to grasp the barrel and as he carries it to the mouth (which is his habit) he fires; should the gun fail to go off, the barrel (that of an ordinary musket, which is thin) is crushed between his teeth, and the encounter soon proves fatal to the hunter.*

Hunters and explorers were to embellish this false description as it made them out to be more daring and heroic in gorilla encounters than was actually the case. The first white man known to have shot a gorilla was the American explorer Paul du Chaillu in 1856 and he made great play on the supposed dangers of encounters with gorillas in his book *Explorations and adventures in equatorial Africa*. Fear of the gorilla was probably taken to its most ridiculous extreme by one fellow of the name Garner who, in 1896, built himself an iron cage and placed it in the forest. In this he sat waiting for 112 days and nights for these "dangerous" beasts to present themselves for observation; needless to say he never caught sight of a gorilla.

It is no wonder that these myths surrounding the gorilla led to the creation of such movie monsters as King Kong. The truth is far removed from this. There are very few authenticated cases of gorillas attacking humans, and those usually occurred when the human intruder turned to flee instead of standing his ground. This is borne out by the fact that the Mandjim Mey people of Cameroon see it as a disgrace to be

**Above:** *Eastern lowland gorilla* (G.g. graueri). Photo: *Louis Slootman, LSDE Photography.*

bitten by a gorilla, for they believe that only a coward would be attacked.

George Schaller's findings on the mountain gorilla, published in 1963, resulted from the first serious and in-depth study undertaken on any of the three gorilla subspecies.

Nearly all that we know of gorilla behaviour and biology is based on studies undertaken on the mountain gorilla, although some researchers have started to delve into the lives of the lowland animals, particularly those in the western populations. Although the forests of the Virunga Volcanoes are not the most pleasant of environments in which to work, it is much more tolerable for researchers than the hot, steamy lowland forests which are home to the two non-montane gorilla subspecies.

Gorillas live in groups ranging in size from two individuals to as many as 37. There is a distinct difference between the eastern and the western populations: those from the western lowlands have smaller group sizes, averaging five members, whereas eastern groups average nine. Each group is dominated by an adult male, referred to as a silverback because of his coat colouring, and includes several adult females and immature animals up to the age of about eight years. The gorilla is an unusual social primate in that both males and females leave the group on reaching maturity. The females join lone males or small groups, and the males remain solitary until they can attract females and establish their own groups.

Gorillas have a relaxed lifestyle, rising relatively late and feeding for about two hours in the morning and a further three to four hours in the afternoon. Then, before nightfall, they settle into their nests which are freshly constructed each night.

Gorillas, because of their bulk, spend most of their time foraging on the ground, although young animals and females, particularly of the lowland subspecies, frequently feed and sleep in trees. Their crude nests are also constructed in trees. Adult males usually construct nests on the ground.

Gorillas do not defend a territory but remain in home ranges which vary from 5 sq km to 35 sq km. Those of western lowland gorillas are generally larger, primarily because of differences in diet. Some studies have shown that there are seasonal differences in range, based primarily on food availability and dietary preferences.

The diet of the eastern and western gorilla populations differs considerably. Eastern animals are predominantly folivorous but those in the west eat great quantities of fruit. Eastern lowland and mountain gorillas feed primarily on herbs, shrubs and vines. The vegetation in their habitat is so lush that they need only cover small distances each day, averaging 0,5 km to 1 km, in order to obtain enough food. The habitat of these gorillas, particularly those in the mountainous east, has been likened to living in a salad bowl.

In the western populations fruits are the most important element in the gorillas' diet, although they also eat leaves, pith and stems. In a study undertaken on one western lowland gorilla group in Gabon it was found that the fruits of at least 95 plant species were utilised. Western gorillas have also been observed wading through shallow pools and swamps to harvest

**Below:** *Typical habitat of the mountain gorilla in the Virunga Volcanoes.* PHOTO: *Harry van Rompaey.*

water plants. They further differ from eastern animals in that they are not averse to including some animal food in their diet. In fact the diet of western lowland gorillas is more like that of the chimpanzee than the diet of the gorillas to the east. Unlike chimpanzees, which use grass stalks or thin twigs to extract termites from their mounds, gorillas simply swipe off the top of a mound: no problem to these most powerful of primates.

## Conservation

Of the three recognised subspecies of gorilla, the one inhabiting the forests of the Virunga Volcanoes, *Gorilla gorilla beringei*, faces the greatest threat. An estimated 600 individuals survive. In the late 1950s it was estimated that there were between 400 and 500 animals but by 1973 only 275 gorillas remained. The number dropped further to about 250 in 1981, most animals being lost from the western slopes in Congo (DR). From then, however, increased international scientific and tourist interest improved the prospects for these gorillas' survival, with about 600 surviving in 1994. Gorillas are present in the Virunga National Park in Congo (DR), Bwindi Impenetrable and Mgahinga Gorilla national parks in south-western Uganda and the Parc National des Volcans in extreme north-western Rwanda, all within the Virunga range. In large measure it is the income from foreign tourists that has allowed this small gorilla population to survive. Some animals are occasionally killed to provide skulls and dried feet for sale to a handful of unthinking tourists, but protection has generally been good.

However, because of increasing human populations people are clearing the forests for cultivation and, in Congo (DR), for cattle ranching. There is also disturbance caused by illegal wood gatherers, smugglers and poachers. The latter are not deliberately setting snares for gorillas as they are not eaten, but young animals are at risk of being caught in snares set for other species. The greatest threat to the continued wellbeing of the mountain gorilla population has been created by the civil war in Rwanda which has caused many hundreds of thousands of starving refugees to pass through and seek resources in the montane forests.

The eastern lowland gorilla *(G.g. graueri)* may number between 3 000 and 5 000 animals but accurate estimates are not available except for a few limited areas. It seems likely that there may be as many as 10 000 individuals in total. These gorillas are entirely restricted to eastern Congo (DR). In a limited survey undertaken in the 1950s it was estimated that there were some 60 population centres within an area of 91 000 sq km, of which only 21 000 sq km was believed occupied, with substantial populations being restricted to some 5 000 sq km. At that time, however, it was generally thought that gorillas did not occur in primary forest. Recent research has shown that primary forest is occupied by gorillas, albeit at low densities, and there is now no certainty as to how far west they extend.

Eastern lowland gorilla populations are present in the 10 000 sq km Maiko National Park but at low densities. In the 6 000 sq km Kahuzi-Biega National Park there are probably no more than 240 individuals. This means that the vast majority of animals occur outside protected areas. Limited clearance of primary forest can be beneficial to eastern lowland gorilla populations, as much of their feeding is undertaken in clearings and secondary forest where herbaceous plants are most abundant. However, extensive clearing and disturbance are detrimental and result in reductions, or extinctions, of gorilla groups. Increasing human populations throughout their range will certainly put these animals under serious threat in the medium to long term unless the area of prime gorilla habitat under protection is increased and they are more actively protected. However, such measures are unlikely to be taken in the near future.

By far the most abundant of the gorilla subspecies is that occupying the western lowland forests, *G.g. gorilla*. It was long thought that numbers were lower than 10 000 individuals but it is now believed that there are at least 35 000 to 45 000 gorillas surviving, with some estimates as high as 100 000. Recent findings have shown that these gorillas also make extensive use of primary forest, and in the light of this it is believed that the total may be considerably higher than the low estimates.

The majority of western lowland gorillas inhabit the country of Gabon, which has about 85% of its land surface covered by forest. Gabon also has one of Africa's lowest human population densities, with vast areas having virtually no people. Gorillas are protected in three reserves in that country, covering several thousand square kilometres, although controls are limited. In the north of the country gorillas are hunted for food, but in the south tribal traditions forbid the killing and eating of these animals. Because of relatively low numbers of commercially exploitable timber trees in Gabon, deforestation does not pose a significant threat.

In the tiny country of Rio Muni (Equatorial Guinea), there are possibly as many as 2 000 gorillas. Small gorilla populations occur in two conservation areas. As most of the human population is concentrated along the coast, the threat to gorillas at this stage is not severe. There is however a need to extend protected areas.

Little is known of the gorilla population in Congo but there are believed to be between 1 000 and 3 000 animals. Only the Odzala National Park is considered adequate for conservation purposes. It has been estimated that between 400 and 600 gorillas are killed each year for food in Congo. If this estimate is correct, the overall population may be higher, possibly as many as 30 000. Apart from gorilla meat for food, there is also a market for gorilla parts, which are used in traditional medicine in several parts of its range.

The population in Cameroon is probably limited to some 1 500 gorillas. Although they occur in several conservation areas, protection is generally inadequate. Extensive logging and clearing of land for plantation cropping pose a major threat, as does the hunting of gorillas for meat.

A small population, estimated at 500, is present in the extreme south-west of Central African Republic but there are the usual threats of logging, forest clearance and hunting.

An isolated gorilla population in south-eastern Nigeria was thought to have been extinct for more than 30 years but in

1987 animals were rediscovered in forests on the Sankwala Mountains within Cross River State, adjoining Cameroon. At that time it was estimated that between three and five sub-populations were scattered over an area of some 750 sq km. However, these animals are under serious threat and are actively hunted by the Bokai people. It is known that in 1986 one community killed eight gorillas, and in 1987 another killed six. The motivation is high as a gorilla carcass sold in the Lagos markets can fetch 300 navra (at present about US $14), a fortune to a peasant hunter. It is obvious that unless drastic measures are taken to conserve these isolated populations there will be no rediscoveries in the future.

# Chimpanzee
## *Pan troglodytes* Ⓓ

### Description and taxonomy

The chimpanzee is so well known that there is little need to give a detailed description. Chimpanzees are relatively heavily built but are much lighter than gorillas. The limbs are long although the legs are noticeably shorter than the arms. When the animal is walking the back slopes down towards the rump. The facial skin may be pinkish or black but this varies considerably between individuals, populations and age groups. This is one character used to separate subspecies, but it does not appear to be consistent. The top of the head and the body are well covered with black hair. Older animals start greying and frequently go bald. Animals from the eastern populations are sometimes called the long-haired race, but it is mainly those groups living in association with montane areas that have

longer hair. The large ears are pinkish to black and stick prominently from the head.

The ancestral origins of the chimpanzee are to be found in the fossil record of the Miocene era in east Africa. These creatures were given the name *Proconsul africanus*. Three species of *Proconsul* are recognised, the largest of which may have been the ancestor of the modern gorilla. The chimpanzee has been known to the non-African world for far longer than has the gorilla, in part because of its more extensive distributional range. Many different species and subspecies of chimpanzee have been described over the years (14 species at the beginning of the 20th century), but only three subspecies are recognised today, namely the western chimpanzee *(Pan troglodytes verus)*, the central chimpanzee *(P.t. troglodytes)* and the eastern chimpanzee *(P.t. schweinfurthi)*.

Given the considerable variation displayed by chimpanzees there is some doubt as to the validity of these subspecies. The western subspecies *verus* is now almost certainly totally isolated from populations of the central chimpanzee, but the level of overlap between the latter and the eastern populations is largely unknown.

The bonobo, or so-called pygmy chimpanzee *(P. paniscus)* used to be classified as a subspecies of the chimpanzee but has now justifiably been raised to full species status.

### Distribution and habitat

The chimpanzee was earlier almost certainly more widely distributed than it is today, with the western, central and eastern populations forming one more or less contiguous population. It also possibly occurred further to the south and east in association with forested areas of the Great Rift.

The western chimpanzee *(Pan troglodytes verus)* occurs in isolated patches from the west bank of the Niger River in central Nigeria to southern Senegal. The bulk of the population is found in Guinea, and there are small populations in Sierra Leone, Ivory Coast, Liberia and Mali. Populations in Senegal and Ghana are so small that they are unlikely to survive for many more years.

Most of the Guinean chimpanzee population is located in the west and the south-east. In Sierra Leone groups are widely distributed but at low densities. In Ivory Coast much of the population is found in the south-west, although it could be more widespread than is generally believed. In Liberia chimpanzees occur widely. Although the Malian population is small and restricted to the south-east it is believed to be quite stable. Ghana has a small number of chimpanzees in the south-west and Senegal has probably fewer than 300 animals in the south-east, in and around the Niokolo-Koba National Park. In recent years this chimpanzee has become extinct in five other west African countries.

The central chimpanzee *(P.t. troglodytes)* occurs in seven countries. It is present in south-eastern Nigeria, the southern areas of Cameroon and throughout Gabon. Its distribution in Congo is poorly known but most reports eminate from the north and west. In Rio Muni (Equatorial Guinea) populations

| CHIMPANZEE | |
| --- | --- |
| Standing height | ♂ 92 cm; ♀ 70 cm |
| Mass | ♂ 40 kg; ♀ 30 kg |
| Sexual maturity | 10-13 years (♂ and ♀) or even later |
| Gestation | about 240 days |
| Birth mass | 1,5-2,0 kg |
| Weaned | usually in the third year |
| Birth interval | about 6 years, occasionally less |
| Life span (wild) | probably 35-45 years |
| **Number surviving** | |
| western chimpanzee: | below 17 000 |
| central chimpanzee: | over 80 000 |
| eastern chimpanzee: | below 100 000 |

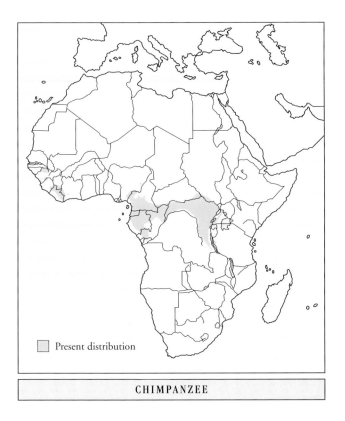

Present distribution

CHIMPANZEE

are small and apparently limited to a few areas with undisturbed primary forests. Some of the most northerly populations of this race are found at low densities in south-western Central African Republic. The Angolan enclave of Cabinda, lying between Congo (DR) and Congo, harbours a tiny population but exact numbers are unknown.

Eastern chimpanzees *(P.t. schweinfurthi)* occur in six countries. Substantial populations are restricted to Congo (DR), where they occur widely to the north and east of the Congo River and as far south as the southern shore of Lake Tanganyika. They are apparently absent from the central Congo Basin, their place being taken by the bonobo. In the north-east they extend into Sudan. They are believed to occur in the south-west of that country, although no recent surveys have been undertaken because of the long-standing civil war. Populations in Uganda are restricted to forest blocks in the west along the Congo (DR) border. In Tanzania they only occur along the shore of Lake Tanganyika. In Burundi small numbers appear to be restricted to Kibira National Park and the Rumango-Bururi Forest Reserve. In the densely populated Rwanda, chimpanzees are found only in the Nyungwe Forest Reserve, with perhaps non-viable groups elsewhere.

The chimpanzee is able to make use of a far greater diversity of habitats than the gorilla. Chimpanzees successfully occupy a wide range of forest and woodland types, including savanna woodland. In some areas they even inhabit open savanna bisected by small gorges and gullies with patches of evergreen forest. This is probably how our ancestors began to disperse and occupy the open grasslands of Africa.

Populations are present from coastal habitats to montane forests, up to an altitude of about 3 000 m in the east. The chimpanzee's ability to live in such a great diversity of habitats seems to be limited only by the availability of surface water and suitable nesting trees.

**Below:** *Despite international laws, young chimpanzees are still captured and sold.*

## Distribution and habitat

The bonobo is entirely restricted to the lowland rainforests between the Congo and Kasai rivers in western Congo (DR). It is apparently absent from the area between the Busira and Momboyo rivers. Even within its range it seems to occur patchily and suggestions that it has a wider range are speculative at this stage. What are considered to be viable populations have been located in only five localities to date but much of their known and presumed range is zoologically poorly known.

The bonobo utilises both primary and secondary forest, with some use being made of seasonally flooded swamp forest. They show no hesitation in wading through shallow water.

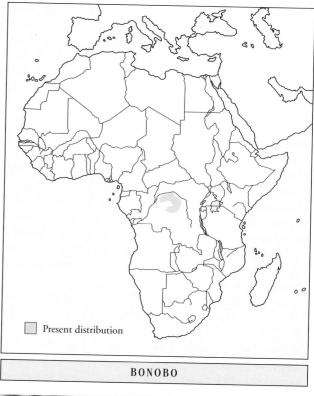

Present distribution

| BONOBO | |
|---|---|
| Standing height | about 1 m (♂ and ♀) |
| Mass | ♂ 45 kg; ♀ 32 kg |
| Sexual maturity | first reproduction 13-14 years |
| Gestation | 230-240 days |
| Birth mass | 1,5 kg |
| Weaned | in the third year |
| Birth interval | average 5 years |
| Life span (wild) | unknown but probably similar to the chimpanzee |
| Number surviving | unknown but probably below 20 000 |

## BONOBO

**Above:** *The bonobo* (Pan paniscus) *is restricted to the lowland forests of Congo (DR), to the south and east of the Congo River. The exact limits of its distributional range are not known, but numbers are lower than was previously thought.* Photo: *Linda van Elsaker.*

## Behaviour

It is only during the last two decades that serious attempts have been made to study the bonobo in the wild, but political upheavals in Congo (DR) in recent years have made life almost impossible for research workers. Studies of bonobos have forced scientists to review their understanding of the evolution of human aggression, sexual behaviour, language and behaviour in general. The bonobo is probably the most intelligent primate after humans.

Bonobos live a relatively peaceful and tranquil life compared to chimpanzees. This can be largely explained by the fact that female bonobos are up to eight times more available to the males for mating, and there are roughly equal numbers of sexually mature males and females in groups. Males do not need to compete for mating rights and sex is an important way of ensuring group stability. Copulatory positions are much more varied than in either the chimpanzee or gorilla, and sexual intercourse is more frequent.

There is no particular birth season. Males remain with their birth group for life but females leave to join another group on reaching maturity.

Groups may number from 30 to 80 individuals but as many as 120 have been recorded. Small subgroups form to forage over the home range. These foraging groups usually include both males and females. One study has shown that only 30% of a bonobo's day is spent feeding. They eat mainly fruit but also other plant parts. Like their chimpanzee relatives they also eat invertebrates and occasionally small mammals.

## Conservation

It has been suggested, based on available suitable habitat, that there may be as many as 200 000 bonobos, but this is now viewed as being highly unlikely as they are known to occur patchily and in low densities. Although much of their range has not been surveyed it has been suggested that a more realistic figure is 10% of the above.

One of the reasons for establishing the Salonga National Park (Congo (DR)) was to protect part of the bonobo population, but it now appears that densities are low here. Given the present instability in Congo (DR) it seems unlikely that further conservation areas will be proclaimed, or the existing one adequately man- aged. The main threats to the long-term survival of the bonobo are loss of habitat and hunting for meat, both on the subsistence and commercial level. Bonobos are also hunted for body parts for the traditional medicine market.

# CERCOPITHECIDAE

## *True monkeys*

This is the most diverse primate family, with the largest number of species. Several of the more common savanna and some forest species have been studied in the wild, but most are still largely unknown.

At least two species, the Salonga and sun-tailed guenons, and as yet undescribed subspecies have been added to the African primate inventory only in recent years. It is therefore quite possible that other additions will come to light.

---

**The following species or subspecies have been classified as endangered:**

Tana River mangabey *Cercocebus galeritus galeritus*
Sanje mangabey *Cercocebus galeritus sanjei*
Drill *Mandrillus leucophaeus*
Preuss's guenon *Cercopithecus preussi*
Red-bellied guenon *Cercopithecus erythrogaster*
Red-eared guenon *Cercopithecus erythrotis*
Sclater's guenon *Cercopithecus erythrotis sclateri*
Golden monkey *Cercopithecus mitis kandti*
Miss Waldron's bay colobus *Procolobus badius waldroni*
Pennant's red colobus *Procolobus pennanti*
Tana River red colobus *Procolobus rufomitratus rufomitratus*
Uhele red colobus *Procolobus gordonorum*
Zanzibar red colobus *Procolobus kirkii*
Black colobus *Colobus satanas*

---

We give a brief overview for each of the above species and subspecies, and cover additional subspecies that fall into other categories. All of the above are restricted to forested habitats, and 60% are restricted to west Africa, where the greatest levels of habitat destruction have taken place.

One of the principal problems facing the adequate conservation of Africa's rich primate fauna, and of course many other biota, is our lack of knowledge of their ecology. Some species and their habitats are under such extreme threat that there is little, or no, hope of their long-term survival.

# Crested mangabey
## *Cercocebus galeritus*

The crested mangabey, also known as the agile mangabey, has its main population centre in west-central Africa in Cameroon, Gabon and into Congo (DR). It occurs primarily north of the Congo River with isolated populations in western Congo (DR). It faces no major threats at this stage. Several subspecies within the main population have been recognised but the species' taxonomy is still poorly understood.

| CRESTED MANGABEY | |
|---|---|
| **Total length** | 1,3 m |
| **Tail length** | 75 cm |
| **Troop size** | 13-36 (Tana River subspecies) |
| | 15-40 (Sanje subspecies) |
| **Sexual maturity** | ♀ 4-5 years (Tana River subspecies) |
| **Diet** | mainly fruit but Tana River subspecies also eats seeds, insects, frogs, lizards |

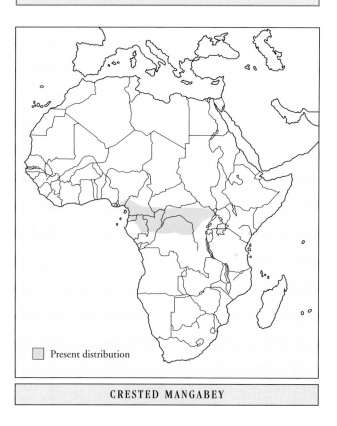

☐ Present distribution

**CRESTED MANGABEY**

The two endangered subspecies are separated from the main population by more than 1 000 km. This indicates how much more extensive the tropical forests once were. During climatic changes these animals became isolated.

## Tana River mangabey
### *Cercocebus galeritus galeritus* Ⓔ

Only very limited information is available on the Tana River mangabey, a subspecies of the crested mangabey.

It is endemic to the gallery forest of the Tana River flood-plain in Kenya over a frontage of less than 60 km. The population is surrounded on three sides by semi-desert country, which is totally unsuitable for the animals, and the Indian Ocean to the east. The population is not contiguous but the troops are patchily distributed, making them especially vulnerable to habitat changes.

In 1972 there were believed to be more than 2 000 individuals but numbers have decreased steadily. By 1985 there were estimated to be fewer than 1 000 Tana River mangabeys.

Although habitat destruction through direct forest clearing for subsistence agriculture and the harvesting of large trees for the production of dug-out canoes have certainly had a major impact on the mangabeys, it is the building of impoundments upstream that has most seriously affected the long-term viability of the gallery forest on which these mangabeys rely.

The bulk of the mangabey population is protected in the Tana River Primate National Reserve, but efforts need to be made to prevent further deterioration of the forest. One subspecies of the red colobus *(Colobus badius rufomitratus)*, with a very limited distribution on the Kenyan coast, is also found in this primate reserve.

## Sanje mangabey
### *Cercocebus galeritus sanjei* Ⓔ

Virtually nothing is known of the Sanje mangabey, another subspecies of the crested mangabey. It was only described for the first time in 1981.

The Sanje mangabey is only known to occur in a small area of forest on the eastern slopes of the Uzungwa Mountains in south-central Tanzania. There are an estimated 1 800 to 3 000 individuals, the majority of which are protected in what used to be the Mwanihana Forest Reserve, and is now the Uzungwa National Park.

Observations indicate that they live in mixed troops and spend much of their time on the ground. Human pressures in the area are considerable and much of the forest below 1 000 m has been cleared for cultivation. The local people also actively hunt all primates as a source of meat.

The Sanje mangabey shares its forest home with a red colobus subspecies, *Colobus badius gordonorum,* which occurs only in the Uzungwa Mountains and in very small numbers.

This is also an important area for rare bird species.

## Drill
### *Mandrillus leucophaeus*

### Description and taxonomy

This large, terrestrial primate is distinguished by its very short, stubby tail, dog-like black face fringed with white hair and a bluish-purple naked posterior.

| DRILL | |
|---|---|
| **Total length** | ♂ about 1 m; ♀ slightly more than 50 cm |
| **Tail length** | 5-12 cm |
| **Mass** | usually 10-22 kg; up to 36 kg (♂ larger than ♀) |
| **Troop size** | up to 20 but temporary groupings up to 200 |
| **Diet** | wide range of plant food, invertebrates, small vertebrates |

The drill is sometimes placed in the genus *Papio* but many authorities are of the opinion that it is distinct enough to be placed in its own genus, which it shares with the mandrill *(Mandrillus sphinx)*. Three subspecies are recognised but their validity is uncertain. One subspecies, *poensis,* was restricted to the island of Bioko in the Gulf of Guinea but it is not known whether any populations survive.

### Distribution and habitat

The drill occurs only in lowland rainforest, coastal and riparian forest in south-eastern Nigeria and western Cameroon. Populations on the mainland occur from the Cross River in Nigeria to the Sanaga River in Cameroon. There is now some doubt whether they ever occurred south of the Sanaga River, where they would have to compete directly with the mandrill. Nigerian populations are limited to montane forest near the Afi River. In Cameroon the drill occurs patchily over a total area of some 75 000 sq km, but no estimate of drill numbers has been made.

### Conservation

The drill is one of Africa's most endangered primates. The principal threats are forest destruction, reafforestation with species of little or no food value, and hunting for the meat market. Deforestation not only results in loss of habitat, but logging roads increase accessibility for settlers and hunters. Drills are very vulnerable as they are easily driven into trees by

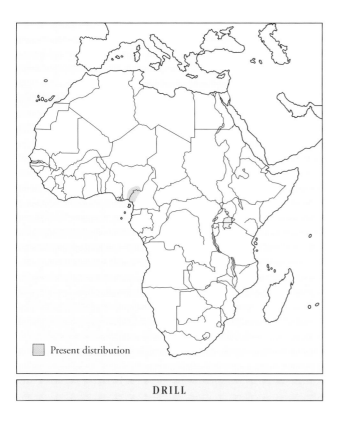

Present distribution

DRILL

Below: *Male drill* (Mandrillus leucophaeus). PHOTO: *Roland Seitre.*

dogs; hunters can then shoot them at will. It is unlikely that the drill will survive in Nigeria unless efforts are made effectively to conserve populations in such areas as Boshi-Okwangwo and the Obudu cattle ranch. Drills are present in the Korup National Park in Cameroon but exact numbers are not known.

# Preuss's guenon
## *Cercopithecus preussi* Ⓔ

### Description and taxonomy

Some authorities regard this monkey as a subspecies of L'Hoest's guenon *(Cercopithecus lhoesti)*. Preuss's and L'Hoest's guenons are similar in appearance, with a dark grey to almost black coat, a brownish to chestnut saddle and dark underparts. The bib is not so distinct in Preuss's guenon and the cheek fur is light grey. The tail is hook-shaped towards the tip.

| PREUSS'S GUENON | |
|---|---|
| **Total length** | 1,7 m (♂ larger than ♀) |
| **Tail length** | 480-800 cm |
| **Mass** | 3-8 kg |
| **Troop size** | 2-9 *(preussi)*; 10-17 or more *(lhoesti)* |
| **Diet** | mixed and opportunistic |

### Distribution and habitat

The main population (L'Hoest's guenon) lives in the border area between Congo (DR), Uganda, Rwanda and Burundi. This eastern population is considered to be vulnerable but not in immediate danger at this stage.

Preuss's guenon occurs in extreme south-eastern Nigeria and into Cameroon as far as the Sanaga River. It is only found in montane forests above 1 000 m. In Cameroon it is found over a total area of less than 15 000 sq km. It does not occur uniformly through the area but is patchily distributed in favoured habitats, where disturbance is lowest. The main population concentration appears to be on Mount Cameroon but no estimate has been made of the total number. In the past it has been recorded as occurring on the island of Bioko but whether it still survives there is unknown.

### Behaviour

Preuss's guenon mixes freely with other species of guenon. Each troop has only one adult male. L'Hoest's guenon also forms polyspecific groupings with other guenons and colobus

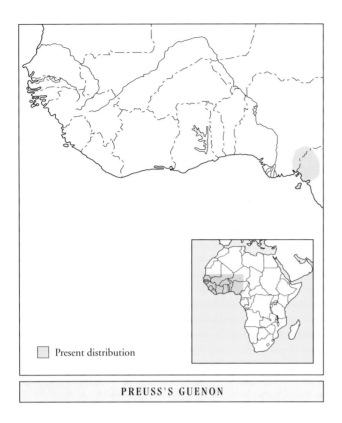

Present distribution

**PREUSS'S GUENON**

monkeys. L'Hoest's guenons have home ranges of about 10 sq km, unusually large for forest monkeys. If this is the case with Preuss's guenon it could be difficult to conserve populations, as large areas would be required.

**Above:** *L'Hoest's guenon* (Cercopithecus lhoesti).

This animal occurs in the notorious elbow between west and central Africa, which has a high concentration of endangered and threatened species.

Destruction of forest, even on Mount Cameroon, is forcing Preuss's guenon and many other species into ever-shrinking habitats. It is believed that the animal survives in the Oban Hills Forest Reserve in south-eastern Nigeria but protection here is minimal. In Cameroon small numbers are believed to occur in some conservation areas but information is lacking.

# Red-bellied guenon
## *Cercopithecus erythrogaster* Ⓔ

The red-bellied, or white-throated, guenon is recognised as two races, which may justify subspecies status. There is a grey-bellied and a red-bellied form. Overall coat colour is brown-agouti, with a black face and a white throat ruff. The belly is either reddish or grey, depending on the race.

This guenon is restricted to lowland rainforest in south-western Nigeria, west of the Niger River. The grey-bellied form is the more widespread but populations are becoming increasingly fragmented. Only two fair-sized populations survive, each made up of a few hundred or thousand animals. One occurs in the Okomu Forest Reserve (1 238 sq km) and the other in the Omo Forest Reserve (some 500 sq km).

The red-bellied form is found only in the dwindling forest

| **RED-BELLIED GUENON** | |
| --- | --- |
| **Total length** | about 1 m |
| **Tail length** | about 60 cm |
| **Mass** | ♂ about 6 kg |
| **Troop size** | 5-30 (poorly known) |

patches of far south-western Nigeria. There are unconfirmed reports of its occurrence in adjacent areas of Benin. Both forms are restricted to high canopy forest, secondary forest and dense vegetation at forest fringes. Virtually nothing is known of their behaviour and needs.

The usual threats of habitat destruction and hunting face these guenons. The fact that Nigeria has Africa's largest human population poses severe survival problems for all biota. Protection of conservation areas is poor. The red-bellied guenon is therefore considered to be one of Africa's most endangered primates and there is little hope for long-term survival. In fact, the rate of forest destruction in Nigeria, and of course the rest of west Africa, could mean the disappearance of several primate species in that region within the next ten to twenty years.

# Red-eared guenon
## *Cercopithecus erythrotis*

This guenon has three subspecies. One, Sclater's guenon *(Cercopithecus erythrotis sclateri)* may deserve full species status. The red-eared guenon is a fairly small monkey with a predominantly blue face. The muzzle is pinkish and the nose spot is brick red to orange in both *erythrotis* and *camerunensis,* but *sclateri* has the spot whitish with a slightly ochre tinge. The amount of red hair on the tail also varies between subspecies.

Virtually nothing is known about these guenons' behaviour, apart from the fact that they have been recorded in multi-male troops in Cameroon and that they form temporary associations with other guenon species. Although their diet is unknown it seems likely that they are mixed feeders with a strong preference for plant parts, particularly fruits.

*C.e. erythrotis* is restricted to the island of Bioko in the Gulf of Guinea, *C.e. camerunensis* occurs in south-eastern Nigeria and northern Cameroon between the Benue and Sanaga rivers and *C.e. sclateri* is found, patchily, only in the Niger Delta and along the lower course of the Niger River.

The status of the animals on Bioko *(erythrotis)* is unknown. *C.e. camerunensis* is present in several reserves, including Korup

**Above:** *Red-bellied guenon* (Cercopithecus erythrogaster).
PHOTO: *Roland Wirth.* **Right:** *The three recognised races of the red-eared guenon* (Cercopithecus erythrotis) *have not been studied in the wild, but the restricted nature of their ranges holds serious consequences for their long-term survival.* PHOTO: *Norman Tomalin, Bruce Coleman Ltd.*

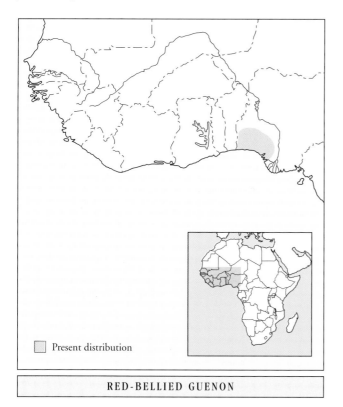

Present distribution

RED-BELLIED GUENON

| RED-EARED GUENON | |
| --- | --- |
| **Total length** | ♂ 1,3 m; ♀ 90 cm |
| **Tail length** | 46-77 cm |
| **Mass** | 2,2-4,2 kg |
| **Troop size** | 4-30 or more |
| **Diet** | unknown |

National Park, but protection is limited.

Sclater's guenon is believed to survive in only five discrete populations. Two of these populations occur close to Igbo villages where they are considered to be sacred and are therefore protected. Each protected group numbers fewer than 250 individuals and increased habitat degradation and reduction in traditional values could result in their eventual eradication. The other populations are located in swamp forest on the Niger River floodplain (where they could be threatened by further expansion of the Akri oil field), in Stubbs

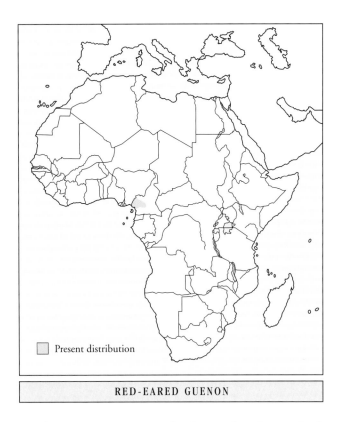

**RED-EARED GUENON**

Creek Forest Reserve in Anambra State and on the west bank of the Cross River near Utuma village. Although Sclater's guenons are present in two forest reserves they are largely unprotected.

Red-eared guenons occupy primary lowland rainforest, seasonal swamp forest, secondary and early development forest.

All three subspecies of this guenon are endangered.

## Red colobus complex

All red colobus species and subspecies are relatively large-bodied and long-limbed. They are leaf-eaters, with a four-chambered stomach to cope with the digestion of this plant food. As their name implies, all have reddish coats, with some black or dark brown colouring. The underparts are generally lighter in colour than the back.

Several of the guenon species groups are taxonomically complex and require considerable study and revision, but the red colobus (*Procolobus*) monkeys are the worst. At present five full species and nine additional subspecies are generally recognised. Some authorities recognise even more. All are placed by some authorities in a super-species, *badius*.

Of these 14 species or subspecies, eight are considered to be endangered, five vulnerable, and one rare. The remaining animals, which some authorities regard as subspecies, are so poorly known that their conservation status cannot be categorised. The issue has become even more complex with the discovery that at least nine subspecies seem to be present in the Congo /Lualaba Basin and the Upper Nile valley alone, as well as two hybrid complexes with a mix of several of these subspecies.

One wonders whether these complexities will ever be unravelled. Amazingly little is known about these agile and handsome primates. Most research work has been undertaken on animals in the Kibale Forest in Uganda (Uganda red colobus *Procolobus rufomitratus tephrosceles*). Troops tend to be fairly stable with several adult males, but mature females seem to migrate between troops. Their leaf food is generally so abundant that troop home ranges overlap considerably and animals only cover short distances each day when foraging.

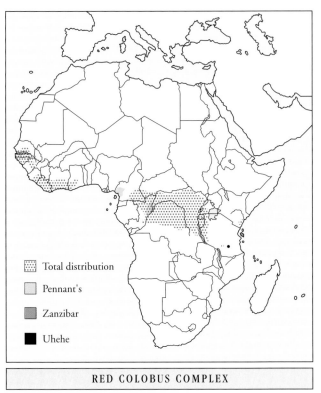

Total distribution
Pennant's
Zanzibar
Uhehe

**RED COLOBUS COMPLEX**

### RED COLOBUS COMPLEX

| | |
|---|---|
| **Total length** | 88-140 cm (sexual dimorphism most marked in western populations) |
| **Tail length** | 42-80 cm |
| **Mass** | 7-13 kg |
| **Home range** | 9-35 ha (not known for many populations) |
| **Troop size** | 25-50; smaller in some populations |
| **Diet** | predominantly leaves; fruits, seeds, perhaps invertebrates |
| **Number surviving** | |
| *bouvieri:* | extremely low |
| *pennanti:* | close to extinction |
| *preussi:* | below 8 000 |

In general the red colobus of west Africa, along with all other biota in that region, are threatened by massive and escalating habitat destruction and a rapidly growing human population.

In discussing the red colobus we have digressed from the conservation category approach of previous sections, primarily to avoid confusion. We will now look briefly at the different populations of the red colobus.

## Western red colobus
### *Procolobus badius*

Of the three subspecies, Miss Waldron's bay colobus *(P.b. waldroni)* is classified as endangered, the bay colobus *(P.b. badius)* is classified as vulnerable, and Temminck's red colobus *(P.b. temminckii)* is classified as rare.

The endangered Miss Waldron's bay colobus occurs only in the high forests of southern Ivory Coast to the east of the Bandama River and into western Ghana. In the past it has been recorded in the Bia and Nini-Souhien national parks but

Above: *Western red colobus* (Procolobus badius), *Senegal.*
PHOTO: *Paul Vercammen.*

its present status in these conservation areas is unknown.

The vulnerable bay colobus occurs patchily in high forest in Sierra Leone, Liberia, Guinea and Ivory Coast. No population estimates are available but habitat destruction has almost certainly resulted in drastic declines.

The rare Temminck's red colobus occurs mainly in coastal forest types in southern Senegal, Gambia, Guinea Bissau and north-western Guinea. The less threatened status of this red colobus is probably indicative of its more flexible habitat requirements. The other two subspecies show a greater preference for more closed forest.

## Pennant's red colobus
### *Procolobus pennanti* Ⓔ

This is another west African group. Its three distinct subspecies are all considered to be endangered. *P.p. preussi* is restricted to lowland evergreen forests in northern Cameroon along the

Nigerian border. The total range covers less than 7 200 sq km. The majority of the population occurs in Korup National Park. *P.p. bouvieri* is only known definitely from the Lefini Reserve but it is possible that small numbers may still occur in pockets in the vicinity.

*P.p. pennanti* is restricted to the island of Bioko. The principal population was centred on the 5 km diameter Caldera de San Carlos in the island's interior but no recent surveys have been done. However, it is generally believed that there has been a recovery in primate populations on the island in recent years.

Apart from the fact that Pennant's red colobus are restricted to established high and gallery forest, little is known about their ecology or requirements. It has been reported that *preussi* is restricted to coastal lowland evergreen forest with rainfall in excess of 1 000 mm. This subspecies at least is said to consort in troops of up to 50 individuals. Habitat loss through logging and hunting for meat pose the principal threats to their survival.

## Eastern red colobus
### *Procolobus rufomitratus* Ⓔ

This group is recognised as a complex of six subspecies which are distinct from the two western populations discussed above. They occur in central and east Africa. Four of the six subspecies are restricted to eastern Congo (DR), namely *P.r. tholloni, foai, foai, ellioti* and *oustaleti. P.r. tephrosceles* has a limited distribution in Uganda and Tanzania and the Tana River red colobus *(P.r. rufomitratus)* is restricted to a portion of the Tana River in Kenya. The Kenyan population is the most endangered. A 1985 survey indicated that there were fewer than 300 individuals surviving, a drop from possibly just under 2 000 in 1972. The total river frontage of forest in which this subspecies occurs is only 52 km, and it faces the same problems of isolation and dwindling habitat that confront the Tana River mangabey (discussed above). It could become extinct in the near future.

The four subspecies from Congo (DR) are so poorly known that we have no idea of their conservation status, although given the remote nature of their range they are probably under

Above: *Eastern red colobus* (Procolobus rufomitratus), *Uganda.*

no immediate threat. The Uganda red colobus *(P.r. tephrosce-les)* is considered to be vulnerable. It is restricted to south-western Uganda and Tanzania, where it occurs in a tiny forest patch on the edge of the Bilharamula Game Reserve and in Birigi Game Reserve. It also occurs in a few isolated forest pockets along the edge of Lake Tanganyika but it is known to have become extinct in a number of such sites in the past four decades. One estimate in 1981 put the total Tanzanian population at fewer than 300 individuals. In Uganda the principal population appears to be centred on the Kibale Forest where densities average an amazing 297 animals per square kilometre.

Populations of the Uganda red colobus occur in troops numbering 25 to 50 animals, with several adult males in each troop. In Kibale, home ranges average 35 ha. Some 80% of this subspecies' diet is made up of leaves and leaf parts. Troops of the Tana River red colobus have an average range of only 9 ha, and leaves form only 64% of their food intake.

Habitat destruction is the major threat to these colobus; hunting appears to be minimal at this stage.

## Uhele red colobus
### *Procolobus gordonorum* Ⓔ

This species, also known as Gordon's or the Iringa red colobus, is only found in the forests on the southern and eastern slopes of the Uzungwa Mountains in south-central Tanzania. It is restricted to riverine and montane forest patches above 550 m. In the Magombero Forest Reserve troops average some 25 individuals but within the Uzungwa Forest troops of between four and six animals have been recorded. In the Uzungwas they commonly associate with black and white colobus monkeys but in Magombero they form polyspecific associations with several forest guenon species.

Despite the fact that the Magombero Forest Reserve has been incorporated into the Selous Game Reserve, the animals still face numerous threats due to inadequate controls. Timber extraction, charcoal production, agricultural expansion, rubber plantations and meat hunting are the major problems.

## Zanzibar red colobus
### *Procolobus kirkii* Ⓔ

This colobus is also classified as endangered because of its restricted distribution. It is an island endemic, occurring at very low population densities in small, isolated forest patches throughout Zanzibar (Unguja). The highest densities occur in four forest pockets: Jozani, Muungwi, the Muyuni coastal strip and the adjacent Uzi Island. There are translocated populations in Masingini, Kichwele and on Pemba Island. Although no recent population survey has been undertaken, in 1981 there were estimated to be at least 1 500 animals. This number seems to have remained constant to 1997. Most animals are found in association with swamp forest, but they also occur in scrub forest and mangrove swamp.

## Black colobus
### *Colobus satanas* Ⓔ

The black colobus is characterised by having a totally black, glossy coat and a crown of semi-erect forward-pointing hairs. No subspecies are recognised. It once occurred in a more or less contiguous belt stretching 1 000 km from the Sanaga to the Congo rivers, over a width of about 240 km, but this has been greatly reduced and fragmented in recent years. It is now definitely known to occur in south-west Cameroon, Rio Muni (Equatorial Guinea) including Bioko, and western and central Gabon. No recent records are available from Congo. Although densities are considered to be relatively high in a few areas, overall distribution and population levels have decreased over the past 30 years. According to the meagre reports that are available the black colobus is largely restricted to dense prima-

| BLACK COLOBUS | |
|---|---|
| **Total length** | 1,2-1,42 m |
| **Tail length** | 60-96 cm |
| **Mass** | 6-11 kg |
| **Home range** | 70 ha (coastal forest); 180 ha (inland forest) |
| **Troop size** | 6-15 |
| **Diet** | young leaves and seeds |

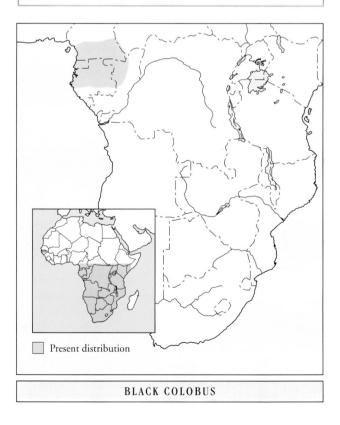

☐ Present distribution

BLACK COLOBUS

Above: *The mist-shrouded forest habitat of the golden monkey.*
Photo: *Harry van Rompaey.*

ry forest, where it frequents the high canopy. The primary threats are habitat destruction and hunting; it has been estimated that up to 1972, 1 000 to 1 500 black colobus were being killed each year in Rio Muni (Equatorial Guinea) for food. This primate is not known to occur in any formal conservation area.

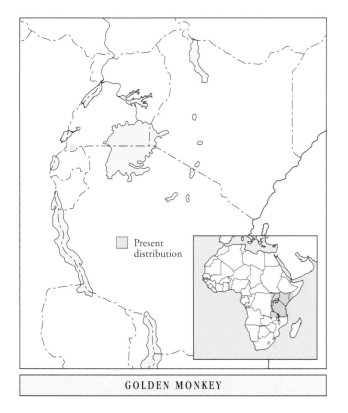

GOLDEN MONKEY

Present distribution

## Golden monkey
*Cercopithecus mitis kandti* **E**

This beautifully coloured subspecies of the "blue" monkey is the most restricted in distribution. Many races and subspecies of the "blue" and "Sykes's" monkeys are recognised (for example *mitis* and *albogularis*). Some have very restricted distributions. This race, *kandti*, coexists with *C.m. doggetti*, which indicates that it may in fact be a full species. It occurs only in the high altitude forest and bamboo belt in the volcanic area of Bufumbira in Kigezi, on the border between south-western Uganda and Rwanda. It numbers only a few hundred individuals.

## VULNERABLE

There are a number of African primates in this category, defined as species that are believed likely to move into the endangered category in the near future unless something is done to halt, or at least drastically reduce, the reasons for their decline.

## Barbary macaque
*Macaca sylvanus* **V**

### Description and taxonomy

The Barbary macaque is a large, tailless monkey with a long-haired grey-yellow to grey-brown coat and a dark pink face.

Above: *Zanzibar red colobus* (Procolobus kirkii). Photo: *John Young.*

## BARBARY MACAQUE

| | |
|---|---|
| **Total length** | 56-70 cm |
| **Mass** | 10-15 kg (occasionally more) |
| **Home range** | 25-1 000 ha or more (dependent on food availability) |
| **Troop size** | 7-40 |
| **Birth season** | February to June |
| **Diet** | fruits, leaves, bulbs, roots, some animal food |

### Distribution and habitat

This is the only primate that occurs to the north of the Sahara Desert. It is the only member of this genus represented on the continent. All other members of the genus, 14 species, are found in Asia. Small numbers occur in the British settlement of Gibraltar at the southern tip of the Iberian Peninsula but their origins are obscure. The Gibraltar population has been supplemented with animals caught in north Africa and it is generally thought that the original stock was introduced. However, it has been suggested that this could be a remnant population with its origins in the pre-glacial era, as old skulls were collected here in the 18th century.

Before the end of the last century these macaques occurred widely over north-western Africa to as far east as western Libya. Populations and ranges shrank during the 1900s but they had already been under pressure over a period of several centuries.

The Barbary macaque is now known only from five regions in the Middle Atlas, High Atlas and Rif in Morocco, and from seven locations in Grande Kabylie and Petite Kabylie in north-western Algeria. These populations are not uniformly distributed, but are scattered and to a large extent isolated from each other. It is now extinct in Tunisia.

Although in the past these primates occupied a wide range of forest types, they are now limited to scrub and forests in the more remote mountains and associated gorges up to an altitude of 3 500 m.

### Behaviour

Each troop has several males and occupies a home range of variable size. Ranges are smallest in areas with the most food and the least human disturbance. Although much time is spent on the ground, these macaques climb readily.

### Conservation

In the early 1970s an estimated 12 000 to 23 000 Barbary macaques survived, of which possibly as much as 80% occur-

**Above:** *Barbary macaques* (Macaca sylvanus) *are the only primates found in north Africa, where they are now threatened by loss of habitat and persecution by humans.* PHOTO: *Mike & Debbie Jordan, Aquila.*

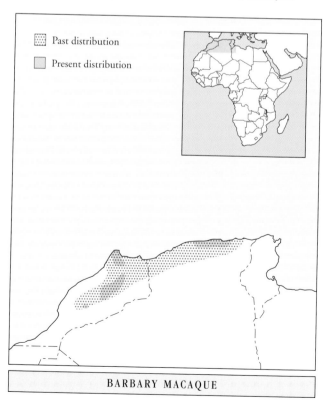

Past distribution

Present distribution

BARBARY MACAQUE

red in the Moroccan Middle Atlas mountains. However, only a small number of animals in Morocco receive adequate protection. Efforts have been made to reintroduce Barbary macaques to areas in Morocco where they had previously occurred, but with mixed results. In Algeria much of the population is protected in national parks. Principal threats include timber harvesting, clearing of forest and killing of these monkeys because they raid crops.

# Red-capped mangabey
## *Cercocebus torquatus* Ⓥ

This large monkey is characterised by bright chestnut-red hair on top of the head.

The species is divided into three subspecies by some authorities *(atys, lunulatus and torquatus)*, but others consider *atys* to be a separate species and *lunulatus* a subspecies of it. All are under threat from habitat loss and considerable hunting pressure.

| RED-CAPPED MANGABEY | |
|---|---|
| **Total length** | 85-140 cm |
| **Tail length** | 40-80 cm |
| **Mass** | 4,5-12 kg (♂ larger than ♀) |
| **Troop size** | 14-23 or more |
| **Diet** | mainly fruit, some animal food; raids crops in some areas |

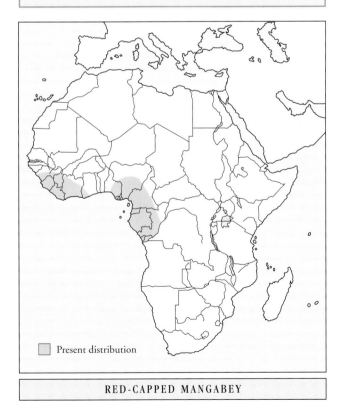

☐ Present distribution

RED-CAPPED MANGABEY

*C.t. torquatus* occurs eastwards from the Dahomey Gap in Nigeria, southern Cameroon, Rio Muni (Equatorial Guinea), Gabon and Congo. It occurs in a wide range of forest habitats, but mainly primary forest. Although it is known from a number of conservation areas, many of these reserves are inadequately protected.

# Mandrill
## *Mandrillus sphinx* Ⓥ

The male mandrill is one of Africa's most dramatically coloured primates. This large, short-tailed animal is distinguished by a long, dog-like face which is brightly coloured in red and blue. The colouring is particularly vivid in adult males. The males' rumps are naked and also impressively coloured.

The mandrill and the drill are sometimes grouped with the baboons in the genus *Papio*. Three subspecies of the mandrill have been described but their validity is uncertain. *M.s. sphinx*

| MANDRILL | |
|---|---|
| **Total length** | ♂ 90 cm; ♀ 55 cm |
| **Tail length** | 7-10 cm |
| **Shoulder height** | ♂ 60 cm; ♀ 45 cm |
| **Mass** | ♂ 30 kg; ♀ 10 kg |
| **Home range** | 30-50 sq km (poorly known) |
| **Troop size** | 15-50 (temporary groups of over 200) |
| **Gestation** | 7,5 months |
| **Diet** | fruits and other plant parts, invertebrates, small vertebrates |

has been reported from north and west of the Sanaga River but we are not aware of any recent records to confirm this. It is now generally accepted that the drill occurs to the north of that river and the mandrill to the south. The subspecies *M.s. insularis* occurs only on the island of Bioko. No recent information is available about any animals on this island.

Current information indicates that the mandrill is only found in the western Congolean forest block to the south of the Sanaga River, in southern Cameroon, Rio Muni (Equatorial Guinea), west Gabon and the south-west of Congo. In Cameroon, at least, populations have been decimated and this could well be the case throughout its range. Gabon is probably its principal refuge, as it is for many other species. The mandrill occurs in a variety of forest types but it is sensitive to disturbance. In many areas it is hunted for its meat. Although it is present in a number of conservation areas, there is minimal or no management of these reserves.

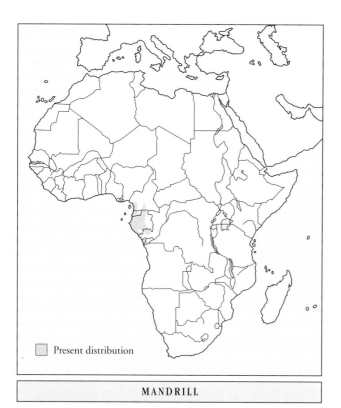

Present distribution

MANDRILL

**Above:** *Male mandrill* (Mandrillus sphinx). PHOTO: *Klaus Rudloff*

The mandrill is not considered to be as seriously threatened as the only other member of its genus, the drill. However, it has been hunted to extinction in some areas and its occurrence in fairly low densities throughout its range means that it could easily become endangered.

# Diana guenon
## *Cercopithecus diana*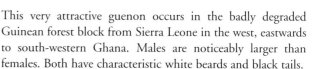

This very attractive guenon occurs in the badly degraded Guinean forest block from Sierra Leone in the west, eastwards to south-western Ghana. Males are noticeably larger than females. Both have characteristic white beards and black tails.

Two subspecies are recognised, *C.d. diana* to the west of the Sassandra River and *C.d. roloway* to the east of this river. The Diana guenon has been considered rare in some areas for many years. Reports of its occurrence to the east of the Benin Gap appear highly unlikely.

This guenon is largely confined to the rapidly disappearing high canopy forest, but it also occurs in mature secondary forest and riparian forest. The threats faced by all other primates in this region apply equally to this guenon. Although it does occur in a few conservation areas, most are subject to high levels of illegal clearing, logging and hunting.

| DIANA GUENON | |
|---|---|
| **Total length** | 90-140 cm |
| **Tail length** | 50-80 cm |
| **Mass** | 2,2-7 kg or more |
| **Home range** | 189 ha in one study |
| **Troop size** | 15-40 (up to 50) |
| **Diet** | fruits, seeds, invertebrates |

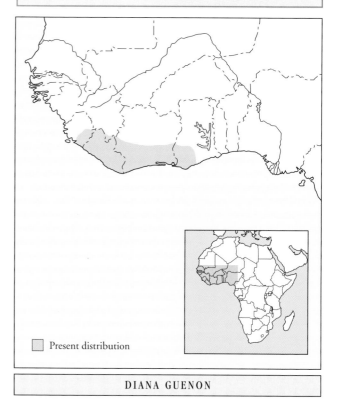

Present distribution

DIANA GUENON

# Salonga guenon
## *Cercopithecus salonga* Ⓥ

This small guenon was first described in 1977 but its validity as a separate species is in question. It is only known from the Wambe Forest in western Congo (DR). It occurs in thickets within secondary forest and occasionally enters swamp forest. Troop sizes range from two to 30 and they associate with other guenon species. It is possible that it has a wider distribution than is presently known.

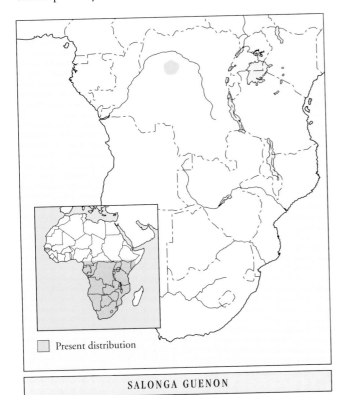

Present distribution

**SALONGA GUENON**

Above: *Owl-faced guenon* (Cercopithecus hamlyni).

# L'Hoest's guenon
## *Cercopithecus lhoesti* Ⓥ

# Owl-faced guenon
## *Cercopithecus hamlyni* Ⓥ

These two species are both dark-coloured. The owl-faced guenon has a distinctive white line down the front of its face. L'Hoest's, also known as the mountain guenon, has a very obvious white bib. They share a similar range. Both species occur in eastern Congo (DR), and L'Hoest's guenon extends marginally into adjacent areas of Uganda and Rwanda.

Virtually nothing is known about the behaviour of the owl-faced guenon in the wild. It has been recorded at altitudes of up to 4 600 m. Although this guenon has been reported to be at least partly nocturnal, this seems unlikely.

Both species occur mainly in montane forests but with some spillover into lower-lying forests.

|  | L'HOEST'S | OWL-FACED |
|---|---|---|
| **Total length** | 0,90-1,5 m | about 1,1 m |
| **Tail length** | 46-80 cm | about 55 cm |
| **Mass** | 3-8 kg | unknown |
| **Troop size** | 10-17 or more | below 10 |
| **Diet** | mainly fruits | poorly known |

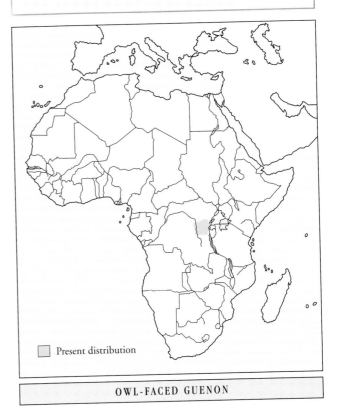

Present distribution

**OWL-FACED GUENON**

## Sun-tailed guenon
### *Cercopithecus solatus* Ⓥ

The sun-tailed guenon, discovered in 1984, was described for the first time in 1988. It is endemic to lowland rainforest in central Gabon over a total range of probably less than 9 000 sq km. Virtually nothing is known about its ecology or conservation requirements.

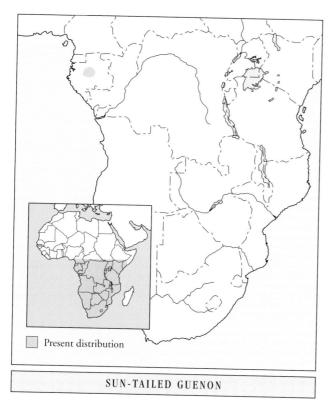

☐ Present distribution

**SUN-TAILED GUENON**

## RARE

In this category there are a number of primate species that at first glance do not appear to be under any major threat, but increasing human populations could push them rapidly into decline. We mention only two briefly.

## Gelada
### *Theropithecus gelada* Ⓡ

## Hamadryas baboon
### *Papio hamadryas* Ⓡ

Both these species occur in north-eastern Africa but their habitat requirements are quite different. The gelada occurs only in the Ethiopian Highlands at altitudes ranging from 2 000 m to 5 000 m where it competes for food with domestic livestock. It is hunted for the impressive capes of the males.

|  | GELADA | HAMADRYAS |
|---|---|---|
| **Total length** | ♂ 1,3 m; ♀ 90 cm | ♂ 1,5 m; ♀ 1,2 m |
| **Tail length** | ♂ 55 cm; ♀ 40 cm | ♂ 70 cm; ♀ 60 cm |
| **Shoulder height** | 40-60 cm | 40-60 cm |
| **Mass** | ♂ 20 kg; ♀ 10 kg | ♂ 20 kg; ♀ 10 kg |
| **Home range** | about 10 sq km | about 30 sq km |
| **Troop size** | loose bands 50-250 | troops up to 600 |
| **Diet** | 90% grass | varied: plant and animal |
| **Number surviving** | about 600 000 | unknown but 90% in Ethiopia |

The hamadryas baboon is restricted to more arid habitats in the Horn of Africa and along the Red Sea coast, with limited populations in the south of the Arabian Peninsula. It has been recorded up to an altitude of 3 300 m in the Simien Mountains in the north of Ethiopia. It occurred previously into Egypt where it was revered as being sacred to Thoth, the moon god, but it is now extinct in that country. The severe droughts in recent decades in both species' distribution areas have surely had a major impact on the populations. They occur in areas of rapidly increasing human populations.

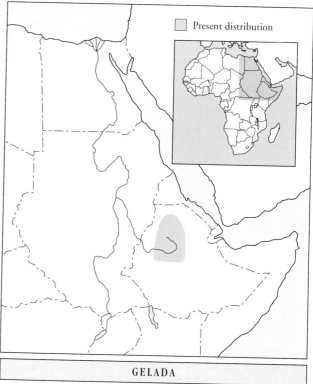

☐ Present distribution

**GELADA**

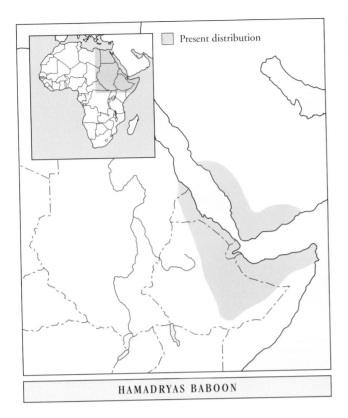

Present distribution

**HAMADRYAS BABOON**

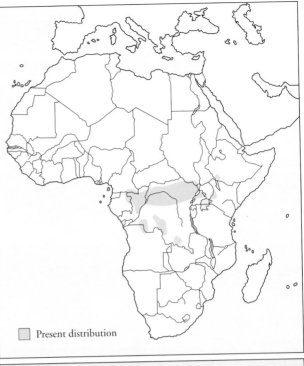

Present distribution

**DE BRAZZA'S MONKEY**

## Other true monkeys

Although no other members of the family Cercopithecidae are threatened over their full range, many local extinctions have undoubtedly taken place even among common species. A number of species are so poorly known that it is impossible to place them in any specific conservation category. Even species such as De Brazza's monkey *(Cercopithecus neglectus)*, which has a wide equatorial distribution in central Africa, is now considered to be seriously endangered in Kenya where it is restricted to forests on the slopes of Mount Elgon and possibly one or two other locations in the far west of the country.

The regular discovery of new species, subspecies and races of cercopithecene monkeys from Africa's tropical forests, particularly in the Congolean block, prompts the question, "What has been lost before it was found?" Many taxonomic problems related to these monkeys remain unresolved. Relationships among many species complexes are poorly understood.

## LORISIDAE

### *Potto and bushbabies*

Sixteen members of this family occur in sub-Saharan Africa. Most are not under any particular known threat, but we know very little about the species and their requirements.

A major problem in determining the conservation status of the bushbabies or galagos is the difficulty in identifying individual species in the field. However, as far as is known each

**Above:** *Gelada* (Theropithecus gelada) *male showing bare breast patch.*

species has a distinctive repertoire of calls which could be useful in establishing species distribution.

Only the Zanzibar galago *(Galago zanzibaricus)* is considered to be vulnerable because of its limited distribution on the island of Zanzibar and in coastal forests along the coasts of Kenya and Tanzania, all of which are being subjected to considerable destruction and disturbance. However, it has been found to occupy disturbed forests, which seems to indicate that it may not be as threatened as has been believed.

# CHAPTER 6

# ANTELOPES

## *Grace on the run*

Discharging both barrels into the retreating phalanx
leaving the ground strewn with the slain.

W. Cornwallis Harris – *Wild sports of southern Africa, 1839*

Africa is truly the continent of the antelope, a loose term that has no taxonomic significance but only serves to separate these hollow-horned hoofed mammals from other ungulates such as cattle, goats and sheep.

There is no certainty as to the exact number of antelope species that roam the savannas, forests and deserts of Africa: totals depend on the whims of taxonomists. Conservatively there are some 79 distinct species and a great number of sub-

species, many of which are of questionable validity. There are, however, a number of subspecies that are quite distinct, such as the two waterbuck, the common (*Kobus ellipsiprymnus ellipsiprymnus*) and the defassa (*K.e. defassa*). They are similar in appearance except that the white ring encircling the rump of the former is incomplete, whereas in the latter it forms a solid white circle. But this apparently easy separation is negated by the fact that there are areas where the two interbreed, and indi-

**Above:** *The red lechwe* (Kobus leche leche) *has a patchy distribution and has suffered a severe reduction in numbers, particularly in the Linyanti Swamp of Namibia.* PHOTO: *Anthony Bannister, ABPL.*
**Right:** *The bontebok* (Damaliscus dorcas dorcas).

food for additional chewing, ensuring maximum digestion.

The modern antelope are separated into several distinct groupings. The tribe Strepciserotini, or spiral-horned antelope, includes nine species of which two, the common eland *(Taurotragus oryx)* and the giant eland *(T. derbianus)*, are the largest living antelope.

The subfamily Cephalophinae is reserved exclusively for the duikers, a predominantly forest-dwelling group, with the notable exception of the abundant and widespread common, or bush, duiker *(Sylvicapra grimmia)*. The duikers are small to medium-sized antelope occurring only in Africa. At least 17 distinct species are recognised. Several species are severely threatened by habitat destruction and hunting, but more of this later.

There are 24 species of predominantly grazing antelope in the subfamily Hippotraginae, whose diverse range includes the reedbuck *(Redunca* spp.), waterbuck, lechwe, puku, kob *(Kobus* spp.), grey rhebok *(Pelea capreolus)*, bontebok, topi, tsessebe *(Damaliscus* spp.), hirola *(Beatragus/Damaliscus hunteri)*, harte-beest *(Alcelaphus* spp.), wildebeest *(Connochaetes* spp.), impala *(Aepyceros melampus)*, roan and sable *(Hippotragus* spp.), addax *(Addax nasomaculatus)* and oryx *(Oryx* spp.).

An even more diverse subfamily is the Antilopinae, with approximately 30 species in Africa. They range in size from the approximately 2 kg royal antelope *(Neotragus pygmaeus)* to the 85 kg male dama gazelle *(Gazella dama)*. The subfamily is divided into two tribes, the so-called dwarf antelopes (tribe Neotragini), which includes the royal, pygmy and suni antelopes *(Neotragus* spp.), the dik-diks *(Madoqua* spp.), klip-springer *(Oreotragus oreotragus)*, steenbok and grysbok *(Raphicerus* spp.), oribi *(Ourebia ourebi)* and the little-known beira *(Dorcatragus megalotis)*. The other tribe (Antilopini) is dominated by the gazelles *(Gazella* spp.), which occur mainly in arid areas. It also has two of the strangest antelope, the gerenuk *(Litocranius walleri)* and the dibatag *(Ammodorcas clarkei)*. Only one member of this tribe, the springbok *(Antidorcas marsupi-alis)*, occurs in southern Africa. The only antelope to occur naturally in Africa and eastwards into Asia, the dorcas gazelle *(Gazella dorcas)*, is also placed in this tribe.

A further six gazelle species occur in the Middle East and into Asia.

A number of Africa's endangered antelope species, such as the addax and scimitar-horned oryx, are more abundant in captivity and on game ranches, the latter par-ticularly in the south-western United States, than they are on their home continent.

Two species of African antelope have become extinct in recent times. The blue buck *(Hip-potragus leucophaeus)* of the southernmost tip of the continent had disappeared by 1799.

viduals within these populations cannot easily be classified as one or the other subspecies. The bontebok and blesbok *(Damaliscus dorcas)* of South Africa are distinct from each other in coloration, although in structure and form they are identical.

In this chapter we cover a number of subspecies threatened with eventual extinction, although the species as a whole may remain fairly secure for the foreseeable future.

The antelopes belong to a large group referred to as the even-toed ungulates, or Artiodactyla, which they share with the pigs, peccaries, hippopotamuses, camels, chevrotains, musk deer, deer, giraffe and wild cattle. The even-toed ungu-lates first appear in the fossil record in the early Eocene, about 54 million years ago, in Eurasia and North America. In Africa they made their first appearance as ruminants ("cud-chewers") some 25 million years ago in the early Miocene era.

The ruminants are specialised herbivores (the present-day antelopes all belong to this group) which have a multi-cham-bered stomach and the ability to regurgitate swallowed plant

The so-called red gazelle *(Gazella rufina)* is only known from specimens obtained towards the end of the 1890s in markets in northern Algeria. No recent specimens have come to light and it is presumed that the species is extinct.

Other species, such as the black wildebeest, or white-tailed gnu, and the bontebok had been brought back from the brink by the timely action of private landowners before wildlife preservation was a considered issue. Later they were given protection in national parks and other conservation areas.

There are several species that are of critical conservation concern, particularly within west Africa, including the arid Sahelian belt. These include such duiker species as Jentink's *(Cephalophus jentinki)* and the zebra duiker *(C. zebra)*, the scimitar-horned oryx *(Oryx dammah)*, the addax *(Addax nasomaculatus)* and all gazelle species. There are also several distinct subspecies that are threatened, for example the western hartebeest *(Alcelaphus buselaphus major)* which survives only in isolated pockets, yet but a few decades ago was probably the most abundant plains antelope from Senegal in the west to Congo in the east. The northernmost hartebeest subspecies, the bubal *(A.b. buselaphus)*, once roamed much of north Africa but is now extinct. In east Africa, of particular concern is the hirola or Hunter's hartebeest *(Damaliscus hunteri)*, which is restricted to a narrow strip of land in an arid region of north-eastern

Kenya. Even seemingly abundant species, such as the blue wildebeest or brindled gnu *(Connochaetes taurinus)*, have declined drastically in some regions although it remains stable in others.

It is in the Sahel, parts of the Sahara and adjacent areas to the north and south where many antelope populations have suffered the greatest impact. Several species in these areas are classified as endangered, and some are on the verge of extinction in the wild.

Even where large numbers of antelope species still occur, pressures caused by humans, such as fencing, increasing human populations, competition with domestic stock for food and water, as well as direct hunting on both a subsistence and commercial scale, leave no place for complacency.

In the following accounts we cover antelopes that are considered to be endangered, threatened, vulnerable or decreasing in numbers, either on the species or subspecies level. But first we take a brief look at the best documented extinct species in Africa, the blue buck.

# HIPPOTRAGINI

*Horse-like antelope*

## Blue buck
### *Hippotragus leucophaeus*  **EXTINCT**

This ungulate belonged to the same genus as the sable and roan antelopes which still roam Africa's wooded savannas. It was first described in a publication by the German businessman Peter Kolb in 1719. His book was translated into English, *The present state of the Cape of Good Hope*, by Medley in 1731. In it Kolb gives a rather fanciful description of this antelope:

> *The Blew Goats are shap'd like the Tame, but are as large as an European Hart. Their Hair is very short and of a delicate Blew; but the colour fades when they are kill'd to a blewish grey. Their beards, which are pretty long, add not a little to their Comliness. Their Hornes are not long in proportion to those of other Goats, but they are very neat, and run very curiously up in Rings till within a lit-*

**Below:** *The southern form of the red or bubal hartebeest* (Alcelaphus buselaphus) *is still abundant, but numbers and range have shrunk dramatically.*

| BLUE BUCK | | |
|---|---|---|
| **Total length** | ♂ 2,5-2,61 m; ♀ 2,37 m | |
| **Tail length** | ♂ 50-55 cm; ♀ 49 cm | |
| **Shoulder height** | ♂ 1,05-1,16 m; ♀ 1,02 m | |
| **Mass** | ♂ 160-170 kg; ♀ 150 kg | |
| **Horns** | ♂ 55-61 cm; ♀ 51-56 cm | |
| **Diet** | browse and graze | |

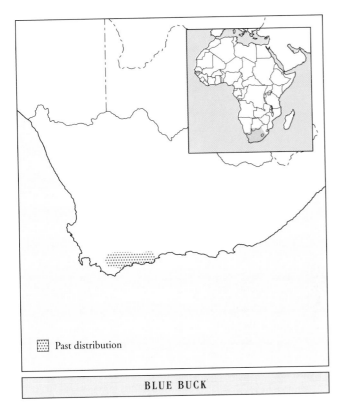

**BLUE BUCK**

that the species had once been more widespread.

By 1774 the famous traveller and naturalist Thunberg noted the increasing rarity of the blue buck ("blaauwbock" to the local Dutch-speaking farmers). Lichtenstein recorded that the last animal had been shot by 1799. Although some reports have the date as 1800, there is little point in quibbling over a discrepancy of a few months.

The blame for the demise of the blue buck is often put on farmers and hunters of European origin, but it seems probable that the decline had been under way since as early as AD 400, when sheep first entered the archaeological record. Sheep would have competed with blue buck for grazing, and no doubt some measure of subsistence hunting was taking place. However, it was the Europeans with their firearms who hammered the final nail in the blue buck's coffin. Today we are left with four faded and moth-eaten museum mounts, a few bones – some of dubious authenticity – and a small selection of sketches, paintings and writings. Let us try to ensure that no more antelope species join the blue buck in being reduced to no more than a handful of relics for future generations.

## Sable antelope
### *Hippotragus niger* **R**

The sable is still fairly common: about 30 000 animals live in Tanzania and several thousand in southern Africa. However, the population in south-eastern Congo (DR) is endangered, as is a remnant group of probably fewer than 300 animals in the Shimba Hills National Reserve in south-eastern Kenya.

A population in north-western Angola is recognised as a distinct subspecies, the giant sable (*H.n. variani*), and is separated by hundreds of kilometres from populations in eastern and southern Africa. In 1970 it was estimated that between 2 000

*tle of the Point; which is streight and smooth. Their Legs are long, but not out of Proportion. Their Flesh is well tast'd but rarely fat. And they are rarely kill'd but for the sake of their Skins; which are as good as those of a Deer. Their Flesh is generally given to the Dogs. These Goats are only to be met with far up in the Country.*

By 1766 the naturalist Peter Simon Pallas had provided the first scientific description of the blue buck, dispelling the myth that it was goat-like, with chin beard.

Piecing together all the evidence and examining the four remaining mounted specimens of the blue buck present us with the picture of an elegant antelope. It was smaller than either the closely related sable or roan antelope, with a shoulder height of between 1 m and 1,2 m. The overall coat colour, as described by Le Vaillant (1790), was faint blue to grey, with dull white underparts. The forehead down to the muzzle was brown, and the sides of the face were paler. A distinct whitish patch was located in front of the eye, from which it gained its specific name, *leucophaeus*. The horns had a slight backward curve and were heavily ridged.

Although some authorities have in the past held the belief that the blue buck was simply a subspecies of the roan (*Hippotragus equinus*) it is now generally accepted that it was distinct enough to be a full species in its own right.

At the time of arrival of the first Europeans at the Cape of Good Hope, the blue buck was apparently restricted to the coastal plain, sandwiched between the mountain chain and the ocean, and roaming areas of suitable habitat over less than 4 000 sq km. Bones of the blue buck have been found along the coastal plain, but at sites over a greater area, which shows

**Below:** *Sable* (Hippotragus niger) *male and female.*

## SABLE ANTELOPE

| | |
|---|---|
| **Total length** | ♂ 2,5-3,3 m; ♀ 2,3-3,05 m |
| **Tail length** | 40-75 cm |
| **Shoulder height** | ♂ 1,3-1,4 m; ♀ 1,17-1,35 m |
| **Mass** | ♂ 200-270 kg; ♀ 190-230 kg |
| **Horns** | ♂ 60-100 cm; ♀ 65-80 cm |
| **Home range** | 240-280 ha |
| **Social structure** | harem herd |
| **Gestation** | 261-281 days |
| **Number of young** | 1 |
| **Birth mass** | 12-14 kg |
| **Diet** | grass |

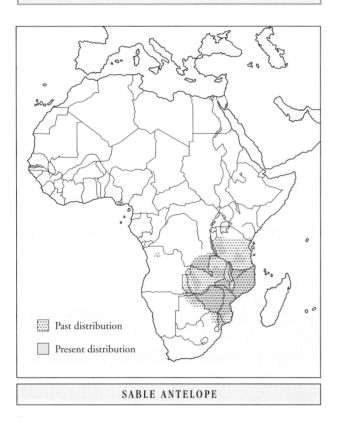

Past distribution

Present distribution

### SABLE ANTELOPE

# Roan antelope
## *Hippotragus equinus*

The roan antelope ranges from west and east Africa southwards to eastern South Africa. It occurs in as many as 29 countries. Although healthy numbers survive – more than 120 000 – roan have disappeared in some areas. In others roan numbers have been greatly reduced and populations fragmented. However, there is no serious threat to the overall population, although this is no reason for complacency. Its large size makes the roan antelope a sought-after poaching target.

## ROAN ANTELOPE

| | |
|---|---|
| **Total length** | ♂ 3,0-3,35 m; ♀ 2,8-3,15 m |
| **Tail length** | 60-70 cm |
| **Shoulder height** | 1,4-1,6 m |
| **Mass** | ♂ 260-300 kg; ♀ 225-275 kg |
| **Horns** | ♂ 70-100 cm; ♀ 60-80 cm |
| **Home range** | 250-300 ha |
| **Social structure** | harem herd |
| **Gestation** | 268-286 days |
| **Birth mass** | 16-18 kg |

**Above:** *Although more widely spread than the sable, the roan antelope* (Hippotragus equinus) *has been reduced to many isolated pockets, particularly in western Africa.*

and 3 000 survived. A count in 1974 came up with 1 000 animals, but the few reports we have recently received indicate that more than 90% have been slaughtered. The survivors cling on in two reserves, Cangandale and Luandu, but an aerial survey (undertaken by W. Delfs of Namibia) in 1990-91 was able to locate only one bull and two cows in Cangandale despite 21 hours of surveying by helicopter. A survey in 1997 counted 253 individuals, indicating that more than 1 000 may survive.

Given the instability in Angola it seems unlikely that the giant sable can survive, if it is not extinct already, and as the conflict continues that country's wildlife has a dim future.

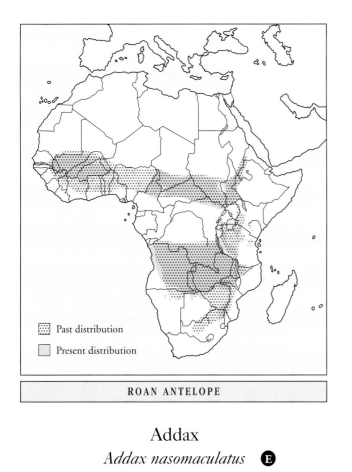

Past distribution

Present distribution

**ROAN ANTELOPE**

| ADDAX | |
|---|---|
| **Total length** | 1,7-2,2 m |
| **Tail length** | 25-35 cm |
| **Shoulder height** | average 1 m (up to 1,15 m) |
| **Mass** | 80-120 kg (♂ heavier than ♀) |
| **Home range** | extensive; dictated by rainfall and grass growth |
| **Social structure** | herds now fewer than 20 |
| **Gestation** | 257-264 days |
| **Diet** | graze and browse |
| **Number surviving** | below 500 in the wild |

# Addax

*Addax nasomaculatus* Ⓔ

### Description and taxonomy

The addax is a fairly large, heavily built antelope with enlarged hoofs, an adaptation for traversing extensive areas of soft sand. Both sexes carry the long, diverging and spiralled horns, but those of the females are noticeably thinner. Overall body colouring is smoky grey, with the rump, underparts and legs white to dirty white. A prominent white band extends across the face below the eyes. Both sexes have a mat of dark brown hair on the forehead. No subspecies are recognised.

### Distribution and habitat

This superbly desert-adapted antelope once ranged widely in the northern limits of the Sahel and in the Sahara Desert, from Mauritania in the west to Sudan in the east.

In Mauritania the latest reports indicate that fewer than 50 addax survive in the border region with Mali, in an area where several hundred animals roamed as recently as 10 years ago. In adjacent areas of Mali it has been estimated that a tiny remnant population survives but it seems likely that these may be the same animals that cross the border from Mauritania. Although there is no recent documentation, the isolated Algerian border region could still hold a few addax. However, it is generally felt that the species is extinct in that country. A remnant population of fewer than 200 addax in Niger is scattered through a

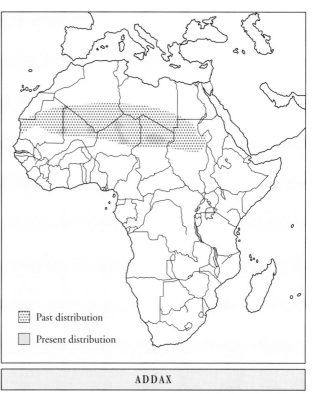

Past distribution

Present distribution

**ADDAX**

narrow belt which runs from the Algerian border towards west-central Chad. It has been estimated that perhaps as many as 50 addax roam the 77 000 sq km Air and Tenere National Nature Reserve. Addax were previously widespread to the north of 15° latitude in Chad, but fewer than 200 are now estimated to remain, down from several thousand just 20 years ago. In the 1970s there were believed to be some 800 addax in the north of the Ouadi Rime-Ouadi Achim Faunal Reserve, extending seasonally northwards towards the Tibesti Mountains, but warfare and uncontrolled poaching have caused catastrophic declines. At the easternmost limit of its range to the west of the Nile River in Sudan, the addax was considered to be relatively common at the beginning of this century, particularly in northern Darfur province. Although no surveys have been undertaken in recent years it is presumed that if still present the addax population is no longer viable and may just consist of animals crossing on occasion from Chad. In the past herds followed the rains into southern Algeria, Libya and Egypt, and ranged throughout the Saharan belt in these countries, reaching the latitude of about 33° north in Algeria. However, by the late 1800s they were already in retreat, and the small size of the population that now remains makes it unlikely that this movement still takes place.

This antelope is able to survive under extremely harsh conditions, including extensive areas of sand dunes. This is the only reason that any addax have been able to survive at all, as hunters in vehicles are unable to enter deep sand regions. Apart from ranging (or more correctly having ranged) over the ergs, or great dune seas, addax also make use of the stony plains.

## Behaviour

In earlier decades the addax formed herds of up to 20 individuals but herd size today is much smaller, and the great aggregations of hundreds, and even up to 1 000 animals, moving in search of fresh grass growth are a phenomenon of the past. Because of the extreme aridity of their chosen habitat they move over considerable distances in search of food. Their diet consists mainly of a variety of grass species but also includes shoots and leaves of acacia species, shrubs and herbaceous plants; a broad diet is essential to survival in the desert. In Niger the single calf is usually dropped between September and January, and this probably applied throughout their once extensive range.

## Conservation

The explorer Nachtigal in 1871 recorded "almost unbelievable" numbers of addax in the area to the north of Lake Chad, but today this highly adapted arid-area antelope is on the verge of extinction. Actual numbers surviving are not known, primarily because of the isolated and inhospitable nature of their remaining range, but it is generally believed that the figure is unlikely to exceed 500 individuals.

With so few animals surviving in the wild, drawing up adequate and meaningful conservation measures is extremely difficult, and is further complicated by continuing poaching. The one glimmer of hope is the strictly controlled nature reserve established

**Left**: *The addax* (Addax nasomaculatus) *is almost extinct in the wild, although substantial numbers are held in captivity.*

specifically for the addax within the Air and Tenere National Nature Reserve in Niger. The addax sanctuary (La Sanctuaire des Addax) covers an area of 12 806 sq km, is closed to human activities and is reported to be regularly patrolled. However, present populations of this antelope are extremely low here, perhaps fewer than 20 animals. It is planned to release some 75 captive-bred addax in this area, with the aim of boosting existing but severely depleted populations and increasing genetic diversity.

Although addax once occurred in substantial numbers in the Chadian Ouadi Rime-Ouadi Achim Faunal Reserve, after 1978 all management and controls came to a halt with the outbreak of civil war and general lawlessness. Today, it is believed, very few addax remain in the reserve, and in Chad as a whole. Although several reserves within their former range would be suitable for reintroductions, before this takes place extensive efforts will have to be made to eradicate the principal causes of their decline. The addax has been reintroduced to the Bou-Hedma National Park in Tunisia, but it remains one of Africa's most endangered large mammals. There are plans to reintroduce addax into other parts of their former range but poor reserve management precludes this at present.

# Scimitar-horned oryx
## *Oryx dammah* Ⓔ

## Description and taxonomy

Unlike those of other oryx species, the horns of this rare antelope are not straight but sweep back in a curve, hence its common name. Overall body colour is white to dirty white, but the neck and chest are brown, with paler brown markings on the rump and hind legs. The extent and shade of the body markings are variable but the face is predominantly white with a brown blaze. The tail is well-haired and somewhat horse-like.

| SCIMITAR-HORNED ORYX | |
|---|---|
| **Shoulder height** | 1,2 m (average) |
| **Mass** | 200 kg (average) |
| **Home range** | very large |
| **Social structure** | herds of 20-40; in the past formed temporary herds of several thousand |
| **Gestation** | 242-256 days |
| **Birth mass** | up to 15 kg |
| **Diet** | grass, browse, wide range of herbaceous plants |
| **Number surviving** | below 500; possibly below 200 |

## Distribution and habitat

Scimitar-horned oryx are known to have occurred throughout the Sahel belt and widely in the Sahara Desert. They are now extinct in Morocco, Western Sahara, Algeria, Tunisia, Libya, Egypt, Senegal, Mauritania, Mali, Niger, Burkina Faso, Nigeria and possibly Sudan. Although a few remnant populations could still survive in perhaps three Sahelian countries, viable numbers are only known to be present in Chad, and even here there are only at best a few hundred. Its position is probably even more precarious than that of the addax in the wild, but many are kept in captive collections, particularly in the United States of America and Europe.

Although this oryx once occurred in some 14 countries, today the only viable population lives in the central regions of Chad, principally between 14° and 16° latitude. A few animals may remain in perhaps three other Sahelian countries, but it is unlikely that they will survive.

In the past this oryx favoured the zone between the Sahara proper and the southern sector of the Sahel, which has low rainfall (up to 150 mm per annum). Except when rain encouraged grass growth, they avoided the arid sand desert and plains utilised by the addax.

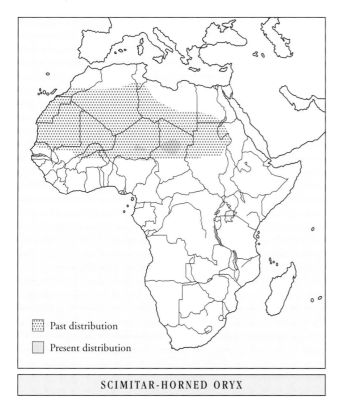

Past distribution

Present distribution

**SCIMITAR-HORNED ORYX**

## Behaviour

Scimitar-horned oryx are highly nomadic animals, in the past congregating in vast herds at feeding grounds, particularly where there was new grass growth. In 1936 one such herd sighted in Chad was said to have numbered 10 000 individuals. Even up to the mid-1970s herds of hundreds were

**Above:** *The scimitar-horned oryx* (Oryx dammah) *is hovering on the brink of extinction.* PHOTO: *Koen de Smet.*

observed in Chad. In Niger births have been recorded throughout the year, but with peaks from February to April and September to November.

Like many arid-area adapted mammals, scimitar-horned oryx are able to survive without drinking water, drawing sufficient moisture from their plant food. Like all oryx, they are predominantly grazers but eat almost any plant food.

## Conservation

Scimitar-horned oryx have proved to be even more vulnerable to human disturbance than the endangered addax, because of their inability to penetrate the harsh desert except when scarce rain has fallen to promote plant growth.

The reasons for their decline include a sequence of severe droughts, uncontrolled hunting, particularly by motorised parties, and competition with domestic livestock for food.

The only hope of saving any animals in the wild is adequate protection of the small numbers in the Ouadi Rime-Ouadi Achim Faunal Reserve in central Chad. However, no one is certain how many animals still remain there now. It was estimated that perhaps as many as 6 000 scimitar-horned oryx survived in this reserve up to 1978, but the outbreak of civil war in Chad put all game species in the central and northern areas under severe pressure. This oryx featured strongly in the diet of rebels and government soldiers alike. It is therefore essential that the international conservation community make every effort to improve conditions in Ouadi.

Scimitar-horned oryx originating from captive-born stock have been released in the Bou-Hedma National Park in Tunisia, which lies within their former north African range.

Some of the recent sightings of scimitar-horned oryx in Niger were made in the Air and Tenere National Nature Reserve, but this conservation area is probably too arid to hold permanent populations of this oryx. It is only suitable at certain times, despite its vast area. Reintroduction of captive-bred animals has been proposed for the Gadabedji Faunal Reserve in Niger, where conditions are more suitable.

There are a number of reserves suitable for reintroduction in parts of the scimitar-horned oryx's former range, but controls and management are lacking or leave much to be desired in most of them. Like the addax, this oryx if reintroduced and carefully managed could in future years provide a valuable source of protein and hides, as well as revenue from sport hunting and tourism.

# GAZELLINAE

## *Gazelles*

The accompanying tables present a summary of Africa's gazelles and two closely related species, the gerenuk and dibatag.

---

### SPRINGBOK

*Antidorcas marsupialis*

| | |
|---|---|
| Shoulder height | 75 cm |
| Mass | ♂ 41 kg; ♀ 37 kg |
| Home range | extensive where animals are not confined |
| Social structure | small herds; at times up to several thousand |
| Gestation | 168 days |
| Birth mass | 3,8 kg |
| Diet | mixed graze and browse; will dig for roots and bulbs |
| Number surviving | over 250 000 |

---

### GRANT'S GAZELLE

*Gazella granti*

| | |
|---|---|
| Shoulder height | ♂ 90 cm; ♀ 84 cm |
| Mass | ♂ up to 80 kg; ♀ up to 50 kg |
| Home range | variable but not large |
| Social structure | herds up to 30; larger herds on occasion |
| Gestation | 198 days |
| Birth mass | 5-7 kg |
| Diet | mixed |
| Number surviving | over 350 000 |

---

### THOMSON'S GAZELLE

*Gazella thomsoni*

| | |
|---|---|
| Shoulder height | 55-65 cm |
| Mass | ♂ up to 30 kg; ♀ up to 22 kg |
| Home range | relatively small when grazing is suitable but large in some seasons |
| Social structure | below 10 to over 100; thousands may gather at green vegetation flushes |
| Gestation | 188 days |
| Birth mass | 2-3 kg |
| Diet | predominantly graze |
| Number surviving | below 1 million |

---

### CUVIER'S GAZELLE

*Gazella cuvieri*

| | |
|---|---|
| Shoulder height | 60-80 cm |
| Mass | ♂ up to 35 kg; ♀ up to 37 kg |
| Home range | probably smaller than for most gazelles |
| Social structure | 3-5; does not form large herds |
| Gestation | unknown |
| Birth mass | 2-3 kg |
| Diet | browse and graze |
| Number surviving | over 1 000 |

**Left:**
*Cuvier's gazelle (Gazella cuvieri).*
PHOTO: *Roland Wirth.*

## RED-FRONTED GAZELLE

*Gazella rufifrons*

| | |
|---|---|
| **Shoulder height** | 65-80 cm |
| **Mass** | ♂ 25-35 kg; ♀ 20-25 kg |
| **Home range** | varies with habitat |
| **Social structure** | herds of 5 or fewer, rarely more |
| **Gestation** | 184-189 days |
| **Birth mass** | 2,5-3 kg |
| **Diet** | mainly grass but also browse |
| **Number surviving** | probably over 10 000 |

## SLENDER-HORNED GAZELLE

*Gazella leptoceros*

| | |
|---|---|
| **Shoulder height** | 65-70 cm |
| **Mass** | 20-30 kg |
| **Home range** | probably fairly large |
| **Social structure** | below 10, usually 1-5 |
| **Gestation** | 156-169 days |
| **Birth mass** | 2 kg |
| **Diet** | mixed |
| **Number surviving** | about 5 000 |

## SOEMMERRING'S GAZELLE

*Gazella soemmerringii*

| | |
|---|---|
| **Shoulder height** | 85-90 cm |
| **Mass** | 35-45 kg |
| **Home range** | not known |
| **Social structure** | herds of 5-20, usually below 10; over 100 on occasion but rarely today |
| **Gestation** | 198 days |
| **Birth mass** | 3-4 kg |
| **Diet** | mixed; mainly grass |
| **Number surviving** | probably about 50 000 |

## DORCAS GAZELLE

*Gazella dorcas*

| | |
|---|---|
| **Shoulder height** | 55-65 cm |
| **Mass** | 15-20 kg or more |
| **Home range** | not known for much of its range |
| **Social structure** | small herds, 5-20, occasionally more but never great aggregations |
| **Gestation** | 170-180 days |
| **Birth mass** | 1,7 kg |
| **Diet** | browse and graze |
| **Number surviving** | over 10 000 in Africa |

## SPEKE'S GAZELLE

*Gazella spekei*

| | |
|---|---|
| **Shoulder height** | 50-60 cm |
| **Mass** | 15-25 kg |
| **Home range** | uncertain; arid habitat so probably fairly large |
| **Social structure** | groups of 5-10 |
| **Gestation** | unknown |
| **Birth mass** | unknown |
| **Diet** | mixed |
| **Number surviving** | probably about 10 000 |

## DAMA GAZELLE

*Gazella dama*

| | |
|---|---|
| **Shoulder height** | 0,90-1,2 m |
| **Mass** | 40-75 kg |
| **Home range** | probably large |
| **Social structure** | 1-15; previously large, temporary migratory herds |
| **Gestation** | unknown |
| **Birth mass** | unknown |
| **Diet** | predominantly browse |
| **Number surviving** | probably below 2 000 |

| GERENUK | |
|---|---|
| *Litocranius walleri* | |
| Shoulder height | up to 1,05 m |
| Mass | ♂ up to 50 kg; ♀ up to 40 kg |
| Home range | up to 6 sq km |
| Social structure | groups of 1-5; never large herds |
| Gestation | 210 days |
| Birth mass | 3 kg |
| Diet | browse |
| Number surviving | about 75 000 |

| DIBATAG | |
|---|---|
| *Ammodorcas clarkei* | |
| Shoulder height | 80-88 cm |
| Mass | 22-35 kg |
| Home range | probably similar to gerenuk but subject to seasonal movement |
| Social structure | groups of 1-5; never large herds |
| Gestation | unknown |
| Birth mass | unknown |
| Diet | browse |
| Number surviving | probably below 5 000 |

The majority of Africa's gazelles occur within the dry areas of the Sahel, Sahara Desert and other parts of north Africa. All have undergone dramatic population and range declines in recent times. Most species can be placed in the endangered category as a result of the same factors that caused the decline of the addax and scimitar-horned oryx: extended droughts, competition with domestic stock and uncontrolled hunting and poaching.

In most cases it has been impossible to establish the size of surviving gazelle populations because of difficult access to their favoured habitats, as well as continuing civil wars and banditry in some areas. Perhaps a number of species do not qualify as endangered in terms of present definitions, but if the conditions detrimental to gazelle populations continue to prevail it is unlikely that viable numbers will survive in the wild very far into the next century.

As most gazelle species require large ranges, many reserves are not adequate for their long-term conservation.

# Red gazelle
## *Gazella rufina* EXTINCT

There is much confusion over the disappearance of the red gazelle from Algeria. Three known specimens were purchased in that country at the end of the 19th century but no other records exist. It has had a patchy taxonomic history but recent taxonomists are convinced that it is or was a distinct species, and not a race of Cuvier's gazelle (the edmi), which is still present in small numbers in northern Algeria. It has been surmised, by Loder in Thomas (1894), that its relatively dark hair coloration makes it unlikely to have been a true desert gazelle, and that it was probably restricted to the area between the Mediterranean Sea and the true desert. We shall never know!

It is of interest that the only two antelope known to have become extinct in recent times occupied the opposite points of the continent, some 9 000 km apart.

# Springbok
## *Antidorcas marsupialis*

Although still occurring in substantial numbers, the only southern gazelle, the springbok, has been reduced to a fraction of its former numerical strength. The great herds, said to have numbered in the hundreds of thousands, which undertook migrations across the arid plains of South Africa, have been well documented by many travellers and hunters of the 19th century. These herds are no more and all that remain are small fenced-in remnant populations. There are perhaps more than

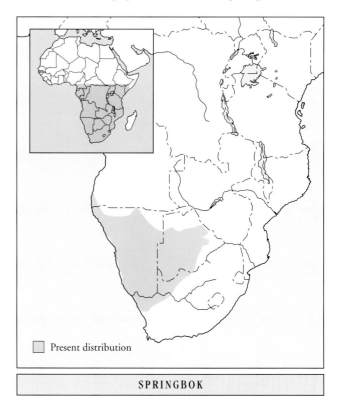

☐ Present distribution

**SPRINGBOK**

250 000 springbok in Botswana and Namibia. At first glance this seems a substantial number, but all evidence points to there having been several million springbok earlier. Their decline has been precipitous.

## Grant's gazelle
### *Gazella granti*

## Thomson's gazelle
### *Gazella thomsonii*

These two common plains gazelles are still abundant in east Africa, with an estimated 360 000 Grant's and almost one million Thomson's gazelles. They occur in many conservation areas and there is little fear of major declines in these sanctuaries. Nevertheless, they have suffered serious declines in some areas, such as in their Somali and Ethiopian ranges.

They are being increasingly influenced by ever-expanding areas falling under cultivation, for example within the Serengeti ecosystem.

**Top**: *Red-fronted gazelle* (Gazella rufifrons). *All gazelle species in the Sahara and Sahel have suffered very serious declines.* PHOTO: *Roland Wirth.* **Right**: *All three subspecies of the dama, or addra, gazelle* (Gazella dama) *are declining. This is the western dama* (G.d. mhorr). **Below right**: *Springbok herd* (Antidorcas marsupialis) *in the Kalahari.* **Bottom**: *Soemmerring's gazelle* (Gazella soemmerringi) *has its population centred on the Horn of Africa. It is one of the continent's largest and most distinctly marked gazelles.*

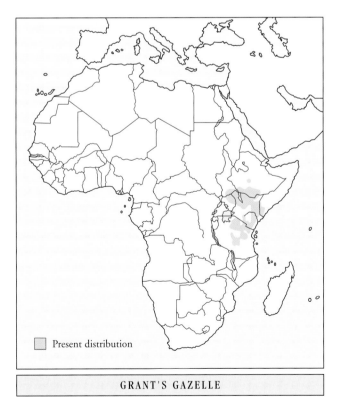

☐ Present distribution

GRANT'S GAZELLE

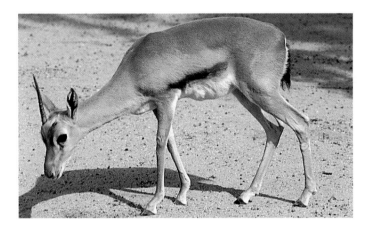

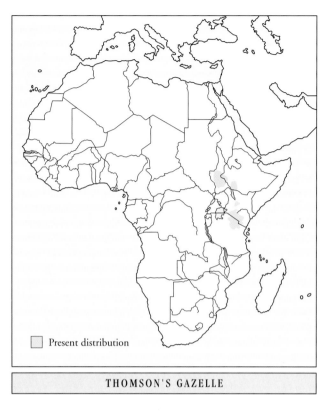

Present distribution

**THOMSON'S GAZELLE**

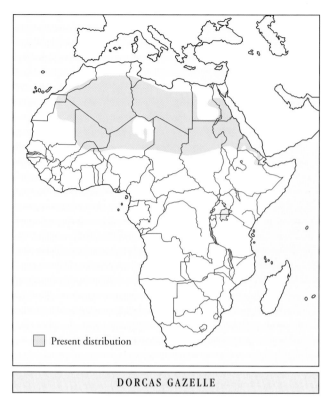

Present distribution

**DORCAS GAZELLE**

## Dorcas gazelle
### *Gazella dorcas*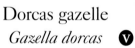

This is the most abundant gazelle in northern Africa. It is the only gazelle in this area not to be endangered – at least at present. However, there is no room for complacency. Massive declines in numbers have taken place and only a small percentage of the animals occur in conservation areas.

The easternmost race of this gazelle, *G.d. pelzelni*, is restricted to the arid coastal strip of the northern Horn of Africa.

The dorcas gazelle is extinct in Senegal and considered to be endangered in Mauritania (fewer than 500), Burkina Faso (remnant), Nigeria (vagrant) and Morocco (fewer than 400; there is a small population in the Sidi Chiker reserve). Overall population size is certainly greater than 10 000 but no one knows by how much. Pressures on this and the other gazelle species continue.

## Red-fronted gazelle
### *Gazella rufifrons*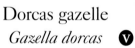

This gazelle once occurred within the Sahelian belt from the Atlantic Ocean to the Red Sea, but populations have become fragmented and greatly diminished. However, it is still present in possibly as many as 15 countries and in a number of conservation areas. The western populations have suffered the greatest declines. It is probably extinct in Ghana, and effectively extinct in Nigeria and Benin. It is considered to be endangered in Mauritania; in Niger probably fewer than 5 000

remain; in Senegal it is considered to be severely threatened; in Burkina Faso there are fewer than 1 500. In several other countries it is, or was, largely of marginal occurrence.

A distinct subspecies, Heuglin's gazelle *(G.r. tilonura)*, is restricted to the east of the Nile River along the Sudanese-Ethiopian border.

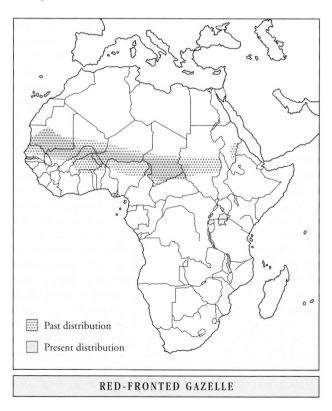

Past distribution

Present distribution

**RED-FRONTED GAZELLE**

# Soemmerring's gazelle
## *Gazella soemmerringii*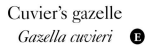

# Speke's gazelle
## *Gazella spekei*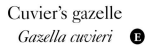

These two species have limited distributions in the arid east, towards the Red Sea. Speke's gazelle also occurs in the Horn of Africa. They are considered vulnerable because of their relatively limited ranges, continuing hunting pressure and growing competition from domestic livestock for limited grazing.

**Above:** *Speke's gazelle* (Gazella spekei), *also known as the "flabby-nosed gazelle", is restricted to the Horn of Africa and has been greatly reduced in numbers. In private collection – Qatar.*

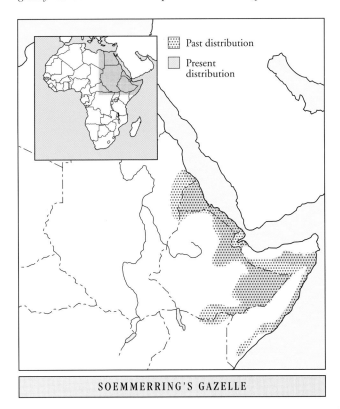

SOEMMERRING'S GAZELLE

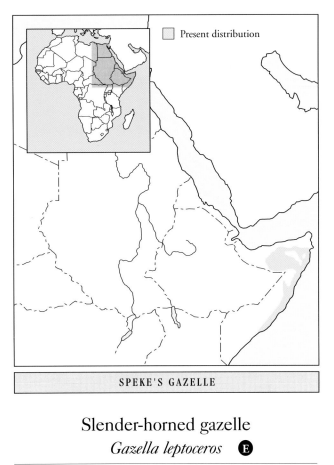

SPEKE'S GAZELLE

# Slender-horned gazelle
## *Gazella leptoceros* Ⓔ

The slender-horned or sand gazelle once had a very wide distribution, from Mauritania in the west to Sudan as far as the Nile River. Today it is restricted to small, isolated populations. There are non-viable numbers in Mauritania and Mali. In Niger the estimated number is fewer than 1 000 gazelles, some of which occur in the Air and Tenere National Nature Reserve. A small number may still occur in the vicinity of the Tibesti Massif in Chad. In Sudan it could be extinct, although no surveys have been recently undertaken. The latest information from north-western Egypt indicates that fewer than 15 individuals survive. If any are still present in Libya and Algeria, these populations are almost certainly non-viable and will become extinct in the near future, as it is in Nigeria. It is almost certainly extinct in Western Sahara.

This is considered to be one of the best desert-adapted of all antelope species, occupying sand dunes as well as stony plains and hills, and able to survive without drinking water.

# Cuvier's gazelle
## *Gazella cuvieri* Ⓔ

Apart from the extinct red gazelle *(G. rufina)*, Cuvier's gazelle, or the edmi, is the only gazelle endemic to the area north of the Sahara. In the past it occurred from Tunisia to the northern region of Western Sahara but it is now extinct in the latter. In Tunisia it is protected in the Djebel Chambi National Park,

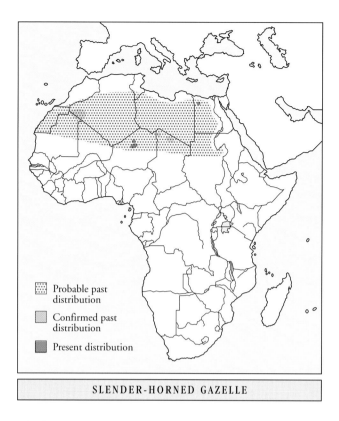

**SLENDER-HORNED GAZELLE**

Probable past distribution

Confirmed past distribution

Present distribution

ductions have been planned for the Belezma and Teniet el Had national parks. Recent unrest in Algeria could place this and other species under increasing pressure, particularly as the gazelle population is scattered in numerous isolated pockets, largely restricted to the hill and mountain ranges. In Morocco only tiny, isolated populations remain, primarily in the mountains and hills centred on the Anti-Atlas and the western extension of the Haut-Atlas.

Unlike most other gazelle species, Cuvier's gazelle is able to utilise a wide range of habitats, from various open forest types with rainfall of some 600 mm per annum to desert on the northern fringes of the Sahara. This adaptability is no doubt the principal reason why this antelope has managed to survive as long as it has where at least one other has become extinct.

# Dama gazelle
## *Gazella dama* **Ⓔ**

The dama gazelle has three distinct subspecies, the western dama *(G.d. mhorr)*, the central dama *(G.d. permista)* and the red-necked gazelle *(G.d. ruficollis)*. It previously occurred widely across northern Africa but numbers have been greatly reduced and all three subspecies are now seriously threatened. It seems likely that no more than 2 000 animals survive in the wild, and possibly considerably fewer than this.

This gazelle is believed to be extinct in Western Sahara, Morocco, Algeria and Libya. The last mhorr, or western dama, was reputedly sighted in the wild in south-western Morocco in the early part of the 1980s.

In the southern Saharan and Sahelian countries the dama

which is adjacent to the Algerian border. Animals move between the two countries here. Algeria holds the largest surviving number of Cuvier's gazelle – probably over 500 – with a well-protected population in the Mergueb Nature Reserve. Researcher Koen de Smet estimated that the gazelle carrying capacity of this reserve could exceed 1 000 animals. Reintro-

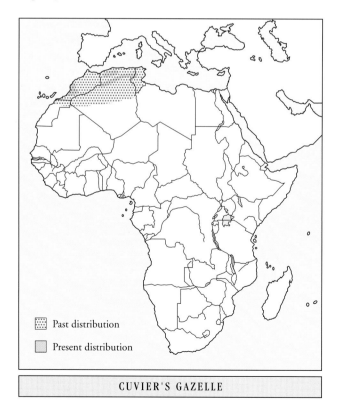

Past distribution

Present distribution

**CUVIER'S GAZELLE**

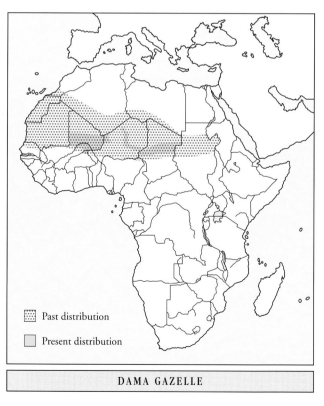

Past distribution

Present distribution

**DAMA GAZELLE**

gazelle is also in dire straits. It is extinct in Mauritania and Senegal, and reduced to at best a few hundred in Mali. Fewer than 1 000 survive in Niger and numbers continue to decline. Possibly the largest population is centred on the Ouadi Rime-Ouadi Achim Faunal Reserve in Chad. Although there may have been as many as 8 000 dama gazelles in this reserve some 20 years ago, it is unlikely that more than a few hundred survive there today. In Burkina Faso the dama gazelle is probably extinct as a viable breeding population, as it is Nigeria, where the species was probably always of marginal occurrence.

Once widely distributed in Sudan west of the Nile River, mainly in the provinces of Northern Darfur, Northern Kordufan and the southern sector of Northern province, today it seems likely that the dama gazelle only survives in very small numbers, in the vicinity of the border with Chad.

Captive herds are maintained at a number of European and North American facilities and if suitable conservation areas in this gazelle's former range can be adequately secured and managed, reintroduction would be feasible. Care should be taken that the three races are not mixed and that releases only take place within their correct ranges. Seven animals were reintroduced from captivity to the Gueumbeul Faunal Reserve in Senegal, and reports indicate that a number of young have been born.

Reintroduction programmes into well-managed and secure conservation areas would bolster any remaining wild populations and improve genetic diversity, as well as establishing new populations.

# Gerenuk
## *Litocranius walleri*

# Dibatag
## *Ammodorcas clarkei* Ⓥ

These two antelope are closely related to the gazelles. They are similar in appearance to each other, with long legs and neck. Both frequently browse by standing up on the hind legs.

The **gerenuk** is sometimes referred to as the giraffe-necked antelope or gazelle. It can be considered secure at present as it occurs in five countries and in a number of well-managed conservation areas. There are probably some 75 000 gerenuk surviving, of which an estimated 45 000 live in Kenya.

The **dibatag** has a very limited distribution within the volatile Horn of Africa. No recent surveys have been undertaken and exact numbers are unknown. It is only found in northern and central Somalia and adjacent areas of eastern Ethiopia. Within its Ethiopian range it is probably secure at present but it has apparently lost some 50% of its range in Somalia. The protracted unrest in that country has undoubtedly placed it under considerable pressure, as it has all other species. Numbers surviving are probably in the low thousands.

Given the arid and restricted nature of the dibatag's habitat their numbers were probably never very high.

**Above:** *Gerenuk* (Litocranius walleri), *Tsavo East National Park.*

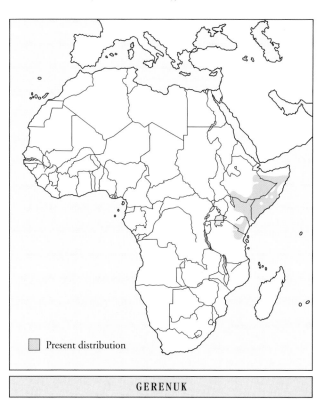

Present distribution

GERENUK

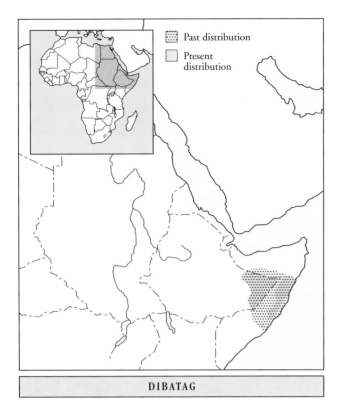

Past distribution

Present distribution

DIBATAG

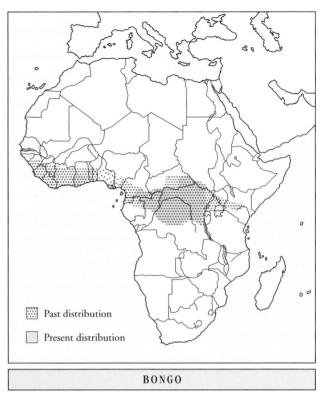

Past distribution

Present distribution

BONGO

# STREPCISEROTINI

## *Spiral-horned antelope*

There are nine species in this antelope tribe. The common eland *(Taurotragus oryx)* and the giant or Lord Derby's eland *(T. derbianus)* are the two largest living antelope. A number of species, such as the bushbuck *(Tragelaphus scriptus)*, the greater kudu *(T. strepsiceros)* and the swamp-dwelling sitatunga *(T. spekei)*, are widespread and under no threat, except on a localised scale. The nyala *(T. angasi)*, lesser kudu *(T. imberbis)* and bongo *(T. euryceros)* have more restricted ranges but are also not considered threatened at this stage. However, the bongo is now very rare in the forests of western Kenya and has disappeared, or been greatly reduced, from increasingly isolated forest pockets in west Africa. It occurs widely in the extensive Congolean forest block, although the population size is unknown. Two species in this tribe are, however, of particular conservation concern: the giant eland and the mountain nyala.

## Giant (Lord Derby's) eland
### *Taurotragus derbianus* Ⓥ

### Description and taxonomy

This massively built antelope is more reddish-brown in colour than the common eland and is distinctly marked with 12 to 15 vertical white body stripes. The horns are massive and tightly spiralled; those of females are smaller. Two races are recognised. The western form *(T.d. derbianus)* is endangered over almost its entire range. The eastern form *(T.d. gigas)*, although more numerous, has undergone serious declines in both range and numbers and is considered to be vulnerable.

### Distribution and habitat

The giant eland once occurred in a wide belt through the savanna woodlands of western and north-central Africa, from Senegal to northern Uganda. The exact limits of the western and eastern races are unknown but the western race has only

**Below:** *Giant eland* (Taurotragus derbianus) *bull in captivity.*

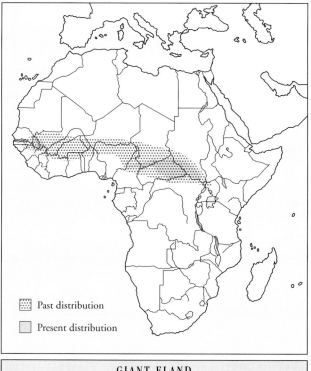

Past distribution

Present distribution

GIANT ELAND

### GIANT (LORD DERBY'S) ELAND

| | |
|---|---|
| **Total length** | 4,35 m |
| **Tail length** | 90 cm |
| **Shoulder height** | up to 1,8 m |
| **Mass** | ♂ up to 1 000 kg; ♀ usually below 500 kg |
| **Home range** | large but possibly smaller than of common eland |
| **Social structure** | herds up to 25; usually smaller, occasionally larger |
| **Gestation** | up to 285 days |
| **Birth mass** | 23-35 kg |
| **Diet** | predominantly browse |
| **Number surviving** | |
| western race: | below 1 200 |
| eastern race: | over 15 000 |

one viable population surviving: in south-eastern Senegal. The bulk of the population occurs in the Niokolo-Koba National Park, comprising about 80% (800 or so animals) of Senegal's total. It is possible that a remnant population survives in Mali but there are no recent records. The giant eland is extinct in Gambia and Guinea. A few possibly survive in Guinea Bissau. It was probably never resident in Sierre Leone, but certainly does not occur there now. It seems likely once to have occurred

in the north of Ivory Coast but this is not certain. The giant eland is extinct in Ghana, Togo and Nigeria.

The eastern giant eland became extinct in northern Uganda in 1970, where it had apparently occurred seasonally and as a small resident population. In Sudan it is restricted to the south-western woodland savanna where in 1977 it was estimated that perhaps as many as 18 000 survived. The figure is believed to be considerably lower today. Once abundant in south-western Chad, the eastern giant eland may now be extinct as a resident species although some movement may be taking place from neighbouring Central African Republic. The latter country probably has the largest remaining eastern giant eland population with some estimates as high as 10 000, even though an outbreak of rinderpest greatly reduced the herds in 1983. The eland are said to have benefited from the reduction of elephant numbers by poaching, which has resulted in bush encroachment. In Central African Republic giant eland occur in the Bamingui-Bangoran and Manovo-Gounda-St Floris national parks. Populations total at least in the high hundreds. This country holds out the best hope for the long-term conservation of this species. In Cameroon it occurs in three national parks (Faro, Boubandjidah and Benoue) and their adjacent areas but the population was apparently badly affected by the 1983 rinderpest outbreak. It may still be present in very small numbers in far northern Congo (DR) but there are no recent records.

#### Conservation

Viable giant eland populations now occur only in Senegal, Central African Republic and Sudan.

Giant eland probably once occurred in numbers of well over 100 000, which gives an indication of how precipitous their decline has been. They are extensively hunted for their meat and hides.

## Mountain nyala
### *Tragelaphus buxtoni*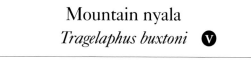

#### Description and taxonomy

Despite its common name, in many ways this species more closely resembles the greater kudu than the nyala of southern Africa. It is a large antelope with a shaggy greyish-brown coat, usually with four indistinct white vertical body stripes and a white chevron between the eyes. There is also a white throat patch and a white band on the upper chest. Only the males carry the long, widely spiralled horns.

#### Distribution and habitat

The mountain nyala was first discovered in 1908 and described in 1910, which is surprising considering its relatively large size. The entire population is restricted to a small area of south-central Ethiopia, which makes them particularly vulnerable to disturbance and outbreaks of disease.

In the past the mountain nyala had a somewhat more extensive range within the Ethiopian Highlands but now isolated populations are restricted to the area between the Bale and Harerghe mountains at altitudes of 3 000 m to 4 200 m. They occur in mixed woodland, montane heath and moorland, generally avoiding areas with low vegetation cover.

| MOUNTAIN NYALA | |
|---|---|
| Total length | 2-2,8 m |
| Tail length | 25 cm |
| Shoulder height | up to 1,35 m |
| Mass | ♂ 300 kg (maximum); ♀ 150-200 kg |
| Home range | relatively small; some seasonal movement |
| Social structure | average group size 9; range is 1-96 but large groups are unusual |
| Gestation | unknown |
| Birth mass | unknown |
| Diet | predominantly browse; occasionally grass and herbs |
| Number surviving | 2 000-4 000 |

## Behaviour

Mountain nyala are subject to some seasonal local movement, favouring thicker vegetation during the dry season. Their activities are probably greatly influenced by human disturbance, particularly outside conservation areas. This may be the cause of their mainly nocturnal life style and frequent use of dense vegetation cover. Most calves (70%) are dropped late in the rainy season.

## Conservation

As many as 1 400 mountain nyala may be protected in the Bale Mountains National Park, but the rest of the population lives outside conservation areas. These animals are vulnerable to hunting and habitat destruction. Hunting pressure is believed to be minimal. Cultivation and grazing by domestic animals, however, are making a major impact on the habitat of the mountain nyala. It seems likely that only those animals in the Bale Mountains will survive in the medium to long term unless a second area is established in which this antelope can be preserved. However, given the human pressures in Ethiopia this seems an unlikely prospect. Unless that country's conservation areas receive protection, this and other species could disappear.

**Above:** *The mountain nyala* (Tragelaphus buxtoni) *more closely resembles the greater kudu than the nyala of south-eastern Africa. It is restricted to a few pockets in the Ethiopian Highlands.*
PHOTO: *Chris & Sheila Hillman, Images of Africa Photobank.*

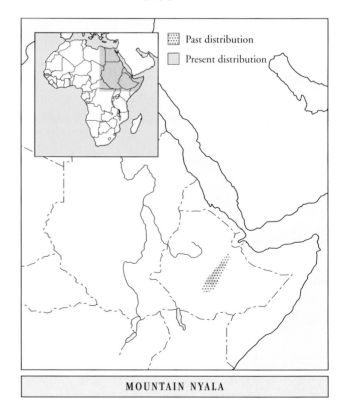

Past distribution

Present distribution

MOUNTAIN NYALA

# CEPHALOPHINAE

## Forest duikers

There are at least 16 species of these predominantly small to medium-sized (4-80 kg) antelopes. Most species are restricted to different forest associations. Taxonomists are uncertain as to how many species of duiker there actually are, primarily because of the great number of geographical variations that exist. It is also possible that new species could be described from poorly explored montane and lowland forests.

If more duiker species are generally acknowledged in future, this would add several species to the vulnerable, and perhaps endangered, categories. For example, the red duiker, which occurs in the high moorland and heath on the Ruwenzori Mountains, is sometimes regarded as a separate species, namely *Cephalophus rubidus*. Despite the proclamation of the Ugandan side of the mountain range as a national park, poaching is known to continue here.

Forest-dwelling duikers all have arched backs and relatively short legs, and the crest of hair at the top of the head often hides the short, spiky horns that are carried by both sexes.

Although a few species, such as the blue duiker *(Cephalophus/Philantomba monticola)* and yellow-backed duiker *(C. sylvicultor)*, have wide distributions, others such as Jentink's duiker *(C. jentinki)* and Ader's duiker *(C. adersi)* have very limited ranges. The most widespread of all the duiker species is the common duiker *(Sylvicapra grimmia)*, which stands alone in its genus.

All species, as far as is known, are either solitary or occur in pairs. A pair may defend a jointly held territory against both males and females. Despite sharing a territory, the male and female have minimal contact with each other.

Home ranges are small, as food is abundant in duikers' forested and woodland habitats. Because most, if not all, species defend territories, competition for food is limited. Apart from a great diversity of plant food, including fungi, fruits, leaves, flowers, shoots and seeds, some species readily feed on animal food, such as insects, small mammals, young birds and carrion. In this they are unique among antelope.

The duikers, particularly those in west Africa and species that occur at high densities, are one of the most critical sources of protein for humans. It has been estimated that blue duikers in one area of Gabon reach densities of 70 individuals per square kilometre. In one study undertaken in the markets of the city of Bukavu in Zaïre over a six-week period it was found that some 46 tons of game meat ("bush meat") were sold, of which 37% was antelope meat, mainly from several duiker species. Similar utilisation of duiker meat has been observed throughout the Guinean-Congolean forest belt.

The potential for farming with certain duiker species, particularly in west Africa, is being investigated by the Chipangali Wildlife Trust, among others. Although at present some of the heavily harvested duiker species appear to be maintaining their population levels, loss of habitat and growing demand for their meat are almost certain to result in short-term range loss and long-term extinction over large areas. Husbandry of duikers could go some way towards alleviating these pressures.

# Jentink's duiker
## *Cephalophus jentinki* Ⓔ

### Description and taxonomy

Jentink's duiker is one of the largest members of its genus – and the most endangered. It is a handsome animal with a black head and neck, and a white band extending across the shoulders. The remainder of the body is grizzled silvery grey. The underparts are slightly paler.

| JENTINK'S DUIKER | |
|---|---|
| Total length | 1,5 m |
| Tail length | 15 cm |
| Shoulder height | 80 cm |
| Mass | up to 70 kg |
| Number surviving | unknown but maybe below 2 000, in isolated pockets |

### Distribution and habitat

This duiker occurs in three west African countries: Sierra Leone, Liberia and Ivory Coast. Although its presence was suspected in Sierra Leone for many years, it was only confirmed in the late 1980s on the southern section of the Freetown Peninsula. Although no estimate of the size of the population has been made, it must be very small and under considerable pressure. It is known that at least five of these duikers were killed here in 1988. Forests of similar structure to those on the

**Right:** *Jentink's duiker* (Cephalophus jentinki) *is one of the largest (up to 70 kg) and most distinctly marked of the duikers, but sadly is one of the most restricted and endangered.*

PHOTO: *Wardene Weisser, Ardea London.*

peninsula are located in the east and south-east of the country and it is conceivable that Jentink's duiker may be present in at least some of these. Unconfirmed reports indicate that it occurs in the Gola Forest close to the Liberian border, and in the Tingi Hills and Loma Mountains close to Sierra Leone's border with Guinea.

Jentink's duiker is believed to occur patchily throughout Liberia, but its presence has been confirmed in Sapo National Park and the Krahn-Bassa, Gola and Gbi national forests. It has been generally presumed that this duiker is restricted to primary lowland forest but in parts of its limited range it is known to utilise forest margins and croplands. The opinion has been expressed that it may be more abundant, particularly in Liberia, than is generally believed, but even so densities are very low and a range of human pressures threaten the continued existence of this and other forest animals.

In Ivory Coast Jentink's duiker is restricted to the forests of the south-west, with known populations occurring in Tai National Park and the forest reserves of Scio, Haut Dodo and Cavally-Gouin. It has only been recorded in primary forest in this country but given its secretive nature and low densities it could have been overlooked.

## Behaviour

Very little is known about the ecology of this rare duiker, but it feeds on a wide range of plant parts, including tubers and roots, oil-palm nuts and cassava. It is said to lie up during the day in hollow logs and among the buttressed roots of large trees in its forest home. As this is the case with most forest species, serious study has not been undertaken.

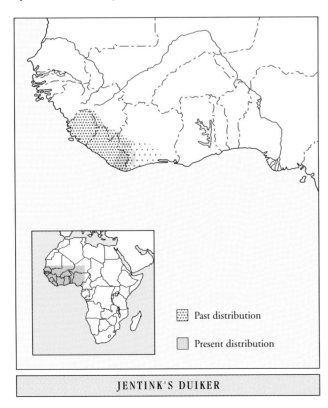

JENTINK'S DUIKER

| Past distribution |
| Present distribution |

## Conservation

Despite this species' endangered status it is still hunted in all three countries, along with other duikers. A detailed study of its ecology, requirements and population status is essential, given the level of habitat destruction throughout its range.

**Above:** *Blue duiker* (Cepholaphus monticola) *fawn licking its mother.*

# Black duiker
## *Cephalophus niger* Ⓔ

# Ogilby's duiker
## *C. ogilbyi* Ⓥ

# Zebra duiker
## *C. zebra* Ⓡ

These three forest duiker species are restricted to west Africa. They are probably the most vulnerable of all duikers in the area to habitat destruction and hunting for "bush meat".

All are associated with lowland forests, although the zebra duiker also occurs in forested hill country. It is likely that the other two duiker species inhabit a wider habitat range than was

|  | BLACK | OGILBY'S | ZEBRA |
|---|---|---|---|
| **Total length** | 0,90-1 m | 0,97-1,3 m | 0,90-1,05 m |
| **Tail length** | 12-14 cm | 12-15 cm | 15 cm |
| **Shoulder height** | 45-50 cm | probably 42-55 cm | 40-50 cm |
| **Mass** | 18-24 kg | 14-18 kg | 15-20 kg |

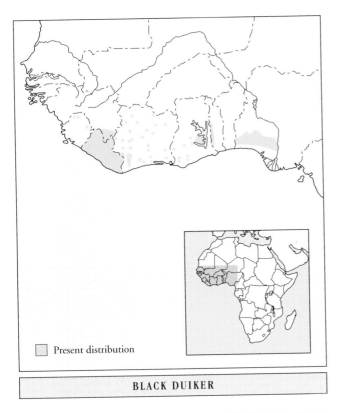

**BLACK DUIKER**

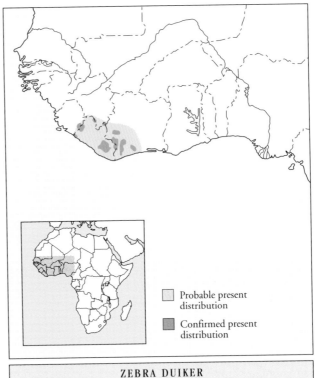

Probable present distribution

Confirmed present distribution

**ZEBRA DUIKER**

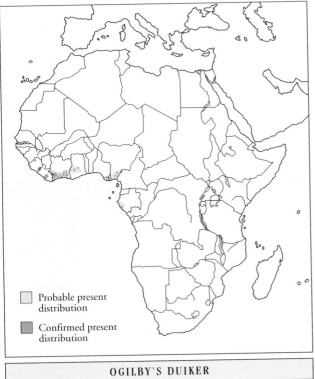

Probable present distribution

Confirmed present distribution

**OGILBY'S DUIKER**

**Above:** *Zebra duiker* (Cephalophus zebra) *in Berlin Zoo.* PHOTO: *Klaus Rudloff.*

previously thought.

The **black duiker**, as its name implies, is uniformly dark in colour, from dark brown to black. The black duiker occurs from Guinea to Nigeria, including Sierra Leone, Liberia, Ivory Coast, Ghana, Togo and possibly Benin. It is considered to be endangered in the easternmost reaches of its range. To the

west, despite heavy hunting pressure, it is apparently safe.

**Ogilby's duiker** is overall reddish-orange, with a dark brown to black dorsal stripe and pale to white "stockings". There is some confusion as to the taxonomic status of this duiker, with some authors being of the opinion that it could be a form of the more widespread bay duiker *(C. dorsalis)*. Ogilby's duiker has a similar range to the black duiker but extends down into Cameroon, Gabon and the island of Bioko in the Gulf of Guinea, and it does not extend as far west as Guinea. It is said to be absent from Togo and Benin, but occurs in Nigeria close to the Cameroon border. The fact that the western and eastern populations of this duiker are separated warrants re-examination of its taxonomic status and its relation to the bay duiker.

The attractive **zebra duiker** is characterised by its reddish-brown coat, with 12 to 15 vertical white stripes on the body, hence its name. The zebra duiker has a similar distribution to Jentink's duiker, in Sierra Leone, Liberia and south-western Ivory Coast. Recent records from Sierra Leone, where the zebra duiker is considered to be endangered, indicate that it may only survive in the Gola Forest adjacent to the western Liberian border. In Liberia its range is now fragmented but it occurs in a number of conservation areas. However, because of civil unrest there is no effective management of reserves. Although it has declined in Liberia, it is still not considered to be endangered there. The Ivory Coast population, centred on the Tai National Park and adjacent forest reserves, has undergone considerable declines and is generally held to be endangered. It is known to be present in four forest reserves.

# Ader's duiker
## *Cephalophus adersi* Ⓔ

# Abbott's duiker
## *Cephalophus spadix* Ⓥ

These two duiker species occur in east Africa. They are decreasing and considered to be vulnerable because of their restricted distributions. Both species are under threat because of habitat destruction and hunting. There is no indication of population sizes but they are probably in the low thousands.

| | ADER'S | ABBOTT'S |
|---|---|---|
| **Total length** | about 75 cm | 1-1,3 m |
| **Tail length** | 9-12 cm | 8-12 cm |
| **Shoulder height** | 30-32 cm | 50-65 cm |
| **Mass** | 6-12 kg | 52-60 kg |

**Above:** *Common duiker* (Sylvicapra grimmia) *ewe and fawn.*

ADER'S DUIKER

ABBOTT'S DUIKER

The small **Ader's duiker** is tawny red with a white band on the rump. It belongs to the taxonomically very complex red duiker group. This species has been recorded as occupying various forest, woodland and thicket types. Ader's duiker occurs only on the Tanzanian island of Zanzibar (Unguja). It is now probably extinct on the mainland. These forests, centred on

Above: *The yellow-backed duiker* (Cephalophus sylvicultor) *is the largest member of its family.*

| HIROLA (HUNTER'S HARTEBEEST) | |
|---|---|
| Total length | 1,5-2,4 m |
| Tail length | 30-45 cm |
| Shoulder height | 98-125 cm |
| Mass | 75-160 kg<br>(♂ larger than ♀) |
| Home range | not known;<br>subject to some<br>local migration |
| Social structure | herds of up to 25<br>individuals; often smaller |
| Gestation | probably about 8 months |
| Birth mass | probably 10 kg |
| Diet | graze |
| Number surviving | below 500 |

the Arabuko-Sokoke block, are becoming increasingly fragmented, and illegal hunting is a constant problem. Forests of similar form and structure occur on the north-eastern Tanzanian coast and in the increasingly degraded Usambara Mountains. No detailed surveys have been undertaken but the presence of this duiker here cannot be entirely ruled out. The population on Zanzibar has been estimated to number about 5 000 but a recent survey suggests that the figure is less than 1500. Because of habitat destruction and hunting Ader's duiker is considered endangered on Zanzibar. In contrast, the only other two species of antelope on Zanzibar, the blue duiker *(C. monticola)* and the suni *(Neotragus moschatus)*, seem to be more adaptable to habitat modification and are still present in fair numbers.

**Abbot's duiker** is dark brown to almost black with no distinguishing features, other than its large size. It is found in a number of isolated montane forests in Tanzania, including those on the Uluguru, Uzungwe, Rungwe and Usambara mountains and Mount Kilimanjaro. It may still occur on zoologically poorly known mountains in the west of Tanzania.

# ALCELAPHINAE

## *"Cow" antelope*

This tribe contains eight species in five genera. Several have wide distributions but a number of subspecies are vulnerable.

Two species, the bontebok *(Damaliscus dorcas)* and the white-tailed gnu or black wildebeest *(Connochaetes gnou)*, were saved from extinction by the actions of private landowners. The hirola, or Hunter's hartebeest, of Kenya is now endangered. Even the abundant brindled gnu, or blue wildebeest, of southern and east Africa faces threats, although there are still more than 1,5 million of these strange-looking antelope.

Above: *The hirola, or Hunter's hartebeest* (Beatragus hunteri), *is restricted to a small area of north-eastern Kenya.* PHOTO: *Antwerp Zoo.*

## Hirola (Hunter's hartebeest)
### *Beatragus hunteri* Ⓔ

### Description and taxonomy

This species has the typical hartebeest build with hindquarters standing lower than the forequarters and a long, narrow head. Overall body colour is tawny yellow, and a distinct but narrow white chevron runs between the eyes. The horns more closely resemble those of impala than of other hartebeest.

Although some scientists classify the hirola as a subspecies of *Damaliscus lunatus*, which includes the topi and tsessebe, it is now generally recognised as a full species in its own right.

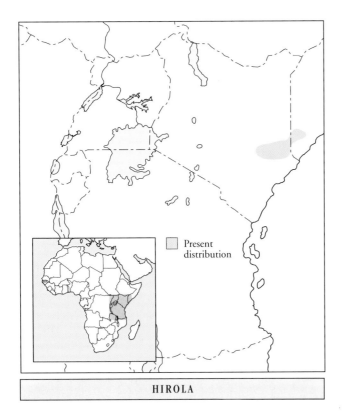

HIROLA

| HARTEBEEST | |
|---|---|
| Total length | 1,8-3,1 m |
| Tail length | 30-70 cm |
| Shoulder height | 1,2-1,5 m |
| Mass | 100-225 kg (♂ larger than ♀) |
| Home range | large; usually nomadic |
| Social structure | herds up to 20; temporary groupings of hundreds and in the past thousands |
| Gestation | 240 days |
| Birth mass | 12-15 kg |
| Diet | grass; occasionally shrubs |
| Number surviving | below 450 000 |

## Distribution and habitat

The hirola has a very restricted range on the narrow strip of grassed plain extending from the coast in south-eastern Kenya, in the districts of eastern Tana River, southern Garissa and western Lamu. It previously extended into Somalia but this part of the population is now most probably extinct.

The range of the hirola in Kenya is estimated at approximately 15 000 sq km. The distribution area seems to have changed little in recent years, but the population numbers have declined dramatically. In 1973 there were an estimated 14 000 hirola in Kenya but by 1993 the total had dropped to fewer than 2 000 and by 1997 less than 500 survived.

## Conservation

The hirola is one of Africa's rarest and most threatened large antelope. Its catastrophic decline is a result of increasing competition for grazing with domestic livestock, aggravated by extended drought and poaching. In the past poaching was primarily a problem in the Somali sector of the hirola's range but it is believed to have increased in Kenya recently as a result of the influx of Somali refugees into that country. Control of poaching by the authorities is difficult because many Somalis are heavily armed and lawlessness is a problem north of Lamu.

The Arawale National Reserve, east of the Tana River, was proclaimed to protect the hirola but the reserve covers only a tiny fraction of its range. In the 1960s a few animals were translocated to Tsavo East National Park, with a further translocation in 1997. The present population is not known, but it is believed there are 100 now.

**Above:** *The kongoni, or Coke's hartebeest* (Alcelaphus buselaphus cokii), *is restricted to Kenya and northern Tanzania.*

# Hartebeest
## *Alcelaphus buselaphus*

This species is divided into numerous more or less distinct sub-species or races. The different races are all similar in build and structure but vary in body coloration, and in particular in the form of the horns. The shoulders stand higher than the rump and the head is long and narrow. Colour varies from pale straw-yellow to a deep glossy reddish-brown, depending on the race, although there is some variation within each subspecies. The only characteristic that is usually reliable is the horn shape and structure.

There are now seven recognised subspecies. Lichtenstein's hartebeest *(Sigmoceros lichtensteini)* is a separate species. In some cases the different races hybridise at their point of meeting.

The bubal or northern hartebeest *(A.b. buselaphus)*, of north Africa, slipped unnoticed into extinction in the early years of this century. It had occurred on the lowland plains from northern Morocco to Egypt. A few may have survived until the early 1930s in Morocco and possibly Algeria.

The hartebeest occurs from Senegal through the savannas of west Africa to Somalia and southwards into east Africa, with a separate population in southern Africa. A number of races still survive in substantial numbers although all have seen their range shrink and their populations decline because of hunting and habitat changes.

The number of **western hartebeest** *(A.b. major)* of west Africa is estimated at more than 45 000. It occurs in at least 14 countries. However, until a few decades ago it occurred in the hundreds of thousands in a more or less contiguous belt from the shores of the Atlantic Ocean to western Central African Republic. The healthiest populations survive in Central African Republic, Senegal, Ivory Coast, Burkina Faso, Benin and Cameroon; elsewhere the western hartebeest is either extinct or highly fragmented.

The **lelwel hartebeest** *(A.b. lelwel)* is probably the most abundant race: there are more than 250 000. It occurs in Sudan (the bulk of the population), Ethiopia (where it is vulnerable), Uganda, north-western Tanzania (vulnerable) and in the north and east of Central African Republic (perhaps as many as 100 000). A small population is present in the far northern and north-eastern reaches of Congo (DR). The lelwel hartebeest is extinct in Kenya.

The kongoni, or **Coke's hartebeest** *(A.b. cokei)*, numbers some 60 000 in Kenya and Tanzania, with large populations in several conservation areas. Like all other races it has lost ground to agriculture, pastoralism and hunting.

The southernmost race, the **red, or Cape, hartebeest**, is now largely restricted to Botswana and Namibia, having once occurred over much of southern Africa. Nevertheless, substantial numbers still survive, and it has been extensively reintroduced onto privately owned game farms in South Africa. As a result of drought and the construction of veterinary cordon fences limiting movements to alternative grazing grounds, Botswana probably lost as much as 70% of its hartebeest population in the late 1980s. Remaining animals are well protected in a number of large national parks and conservation areas.

Of particular conservation concern are the Tora hartebeest *(A.b. tora)*, which is endangered, and Swayne's hartebeest *(A.b. swaynei)*, which is also endangered.

The **Tora hartebeest** population formerly straddled the bor-

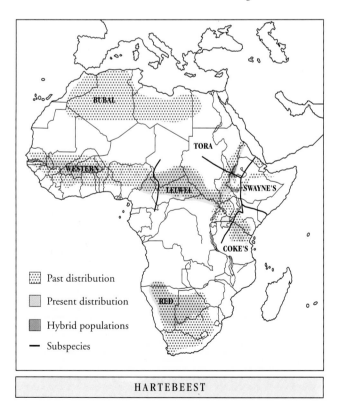

**HARTEBEEST**

Past distribution

Present distribution

Hybrid populations

— Subspecies

**Below:** *One of several recognised subspecies of hartebeest, Swayne's hartebeest* (A.b. swaynei) *has experienced drastic declines within the Rift Valley of Ethiopia today.*

PHOTO: *Chris & Sheila Hillman, Images of Africa Photobank.*

der of Sudan and Ethiopia, occurring in Sudan's Blue Nile and Kassala provinces and the north-west lowlands of Ethiopia. In the early part of this century this race was said to have been numerous on the Setit, the upper Atbara and Blue Nile tributaries in Sudan, and from the Blue Nile to the Lake Tana region in Ethiopia. Today only remnant populations survive. Although no accurate count is available, numbers are known to be dangerously low. Some animals may survive in the now independent state of Eritrea, formerly a province of Ethiopia.

**Swayne's hartebeest** is restricted to scattered populations in the Ethiopian Rift Valley, where it was once widespread and extended into Somalia. Four of the five surviving populations are in conservation areas but high human populations place direct and indirect pressures on all Ethiopian sanctuaries. Swayne (1895) described the plains of the Haud Plateau as being covered with hartebeest, estimating that there were perhaps a dozen herds in sight at one time and each herd contained 300 to 400 individuals; more than the entire population surviving today!

## Topi, tsessebe, tiang, korrigum
### *Damaliscus lunatus/korrigum* Ⓓ

These animals have the high shoulders, low rump and long, narrow head typical of the Alcelaphini. Colour ranges from pale uniform brown to brown with a dark glossy sheen over varying areas of the body. As in the hartebeest races, horn form is an important identifying character.

The topi, tsessebe, tiang and korrigum are all grouped under the species blanket *Damaliscus lunatus* by some taxonomists; others place only the tsessebe under that label and the remaining three under *D. korrigum*. Whatever taxonomic classification one follows, all forms are closely related.

Although most races still survive in substantial numbers, there have been massive declines in populations and overall range. The causes of these declines are in most cases still in place, which means that populations will continue to shrink to the point of extinction unless something is done to stop the slide. For example, although the overall population of the tiang *(D.l. tiang)* may be as high as 700 000, in Central African Republic in the space of eight years (1978-85) the population crashed from an estimated 55 900 animals to 5 400.

**Top**: *The tsessebe* (Damaliscus lunatus) *has a patchy distribution. It is sometimes placed together with the more widespread and abundant topi* (D. korrigum). *However, even this species has seen serious declines, particularly in western Africa.*
**Above**: *A young topi* (D. korrigum) *standing on top of a termite mound, a habit characteristic of this species.*

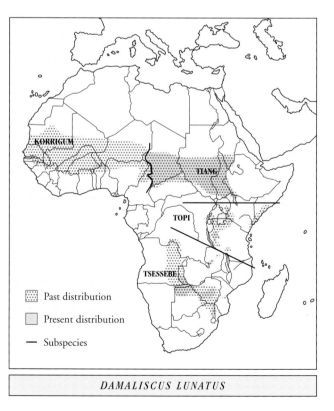

Past distribution
Present distribution
— Subspecies

*DAMALISCUS LUNATUS*

| TOPI, TSESSEBE, TIANG, KORRIGUM | |
|---|---|
| Total length | 1,9-2,6 m |
| Tail length | 40-60 cm |
| Shoulder height | 1-1,3 m |
| Mass | 75-160 kg |
| Home range | tsessebe about 4 sq km; some more nomadic with larger ranges, depending on habitat |
| Social structure | herds of 5-30; temporary groupings of hundreds, previously many thousands |
| Gestation | 240 days |
| Birth mass | 10-12 kg |
| Diet | graze |
| Number surviving | below 1 million |

The korrigum (D.l. korrigum) of west Africa numbers only 2 000-4 000 animals. It can be considered vulnerable and may soon become endangered. The largest free-ranging population lives on the riverine grasslands of south-eastern Burkina Faso, south-western Niger, northern Togo and northern Benin. This region is well served with conservation areas but their management is generally poor and they afford their inhabitants little protection. The remaining population is located in Cameroon, where small numbers occur in several national parks. In the early 1960s it was estimated that as many as 20 000 korrigum inhabited the Waza National Park in Cameroon but by 1977 only 600 to 800 remained.

## Bontebok, blesbok
### Damaliscus dorcas Ⓥ

The bontebok has a rich, dark brown coat with a purple gloss on the sides and upper legs, this being particularly well developed in rams. The buttocks, underparts and lower limbs are white, as is a distinct facial blaze. The blesbok is overall reddish-brown, with no gloss. Only the facial blaze is white; the buttocks and the underparts are paler but rarely white.

The bontebok and blesbok are both subspecies of Damaliscus dorcas and are restricted to South Africa. The bontebok (D.d. dorcas) occurs in a very limited area of the southern coastal plain in Western Cape province. The more numerous open-grassland blesbok (D.d. phillipsi) is restricted to the interior plains.

Even in historical times the bontebok was restricted to the southern coastal plain of South Africa. Today it occurs only in a few conservation areas, including the Bontebok National Park with about 200 individuals, and on private farms. Despite

its small distributional range at the time of arrival of the first European settlers in the Cape, reports indicate that it occurred in substantial numbers. For example, the traveller William Paterson in 1777 recorded that the country between Botrivier and Caledon "abounds with game, in particular bontebok." There are similar reports for following years but by the end of the 18th century and in the early 19th century travellers were reporting massive declines as a result of hunting. In 1899, the hunter Selous expressed the opinion that no more than 300 bontebok survived.

Efforts to conserve bontebok populations were implemented as early as 1837, when Alexander van der Byl of the farm

**Above:** *The bontebok* (Damaliscus dorcas dorcas) *is restricted to Western Cape province, South Africa. It had come to the verge of extinction but today, as a result of rigid protection, about 1 700 animals survive in reserves and on private farms.*

| BONTEBOK, BLESBOK | | |
|---|---|---|
| Total length | 1,7-2 m | |
| Tail length | 30-45 cm | |
| Shoulder height | 90 cm | |
| Mass | ♂ average 62 kg; ♀ lighter | |
| Home range | | |
| bontebok: | small, fixed | |
| blesbok: | larger, fixed and mobile | |
| Social structure | | |
| bontebok: | herds of 6-10 | |
| blesbok: | herds of 2-25; larger when not breeding | |
| Gestation | 240 days | |
| Birth mass | 6-7 kg | |
| Diet | grass; occasionally browse | |
| Number surviving | | |
| bontebok: | below 2 000 | |
| blesbok: | over 50 000 | |

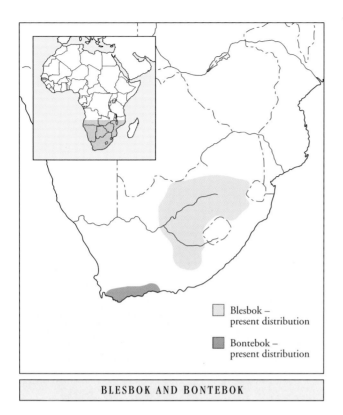

**BLESBOK AND BONTEBOK**

Blesbok – present distribution

Bontebok – present distribution

**Below:** *The black wildebeest* (Connochaetes gnou) *once roamed in great numbers across the South African plains in company with the quagga. The latter species became extinct but a few enlightened farmers saved this wildebeest from the same fate. It now occurs on a number of reserves and game farms.*

*Nacht Wacht* enclosed 27 bontebok within 2 428 ha of ground. Three other farmers were to follow his lead in later years. In 1927 it was estimated that 121 bontebok survived; by 1961 there were some 525; in 1979 the population had grown to slightly more than 1 100; today it stands at almost 2 000. A high proportion of animals occur outside the species' natural range on private farms.

In the early part of this century one farmer is said to have supplemented his bontebok herd with blesbok. In recent years the purity of all bontebok populations has been questioned, as other small groups of blesbok were introduced into their distribution area. Bontebok and blesbok were freely moved around outside their natural range until fairly recently, and consequently genetic mixing has taken place. Conservation authorities have attempted to identify mixed populations and remove blesbok from the natural range of the bontebok. Although confidence has been expressed that the problem is well under control, there will always be a measure of doubt about the bontebok's genetic purity.

The fact that there are almost 2 000 bontebok, a fair percentage in well-managed conservation areas, is no guarantee of their long-term survival. Apart from the uncertainty about the purity of some populations, many animals live in non-viable groups. Even the three largest groups, located in formal conservation areas – the Bontebok National Park, De Hoop Nature Reserve and the Cape of Good Hope Nature Reserve – each numbers well below the 500 individuals generally believed to be required to protect long-term genetic viability. It is unlikely that existing reserves could be expanded to accommodate the large numbers believed to be required, which

means that these populations will have to be extremely carefully managed.

The blesbok appears to have always been restricted to the grasslands of the South African interior. Although it was heavily hunted, it still occurs widely on reserves and farms throughout its range. All populations are now confined. The blesbok also occurs on game farms outside its natural range.

# Black wildebeest
## *Connochaetes gnou* Ⓥ

# Blue wildebeest
## *Connochaetes taurinus* Ⓓ

### Description and taxonomy

As its name implies, the black wildebeest is dark brown to black overall, with a white, horse-like tail. The face is covered with a brush-like tuft of hairs. A fringe of long hair extends from the chin to the chest and a long-haired, erect mane runs down the neck to the shoulders. The horns are present in both sexes and they are sharply curved downwards, forwards and upwards. The shoulders of the blue wildebeest are noticeably higher than its hindquarters. Overall body colour ranges from dark grey to grey-brown. There are darker vertical bands on the body, but these are not always distinct. A mane of fairly long black hair extends down the neck and onto the shoulders. The extended "beard" is black in southern populations and white in north-eastern populations.

**Above:** *Blue wildebeest* (Connochaetes taurinus) *or brindled gnu crossing the Mara River in southern Kenya.*

No subspecies or races of the black wildebeest, or white-tailed gnu, are recognised. Five have been described for the blue wildebeest, or brindled gnu, of which the white-bearded *(C.t. mearnsi)* of east Africa, the blue or black-bearded *(C.t. taurinus)* of southern Africa and Cookson's *(C.t. cooksoni)* of the Luangwa Valley in Zambia are clearly recognisable.

| | BLACK | BLUE |
|---|---|---|
| **Total length** | 2,6-3,2 m | 2,35-3,3 m |
| **Tail length** | 90-100 cm | 60-100 cm |
| **Shoulder height** | 1,2 m | 1,4 m |
| **Mass** | 100-180 kg (♂ larger than ♀) | 180-250 kg (♂ larger than ♀) |
| **Home range** | confined | very large |
| **Social structure** | small herds | herds up to 30 |
| **Gestation** | 250 days | 250 days |
| **Birth mass** | 14 kg | 22 kg |
| **Diet** | grass; occasionally browse | grass; occasionally browse |
| **Number surviving** | over 4 000 | about 1,7 million |

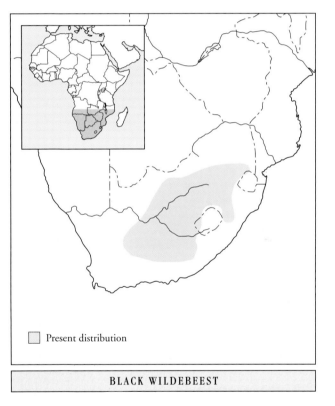

☐ Present distribution

**BLACK WILDEBEEST**

### Distribution and habitat

The black wildebeest has always been limited to the area of low scrub and grassland in the interior of South Africa. Blue wildebeest occur in two separate populations, one in eastern and the other in southern Africa, with a small, isolated population in the Luangwa Valley of Zambia. Wherever they occur they are associated with open grassland and savanna woodland. This species is absent from much of central Africa and has never

occurred in west Africa. Most of the east African population (almost 90%) is centred on north-western Tanzania and adjacent areas of south-western Kenya, with smaller populations centred on the Athi Plains (including Nairobi National Park) and Amboseli in Kenya, and Tarangire National Park or Simanjiro Plains and Selous Game Reserve or Mikumi National Park in Tanzania. In southern Africa the last free-ranging blue wildebeest populations occur in Botswana and to a lesser extent Zimbabwe; elsewhere they are mainly confined within conservation areas and on game farms.

The Ngorongoro-Serengeti-Mara population (the race here is *C.t. mearnsi,* whereas to the east of the Gregory Rift the race *C.t. albojubatus* is recognised by some authorities) numbered some 260 000 in 1961. The number climbed to about 1,3 million by 1977 and now fluctuates between 1 million and 1,5 million. This dramatic increase makes a pleasant change from the usual tales of decline and extinction. One reason for it is that since the early 1960s there has been no outbreak of rinderpest, a disease that decimates this species. Changes in seasonal rainfall have also resulted in increased grazing. The migratory population (20 000 animals) that spends the dry season in the Nairobi National Park and in the wet season moves out of the conservation area onto the Athi-Kaputei Plains is threatened by increasing development, including fencing of the plains, which would disrupt the animals' movements. Only a much smaller population could be permanently accommodated in

**Above:** *The impala* (Aepycerus melampus) *is common but one subspecies, the black-faced impala* (A.m. petersi), *is threatened.*

the Nairobi National Park.

The race *C.t. johnstoni* occurs in substantial numbers – about 80 000 individuals – in southern Tanzania but is now extinct within its former range in Mozambique and Malawi.

The largest blue wildebeest populations in South Africa are located in the Kruger National Park (about 15 000), Kalahari Gemsbok National Park and a number of KwaZulu-Natal reserves. The Namibian wildebeest herds are mostly restricted to the Etosha National Park in the north. Zimbabwean populations are limited to the north-west (Hwange National Park) and the south. Of greatest concern is the dramatic decline suffered by the Botswanan wildebeest herds, particularly in the central and southern areas. This is an example of how a once abundant species, considered a pest in some circles, can decline to near extinction because of drought and veterinary fences that prevent migration to water and fresh pastures. Although drought had regularly caused high mortality before the erection of the extensive cordon-fence network, the wildebeest populations were soon able to recover when conditions again became favourable. The fences now obstructed the herds' traditional migration routes and the population was decimated. In 1963 an estimated 300 000 wildebeest died, and in 1983 possibly as many as 80 000.

### Behaviour

The black wildebeest previously formed temporary migratory herds of many thousands. The blue wildebeest in parts of its range, particularly in east Africa, still migrate in hundreds of thousands of animals along age-old migration routes.

### Conservation

The black wildebeest is another species that almost entered the annals of extinction but for the intervention of private landowners on the interior plains of South Africa. Many readers will no doubt question the inclusion in this book of the blue wildebeest, given that 1,5 million of these animals tread the grazing circuit of the Ngorongoro-Serengeti-Mara in Tanzania and Kenya. However, all is not well with this and other populations.

The black wildebeest, along with all other plains game in South Africa, was heavily hunted for meat and hides, and because they were competing for food with domestic stock. An indication of the extent of the slaughter can be gleaned from the fact that in 1866, one Orange Free State firm exported 157 000 wildebeest and blesbok skins. During 1870-71, 485 786 hides of zebra, wildebeest (probably black) and blesbok were exported from the port of Durban. The bulk of these skins would have been collected in the eastern Orange Free State and to a lesser extent Natal.

By the end of the 19th century the black wildebeest, numbering no more than 600 animals, was restricted to what was then the Orange Free State and southern Transvaal. It was extinct in the then Cape Province. The population was further reduced during the Anglo-Boer War. However, small populations were conserved on farms and by 1946 numbers had increased to just over 1 000 animals. In 1971 there were 3 100 black wildebeest, and in 1994 more than 4 000. The largest single population is located in the Willem Pretorius Game Reserve in the Free State, where there were more than 500 animals in 1992. Another reserve in this province, Tussen-die-Riviere, also has a large population but hybridisation has taken place between this and the blue wildebeest, making the population unsuitable as a source of genetic reserve stock.

## Black-faced impala
### *Aepyceros melampus petersi* **(V)**

This graceful, slender-limbed antelope has an overall reddish-brown coat, paling to fawn on the flanks. It has white underparts and a distinct black vertical stripe on each buttock. The rams have long lyre-shaped horns. The black-faced impala differs from the other races in having a distinct black facial blaze and somewhat bushier tail.

The impala occurs widely in south-eastern and east Africa. Probably well over 500 000 animals inhabit the open savanna woodlands. Six subspecies are recognised, of which only the black-faced impala of extreme north-western Namibia and

| BLACK-FACED IMPALA | |
|---|---|
| **Total length** | 1,5-2 m |
| **Tail length** | 28 cm |
| **Shoulder height** | 90 cm |
| **Mass** | ♂ over 50 kg; ♀ over 40 kg |
| **Social structure** | herds of 3-15 |
| **Gestation** | 196 days |
| **Birth mass** | 5 kg |
| **Diet** | browse and graze |
| **Number surviving** | |
| all impala: | over 500 000 |
| black-faced impala: | below 3 000 |

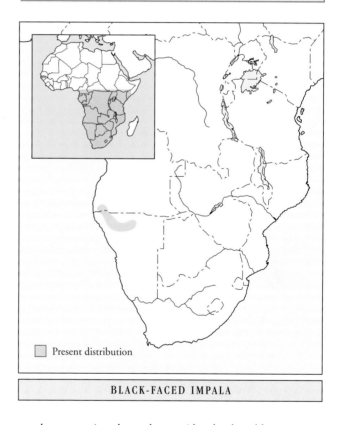

Present distribution

**BLACK-FACED IMPALA**

south-western Angola can be considered vulnerable.

The bulk of the black-faced impala population is protected in the Etosha National Park in Namibia, where they occupy mixed woodlands, avoiding open plains. Their status outside this reserve is precarious. Already in 1973 the black-faced impala was considered to be endangered in Angola, with probably fewer than 800 then surviving. Given the protracted war in that country it is certain that the situation has deteriorated further. In some circles it is believed that not only the black-faced impala, but several other species as well may now be extinct in the Iona National Park in south-western Angola.

# REDUNCINAE

*Reedbuck and waterbuck types*

## Lechwe
### *Kobus leche* Ⓥ

The lechwe is characterised by the hindquarters being noticeably higher than the shoulders. Only the rams carry the long, strongly ridged, lyre-shaped horns. Coat colour varies among the different races from chestnut brown to dark brown, with a varying extent of black. The least black is seen in the red lechwe and the most in rams of the black lechwe. The ewes of the different races are more uniform in colour.

Four races are recognised: the extinct *K.l. robertsi*, which occurred on the Luongo River in north-western Zambia; the red lechwe *(K.l. leche)* of western Zambia, northern Botswana, the Caprivi Strip of Namibia and possibly marginally into Angola and south-eastern Zaïre; the Kafue lechwe *(K.l. kafuensis)* from the Kafue Flats in south-western Zambia; and the black lechwe *(K.l. smithemani)* of the Bangweulu Swamp region in north-eastern Zambia.

A distinct species, the Nile lechwe *(K. megaceros)*, is restricted to the Sudd and associated swamps in southern Sudan and western Ethiopia. The Nile lechwe ram is particularly striking, with a very dark coat and a strongly contrasting white patch on the nape and shoulders. The lechwe has lost much of its former range. The three surviving subspecies occur in isolated pockets in Zambia, Namibia, Botswana, Congo (DR) and possibly Angola. This antelope is particularly vulnerable to poaching: because it occupies open floodplains and swamp fringes, motorised access is easy and animals have nowhere to hide.

**Above:** *Of the three recognised lechwe races, the Kafue* (Kobus leche kafuensis) *is the most abundant but it has been greatly reduced by both subsistence and commercial meat hunting.* PHOTO: *N. Plewman.*

After the sitatunga, the lechwe is the most water-loving antelope. Its habitat is floodplains and seasonally inundated grasslands. It frequently feeds in shallow water and will submerge if threatened. Rams form very small territories during the rut, in which they attempt to hold small groups of ewes with which they mate. Although lechwe usually run in herds of approximately 30 animals, several thousand may gather together on the floodplains. There are, however, few places where such aggregations can be observed today.

The Blue Lagoon and Lochinvar national parks of south-western Zambia hold the largest concentrations of the **Kafue lechwe** and it is here that herds numbering hundreds can be observed. Sadly, the Blue Lagoon population has been under severe poaching pressure in recent years and this continues. The flat, open plains are conducive to commercial motorised hunting. Although large herds can still be seen here they are very timid and much greater control of this and all other Zambian conservation areas is required.

The most serious population declines have been suffered by the **red lechwe**. This is also the subspecies with the lowest number, a meagre 8 000 animals. Until the late 1980s tens of thousands of red lechwe occupied the floodplains and marshes of the Eastern Caprivi district of Namibia, but as a direct result of poaching there are now believed to be fewer than 1 000 animals. Two new conservation areas have been proclaimed within their principal range, but changes in vegetation structure and excessive pressure from a burgeoning human and cattle population are likely to prevent any major recovery.

It is unlikely that red lechwe survive in the south-east of Angola, as the scorched earth policy carried out here by the South African Defence Force and the UNITA guerrilla forces

| LECHWE | |
|---|---|
| **Total length** | 1,6-2,2 m |
| **Tail length** | 30-45 cm |
| **Shoulder height** | 1 m |
| **Mass** | ♂ 100 kg; ♀ 80 kg |
| **Home range** | small; animals occur at high densities |
| **Social structure** | herds of about 30; often hundreds or even thousands |
| **Gestation** | 225 days |
| **Birth mass** | 5 kg |
| **Diet** | mainly semi-aquatic grasses |
| **Number surviving** | |
| Kafue lechwe: | 40 000 |
| black lechwe: | below 30 000 |
| red lechwe: | about 8 000 |
| Nile lechwe: | 30 000-40 000 |

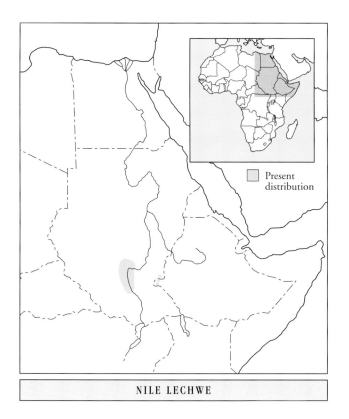

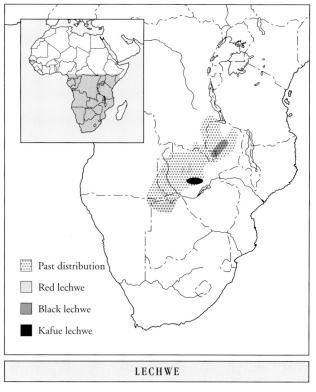

| NILE LECHWE | LECHWE |

during the conflicts of the 1980s included the shooting of game. The population in extreme south-eastern Congo (DR) is classified as endangered. The subspecies is almost extinct in most locations. In the early 1970s several thousand red lechwe survived along the Lualaba River, to the west of the Upemba National Park, but heavy commercial poaching has no doubt greatly reduced, or even eradicated, this population.

The **black lechwe** is concentrated in the Bangweulu swamplands and floodplain of Zambia. Estimated population size was 30 000 in 1991, but heavy poaching in 1992 may have greatly reduced numbers. No more recent figures are available.

**Below:** *The black lechwe* (Kobus leche smithemani) *is restricted to a few populations in Zambia.* Photo: *Phil Berry.*

# NEOTRAGINAE

## Dwarf antelope

## Oribi
### Ourebia ourebi

The oribi is a small and dainty antelope. Small groups, each with one ram, live in short grassland over large areas of sub-Saharan Africa. It is estimated that some 100 000 survive in west and northern central Africa, with perhaps 50 000 in east Africa. The number in southern Africa is unknown but prob-

**Above:** *In South Africa the oribi* (Ourebia ourebi) *is now restricted to a few isolated islands of suitable habitat. Modification and loss of habitat are the main reasons for its decline.*

ably fewer than 20 000. In some areas the oribi is not under any major threat but some populations have suffered serious declines. One subspecies, *O.o. keniae*, which occurred on the lower slopes of Mount Kenya, is probably extinct. There have been dramatic declines in the numbers of oribi in South Africa and Zimbabwe and populations are severely fragmented. For example, in the 1950s the oribi had a fairly extensive distribution on the eastern coastal plain of the then Cape Province (South Africa) and was probably several thousand strong. Today the entire population is restricted to a handful of farms within an area of less than 200 sq km.

With changes in land use and growing human populations it seems certain these animals will not survive in the long term.

## Beira
### Dorcatragus megalotis

This small antelope bears a strong resemblance to the steenbok (*Raphicerus campestris*) but their ranges do not overlap. It differs from the steenbok in having a short but bushy tail and a dark stripe on the flanks. The beira is restricted to a tiny area

| ORIBI | |
|---|---|
| Total length | 92-140 cm |
| Tail length | 6-15 cm |
| Shoulder height | 54-67 cm |
| Mass | ♂ 14-19 kg; ♀ 15-21 kg |
| Home range | variable, usually 4-6 ha |
| Social structure | groups of one male and one or more females |
| Gestation | about 195 days |
| Birth mass | 1,6-2,2 kg |
| Diet | predominantly grass |

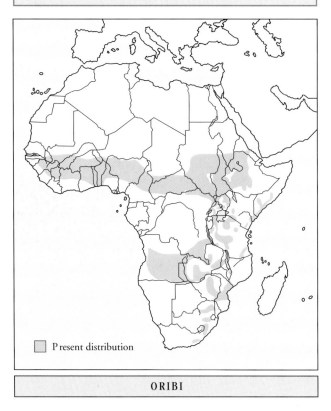

P resent distribution

ORIBI

| BEIRA | |
|---|---|
| Total length | 80-86 cm |
| Tail length | 6-7,5 cm |
| Shoulder height | 50-65 cm |
| Mass | 9-11,5 kg |
| Social structure | family groups, occasionally 2-3 families |
| Diet | succulents, grass, herbs |

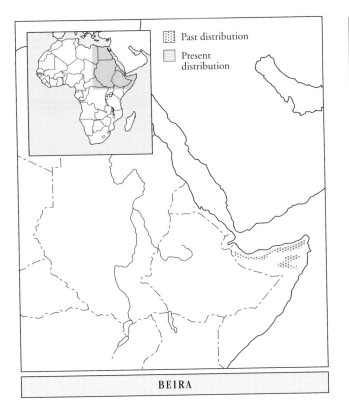

| Past distribution |
| Present distribution |

**BEIRA**

| DIK-DIKS | |
|---|---|
| Total length | 52-72 cm |
| Tail length | 3,5-5,6 cm |
| Shoulder height | 34-43 cm |
| Mass | 2,7-7,2 kg |
| Home range | 2-6 ha |
| Social structure | one male with one or more females |
| Gestation | 155-177 days |
| Birth mass | 500-800 g |
| Diet | principally browse |
| Habitat | semi-arid bushlands |

of eastern Ethiopia in the Marmar Mountains, and to the arid ranges in Somalia north of the Nugaal Valley. With the exception of the tropical forest duikers, the beira is one of the least known African antelope. It lives in pairs or small groups and is a mixed feeder. The beira exhibits considerable agility when moving through the rugged, rocky country it inhabits. The few historical records that are available indicate that this was never a very common species, but the combination of drought, competition with domestic stock and hunting has caused declines. There is no indication of surviving numbers.

## Dik-diks

Four or five species are recognised in this group of tiny antelope. Their centre of evolutionary development is in the Horn of Africa, and it is important to conserve this stock before major declines occur. In some areas they occur at high densities, for example Kirk's or the Damara dik-dik *(Madoqua kirkii)*, in both its east and south-west African populations. Although numbers have no doubt declined in areas of high human density, no dik-dik species appears to be under particular threat at the moment.

These antelope are particularly vulnerable to hunting pressure by humans, competition with domestic stock and modification and manipulation of habitats. Some species are able to cope with these pressures better than others. Although many of Africa's antelope species occur in conservation areas, management and control of poaching is minimal to non-existent in many reserves. This is especially prevalent in the western and north-eastern regions of the continent.

**Top:** *Günther's dik-dik* (Madoqua guentheri) *ewe and fawn in Samburu, Kenya.* **Above:** *Female Kirk's dik-dik* (M. kirkii) *in Etosha, Namibia.*

# CHAPTER 7

# OTHER MAMMALS

## *All creatures great & small*

Habitat reduction is the major threat, as it reduces available space
for non-human mammals and other biota. Hunting is also a problem, as
many wild species are people's only source of protein.

In this chapter we have something of a mixed bag: we cover
the non-antelope ungulates, three coastal species, one rabbit,
a number of insectivores and some bats. Very few species have
escaped some decline in numbers or range, or both, so the
choice of which to cover and which to leave out is quite sub-
jective. Species are under particular pressure in heavily populated regions such as much of west Africa and parts of eastern
and southern Africa. Habitat destruction is the major threat, as
it reduces available space for non-human mammals and other
biota. Hunting is also a problem, as many wild animal species
are people's only source of protein. In many cases our lack of
information prevents adequate conservation action.

# CAPRINI

## *Goat antelope*

### Ibex
### *Capra ibex* **E**

This wild goat is fairly stocky, with a typical goat-like build. It has a short, tuft-tipped tail and males have a characteristic beard. Both sexes carry horns but those of the males are sabre-shaped, massive and heavily ridged. Males are much larger than females. The Walia ibex is on average slightly larger than the Nubian. General body colour is yellowish-fawn to brown but the Walia ibex is darker chestnut-brown. Both races have paler underparts, dark brown to black markings on the legs and a dark streak down the back.

This is the only species of wild goat on the African continent. Two subspecies are recognised, the Walia *(C.i. walie)* and the Nubian *(C.i. nubiana)* ibex. There has been considerable controversy over the taxonomic standing of the Walia ibex. It is distinctive enough for subspecies status but probably not to be raised to species level. A few authorities consider that even the Nubian ibex qualifies as a separate species and should not be lumped with other ibex. However, it is probably best to accept that both African ibex are representatives of the widespread Palaearctic ibex *(C. ibex)*.

The Walia ibex is endangered and only found in and around the Simien National Park in the northern Ethiopian Highlands above 2 800 m. In 1989 there were estimated to be fewer than 400 animals. By 1993 the total was estimated to have fallen

| IBEX | |
|---|---|
| Total length | 1,5-1,9 m |
| Tail length | 15-25 cm |
| Shoulder height | 65-110 cm |
| Mass | 50-125 kg |
| Home range | about 10 sq km (Walia) |
| Social structure | small groups; males and females with young |
| Gestation | 150-165 days |
| Diet | graze and browse |

**Above left:** *Thornicroft's giraffe* (G.c. thornicrofti) *is restricted to the Luangwa Valley, Zambia.* PHOTO: *Phil Berry.*
**Above:** *Walia ibex* (Capra ibex walie) *ram in Simien National Park, Ethiopia.* PHOTO: *Prof. B. Nievergelt.*
**Below left:** *A common hippo* (Hippopotamus amphibius) *– the super keystone species of Africa's freshwater systems.* PHOTO: *M. Philip, ABPL.*

well below this figure. No animals were observed within the Simien National Park in 1993.

The Nubian ibex is more widespread, living at lower altitudes and under drier conditions. Numbers are nevertheless very low, although several areas have not been surveyed for years because of civil war, particularly in Ethiopia and Eritrea.

This ibex is believed to be present in small numbers in northern Eritrea near the Sudanese border and definitely along the coastal hills of Sudan, but numbers are unknown. In Egypt the Nubian ibex occurs in the Sinai Peninsula (small populations occur elsewhere in the Middle East) with about 400 animals, and down the broken desert country that fringes the Red Sea coast. Accurate population numbers are not known but they are probably low.

Threats to the ibex include hunting, competition with livestock and feral camels, and growing human populations.

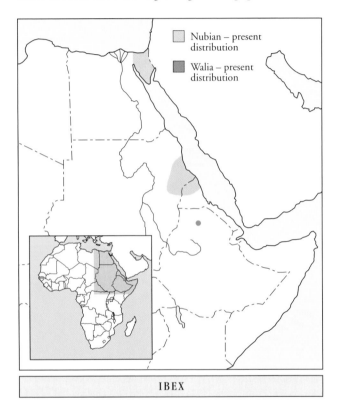

IBEX

# Barbary sheep
## *Ammotragus lervia* **V**

The Barbary is a large, stocky sheep. Rams are larger than ewes. Both have a fringe of long hair on the throat, chest and forelegs and a long, well-haired tail. The fringe is not as well developed in the ewe as in the ram. The horns of the ram are very stout and curved; those of the ewe are much lighter. Overall coat colour is sandy brown, with lighter underparts.

The Barbary sheep, or aoudad, is Africa's only wild sheep, and although it has a wide distribution in north Africa numbers have declined drastically in the past 30 years. Several races have been recognised but differences are minor and overall appearance is similar.

The Barbary sheep occurs patchily throughout the Sahara Desert from the southern slopes of the Atlas Mountains eastwards to the Red Sea hills in Sudan. It is found in 11 countries. It occupies mountainous and hilly terrain within the desert. The total population in Morocco is believed to number 800 to

| BARBARY SHEEP | |
|---|---|
| Total length | 1,4-1,8 m |
| Tail length | 15-25 cm |
| Shoulder height | 75-120 cm |
| Mass | ♂ 100-140 kg; ♀ 40-55 kg |
| Horns | ♂ 80 cm; ♀ 40 cm |
| Social structure | 3-6 (up to 20) |
| Gestation | 150-165 days |
| Number of young | 1-3 (usually 1-2) |
| Diet | mainly browse |
| Number surviving | below 50 000 |

1 000. No estimate has been made for Western Sahara but populations are believed to be small. Mauritanian numbers are probably very low, with the largest population being centred on the Adrar Mountains. Algeria is believed to have several thousand animals, with the healthiest populations in the south and a good number of animals protected in two national parks. Only remnant populations occur in Tunisia. Barbary sheep are probably highly threatened in Libya, but little recent information on any wildlife is available from that country. The Barbary sheep is extinct in Egypt but a reintroduction programme is being planned. Unknown numbers of these sheep occur in northern Chad, Mali and Sudan but they are almost certainly few and declining. In Niger, healthy populations (about 3 600 animals in 1990) are present in the Air Mountains and the Termit Massif. This represents some 70% of all the Barbary sheep in this country. Hunting is a major threat throughout the Barbary sheep's range but desertification, competition with domestic livestock and general disturbance are also major fac-

**Below:** *Male Barbary sheep* (Ammotragus lervia).

tors affecting this and other Saharan wild ungulates. The presence of the Barbary sheep in a number of national parks is no guarantee of long-term protection as many conservation areas are poorly managed, with little control over poaching and human and livestock movements.

| **BARBARY RED DEER** | |
| --- | --- |
| **Shoulder height** | ♂ 1,12 m; ♀ 0,90-1,1 m |
| **Mass** | ♂ 150-220 kg; <br> ♀ 100-150 kg |
| **Number surviving** | about 4 000 |

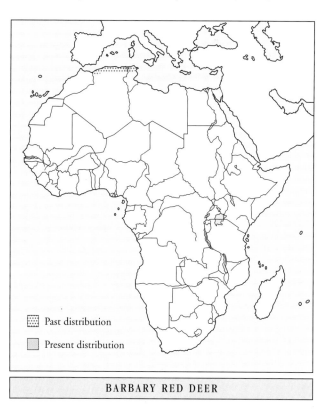

Above: *Barbary red deer* (Cervus elaphus barbarus). PHOTO: *James Dolan.*

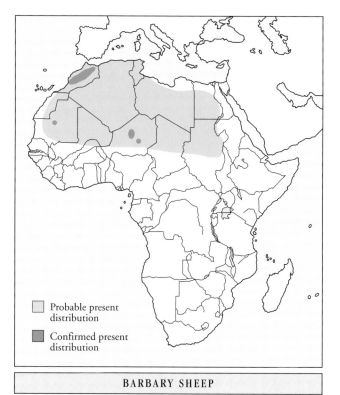

Probable present distribution

Confirmed present distribution

**BARBARY SHEEP**

# CERVIDAE

*Deer*

## Barbary red deer
*Cervus elaphus barbarus* Ⓥ

This is one of the smaller red deer races. Stags are distinguished by the lack of a bez, or second tine, on each antler. The winter coat is dark brown with faint white spotting; the summer coat is yellowish-brown to reddish-brown and the white spotting is more pronounced. Typical of deer, only the stags carry antlers, dropping them for part of the year.

The only deer that now occurs naturally in Africa is the Barbary red deer, one of many subspecies that occur widely in the Northern Hemisphere.

The fallow deer *(Cervus dama)* once occurred in north Africa along the Mediterranean coastline, but it has been extinct for several centuries. Small surviving populations apparently descend from introduced animals, but no documentation exists. Fallow deer of European origin have been introduced on numerous farms in South Africa.

Although there is some mention in the literature that the

Past distribution

Present distribution

**BARBARY RED DEER**

Barbary red deer occurred in Morocco up to the time of Roman colonisation, recent authors accept its distribution as having been only to the Algerian-Moroccan border. Red deer found in Morocco today are introductions from Europe.

Barbary red deer were widely distributed in woodland along the Mediterranean seaboard in Algeria and Tunisia during the Roman occupation, as evidenced from their depiction in many mosaics of that period. Numerous skeletal remains have also been found. The decline in deer numbers can be correlated with the arrival of European colonisers in the 19th and the early part of the 20th century. By 1960 the red deer only survived in north-eastern Constantine in Algeria and the adjacent area of north-western Tunisia. Tunisia's entire population in 1961 numbered only 10 animals, but during the war of independence in Algeria additional animals crossed from Algeria into Tunisia. The Tunisian government established a reserve for the deer in 1963, and in 1966 an additional area was set aside. Red deer now occupy an area of some 200 sq km in north-western Tunisia. In just over 30 years they increased from 10 animals to an amazing 2 000. Although there is now an estimated total of 4 000 animals, their concentration in a small area makes them highly susceptible to any outbreak of disease and to being killed by forest fires, which are frequent in the Mediterranean-type vegetation of their habitat.

# GIRAFFIDAE

### *Giraffe and okapi*

## Giraffe
### *Giraffa camelopardalis* Ⓓ

The giraffe, the world's tallest mammal, is so well known that it needs no description. A number of distinctly marked and coloured races (at least six) are recognised. Visitors to Africa's great savanna national parks and game reserves will no doubt wonder why we should include the giraffe in a book on vanishing wildlife. The reason is that although some races are still abundant in conservation areas, such as the southern giraffe (*G.c. giraffa*), the Kenyan or Masai giraffe (*G.c. tippelkirchi*) and the reticulated giraffe (*G.c. reticulata*), all races have declined dramatically both in range and overall numbers. For example, Rothschild's giraffe (*G.c. rothschildi*) has a very limited distribution in Kenya. Races from western Africa are now greatly reduced and populations seriously fragmented.

The giraffe once occurred wherever there was suitable open woodland and dry acacia savanna, even into desert areas. Not long ago it was found virtually throughout Africa, with the exception of high mountains and forested country. In historical times the giraffe occurred as far north as Morocco and in parts of the Sahara Desert. It is now extinct above the latitude of 15° north. It has disappeared from much of west Africa; in southern Africa as much as 90% of the population is restricted to conservation areas. The eastern and southern popula-

| GIRAFFE | |
| --- | --- |
| Total length | 3,5-5,4 m |
| Tail length | 75-150 cm |
| Total height | ♂ 3,9-5,2 m; ♀ 3,7-4,7 m |
| Shoulder height | ♂ 2,6-3,5 m; ♀ 2,0-3,0 m |
| Mass | ♂ 970-1 400 kg; ♀ 700-950 kg |
| Home range | 20-85 sq km |
| Social structure | herds of 4-30 (variable) |
| Gestation | 450 days |
| Birth mass | 100 kg |
| Diet | browse |

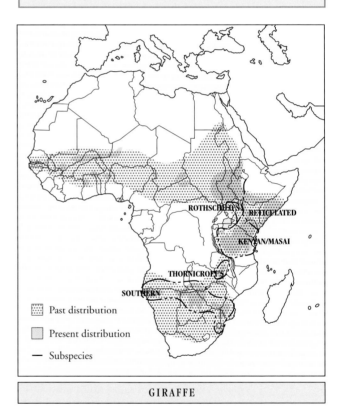

GIRAFFE

Past distribution
Present distribution
— Subspecies

tions are separated by a considerable distance, with a completely isolated population living in the Luangwa Valley of Zambia. This race is called Thornicroft's giraffe.

The giraffe's decline can be attributed in large part to hunting, both for its meat and tough leather, which was used in the past for making, among other things, hide rope, whips and sandals. Increased desertification, destruction of woodland, disturbance at waterholes and expanding agriculture and animal husbandry have placed giraffe populations under considerable pressure. Today these animals are largely confined to conservation areas, and it is doubtful whether they will survive in the long term outside these areas.

**Above:** *Rothschild's giraffe* (C.c. rothschildi) *has very distinct markings and coloration. Its distribution is now very limited.*

# Okapi
## *Okapia johnstoni*

### Description and taxonomy

The okapi has a superficially giraffe-like appearance but the neck is proportionally shorter. The short velvety coat has a rich chocolate brown colour with a distinct reddish or purplish sheen. The most eye-catching feature is the transverse white striping on the upper legs and the rump. The face is creamy-white but the muzzle is dark. The males carry short, hair-covered horns. With its long neck and long legs the okapi is able to reach tree leaves, on which it feeds, at higher levels than other forest ungulates. This reach is further aided by an extremely long (about 35 cm) and dexterous black tongue.

This unusual but attractive forest ungulate, sometimes re-

| OKAPI | |
|---|---|
| **Total length** | 2,5 m |
| **Tail length** | 40 cm |
| **Total height** | 1,7-1,8 m |
| **Shoulder height** | 1,5-1,6 m |
| **Mass** | 200-275 kg |
| **Home range** | 1,9-10,5 sq km (in Ituri Forest) |
| **Social structure** | solitary |
| **Gestation** | 421-457 days |
| **Diet** | browse |

ferred to as the "forest giraffe", was only discovered by the scientific world in 1900. There had been vague reports for a number of years of a large and mysterious animal living in the tropical forests of the northern Congo. The explorer Stanley came up with the first pieced-together descriptions. His report caught the interest of Sir Harry Johnston, whose name the species now bears. Johnston's efforts to find the animal eventually bore fruit when he obtained first some scraps of skin and later a complete skin and two skulls. This was the first hard evidence that a giraffe-like species previously unknown to science did indeed occupy the Congolean forests.

### Distribution and habitat

The okapi occurs only in Congo (DR), in forests north and north-east of the Congo River and at least marginally into the central Congo (DR) Basin in the north-east. There are reports of its occurrence in other parts of the forest block but surveys need to be undertaken to confirm this. It once occurred in the forests of western Uganda but it is now extinct there. Populations are known to be present in the Virunga and Maiko national parks in north-eastern Congo (DR) but in the former it probably does not occur in viable numbers. Its occurrence in Salonga National Park in west-central Congo (DR) still needs confirmation. The best known and possibly the largest population is located in the Ituri Forest.

Okapis occur in montane forests and lowland swamp forests. They will feed in small new-growth glades but they avoid larger open areas.

### Behaviour

Although some animals are kept in captivity, much about okapi behaviour in the wild is still unknown. The first determined effort to study the okapi in its forest home only began in 1986. Research in the Ituri Forest has shown okapis to be mainly diurnal. They move relatively short distances each day when feeding, an indication of the abundance of their food.

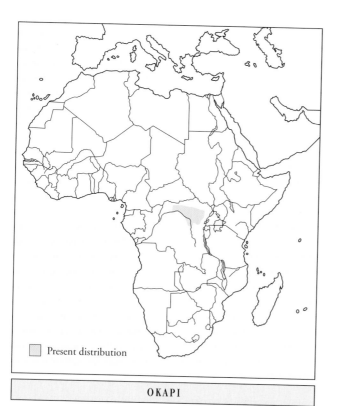

Present distribution

**OKAPI**

**Above:** *The okapi* (Okapia johnstoni). PHOTO: *Klaus Rudloff.*

# EQUIDAE

## *Wild horses*

All zebras are horse-like in appearance. They are characterised by their black and white striping, which differs between species. The greatest variation occurs between the subspecies of the plains zebra. Some races of the plains zebra have "shadow stripes" lying on the white stripes. The two mountain zebra subspecies have distinct dewlaps on the throat and a clear grid-iron pattern above the root of the tail. Grevy's zebra has narrow stripes and a broad, dark stripe runs along the spine.

The three species of zebra have a total of eight subspecies. Only one species, the plains zebra *(Equus burchelli)*, remains abundant on the savanna grasslands of southern, central and east Africa. One subspecies, the quagga *(E.b. quagga)*, occurred in the central plains of South Africa but was hunted to extinction in the 19th century. Some authorities still accord the quagga full species status.

Africa is home to one species of wild ass. It has three recognised subspecies of which one is extinct. All domestic asses, or donkeys, are derived from one or more of the subspecies of African wild ass *(E. africanus)*. From Africa they spread all over

| WILD HORSES | | | | |
|---|---|---|---|---|
| | **MOUNTAIN ZEBRA** | **PLAINS ZEBRA** | **GREVY'S ZEBRA** | **WILD ASS** |
| **Shoulder height** | 1,3-1,5 m | 1,3 m | 1,5 m | 1,1-1,2 m |
| **Mass** | 250-350 kg | 290-340 kg | 350-430 kg | unknown |
| **Number surviving** | below 8 000 | below 700 000 | below 6 000 | 1 000-2 000 |

## Conservation

Although okapi populations in some areas appear to be viable and stable, in other areas they have completely disappeared, mainly as a result of the destruction of their forest habitat. Okapis are also under hunting pressure in parts of their range. Okapi populations are not uniformly distributed and densities in certain forest types can be very low, for example forests dominated by *Gilbertiodendron dewevrei*. Okapis are totally absent from some seemingly suitable areas. Populations in the Ebola River Forest have been greatly reduced by hunting. In the Tchabi and Erengeti regions of North Kivu they may be extinct. Other than humans, leopards seem to be significant predators of okapis, even killing adults. Information on their distribution and conservation status is lacking from most areas.

the world and have served as beasts of burden since the Mesopotamian civilisation of some 2500 BC.

The equids are able to make more efficient use of coarse grasses than the bovids but access to surface water is essential. The plains and mountain zebras *(E. zebra)* form small, permanent family groups (harems). The wild ass and Grevy's zebra *(E. grevyi)* stallions establish territories and mate with mares entering their defended areas; long-term relationships only occur between mares and offspring up to the age of about two years. Large zebra herds may gather temporarily. In the case of the plains zebras many thousands may form loose associations but the integrity of the harem groups is maintained.

Efforts to domesticate zebras have consistently met with failure. There are several references to attempts to tame zebras to saddle and harness.

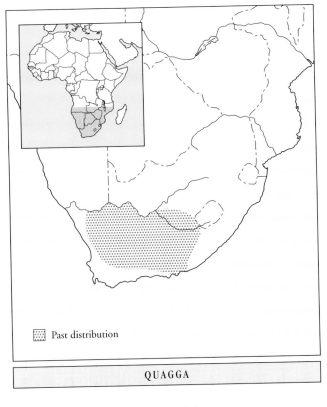

Past distribution

QUAGGA

# African wild ass
*Equus africanus* **E**

This species is divided into three subspecies. One, the Atlas wild ass *(E.a. atlanticus)* is extinct. Both surviving subspecies, the Nubian wild ass *(E.a. africanus)* and the Somali wild ass *(E.a. somaliensis)* are seriously endangered.

The wild ass once occurred from the Moroccan Atlas Mountains across Saharan and possibly Sahelian Africa to the Red Sea and the Indian Ocean coast in Somalia. There is some evidence that they were also present in the Arabian Peninsula. Wild asses have been reported in recent years from northern Chad and the Hoggar Massif in the central Sahara but it is almost certain that these are feral donkeys.

Their remaining range is southern Eritrea and Ethiopia from the Danakil Desert, along the Awash River and extending into the Ogaden, marginally into Djibouti and into northern Somalia, and eastwards as far as the Nogal Valley. The habitat of the African wild ass consists mainly of arid, broken hill country and barren plains.

Wild asses occur in no national parks. The recent warfare virtually throughout their limited range has certainly had a negative impact on the small, isolated populations. Most worrying is the widely scattered nature of the herds and the large number of feral donkeys which interbreed with the wild asses. Surveys undertaken in the mid-1970s indicate that there are many asses of mixed origins.

Wild asses are hunted for food and for medicinal purposes. Growing herds and flocks of domestic animals increase competition for scarce grazing and for access to the few water

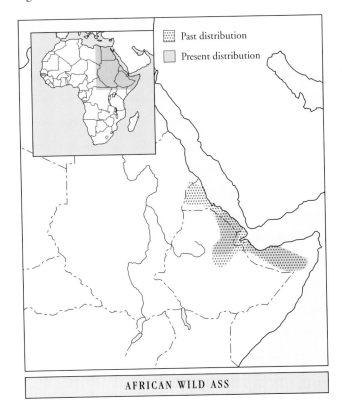

**Above:** *The Somali wild ass* (E.a. somaliensis). PHOTO: *Klaus Rudloff.*

points. Extended periods of drought have probably also impacted on the ass populations. It has been suggested that, on the contrary, the asses, with their adaptation to arid conditions, may in fact benefit from drought: as domestic stock animals succumb, they leave more space for the asses. However, this is just conjecture.

These members of the horse family, progenitors of one of the Third World's principal beasts of burden, are now teetering on the brink of extinction.

Past distribution

Present distribution

AFRICAN WILD ASS

# Grevy's zebra
## *Equus grevyi* Ⓔ

This is the largest of all the wild equids. These zebras move through vast home ranges of up to 10 000 sq km in semi-arid scrub and grassland. In the past they occupied desert where there was access to surface water. They are more resistant to drought than the plains zebra, which shares part of their range.

In the past they occurred virtually throughout Kenya east of the Rift Valley and Lake Turkana, and north of Mount Kenya, as well as in southern Somalia inland from the coastal plain, and through the Ogaden and Awash Valley in Ethiopia. Today Grevy's zebra is extinct in Somalia. It is restricted to three small areas in Ethiopia: north-east of Awash National Park, on the Sarite Plain and in the vicinity of Lake Chew Bahar near the Kenyan border. No recent counts have been undertaken in Ethiopia. In 1980 it was estimated that only about 1 500 survived there, but it is certain that the figure is now considerably lower. Probably the only viable populations survive in Kenya. Here they still occur over much of their former range but in greatly reduced numbers, except in a few conservation areas. It has been estimated that in some areas there has been a 90% decline since the 1960s. A 1977 survey arrived at a figure of 13 718 Grevy's zebras in Kenya, but by 1988 the figure was 4 276 animals – a drop of 70%. The largest protected population, some 1 500 animals, is centred on the Samburu-Buffalo Springs-Shaba national reserves, with smaller numbers in Marsabit, Sibiloi and Losai. They also occur on a few private ranches and open land.

**Below:** *The main population of Grevy's zebra* (Equus grevyi) *is restricted to the dry savanna in northern Kenya. The largest numbers occur in Samburu National Reserve.*

Until the mid-1970s Grevy's zebras were heavily hunted for their skins, which were popular, but there is now no longer a market for them. Like many game species, they face stiff competition from domestic stock for grazing and water. The settling of former nomads near water points previously relied on by the zebras has had a serious impact on them. Reduced river flow, due to irrigation, has decreased the availability of surface water in parts of their Kenyan range, including in the critical Buffalo Springs area. Another threat in the principal core area

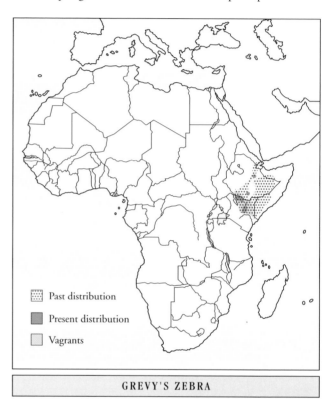

Past distribution

Present distribution

Vagrants

**GREVY'S ZEBRA**

**Above:** *The Cape mountain zebra* (Equus zebra zebra) *is now restricted to a few small reserves and private farms.*

of the three reserves is uncontrolled tourism, which results in disturbance and destruction of vegetation. These national reserves are controlled by the Samburu people and not by the more disciplined Kenya Wildlife Service – a serious obstacle to implementing optimal management practices. It has been predicted that if adequate conservation plans are not soon implemented, Grevy's zebra could become extinct in the wild within 50 years.

# Cape mountain zebra
## *Equus zebra zebra* **Ⓔ**

# Hartmann's mountain zebra
## *Equus zebra hartmannae* **Ⓥ**

During historical times mountain zebras occurred in a more or less contiguous belt from Moçamedes in south-western Angola, along the escarpment and adjacent areas of Namibia, southwards to Western Cape province (South Africa) and through the southern Karoo mountains to Eastern Cape province. Many place names in the Cape provinces carry references to the past presence of "wild horses", meaning mountain zebras. The two subspecies are recognised by most authorities; they differ in aspects of striping and minor size disparity.

By the early 1930s it became apparent that if steps were not taken the Cape mountain zebra would become extinct. In 1937 the state proclaimed the farm *Babylonstoren* in the Cradock district a national park. There were five stallions and a single young mare in the park at that time but by 1946 only two stallions survived. In 1950 a neighbouring farmer donated five stallions and six mares, and by 1964 the herd had grown to 25 individuals. In the same year additional farms were purchased and a further 30 animals fell under the protective umbrella. The Cape mountain zebra in 1992 numbered some 560 to 590 animals in 22 separate populations, of which nine contained fewer than 10 animals. One 1993 estimate put the total at 750. Inbreeding depression in the small popula-

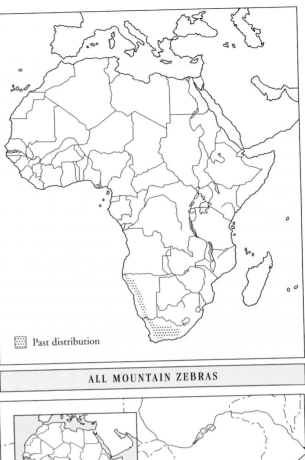

▦ Past distribution

**ALL MOUNTAIN ZEBRAS**

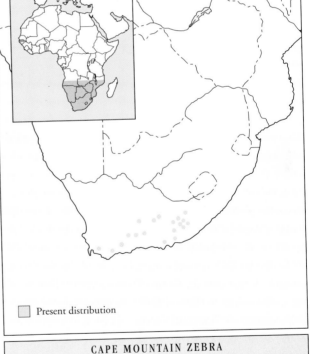

▦ Present distribution

**CAPE MOUNTAIN ZEBRA**

tions is a potential problem. The Cape mountain zebra occurs in four national parks, with the largest numbers in the Mountain Zebra National Park (about 200) and the Karoo National Park (about 80). The largest population outside a national park is in De Hoop Nature Reserve, which has over 30 individuals. More than 90% of Cape mountain zebras are now located in formally proclaimed conservation areas. These numbers are still critically low and outbreaks of disease could have extremely serious consequences.

The policy at present is to spread these zebras into suitable habitat throughout their former range. Although hunting brought the Cape mountain zebra to the brink of extinction, this no longer poses a problem. Apart from the risk of disease, a concern is that the populations are too small to maintain genetic diversity in the long term. The introduction of Hartmann's mountain zebras into traditional areas of the Cape subspecies posed a threat of hybridisation and loss of genetic diversity, but this problem is now largely under control.

Viable populations of Hartmann's mountain zebra within its natural range are now restricted to the Namibian escarpment and vicinity. There is a possibility of remnant herds in south-western Angola. In the early 1950s it was estimated that the Hartmann's population exceeded 50 000 zebras but by 1972 the number had dropped to an estimated 16 400, and by 1982 to 13 300. Today there are about 7 000, of which some 4 000 occur in conservation areas. The largest number, some 2 200, occur in the Namib-Naukluft Park, with about 1 500 in western Etosha National Park.

Various factors have played a role in this drastic decline in numbers, including legal as well as illegal hunting outside conservation areas, and the erection of fences across migration routes, which kill large numbers of animals in times of drought by limiting access to alternative sources of grazing and water. Farmers in the semi-arid Pro-Namib zone tend to be intolerant of zebras on their properties, but this situation is improving with the establishment of game ranches. The long-term future of these zebras will depend on continued protection in the few conservation areas in which they occur.

Present distribution

**HARTMANN'S MOUNTAIN ZEBRA**

## Plains zebra subspecies

Although the plains zebra is still by far the most abundant and widespread of all Africa's equids, several subspecies occur at low population levels and several are in decline. The most abundant by far is Grant's zebra (*E.b. boehmi*) of east Africa. However, its numbers in Ethiopia (2 000 animals) and Somalia (1 000) have decreased dramatically in recent years, in part because of incessant civil war and the ready availability of modern firearms. The upper Zambezi zebra (*E.b. zambeziensis*) of Congo (DR), Angola and western Zambia is in overall decline but numbers are not known. The only stable or increasing populations irrespective of subspecies are located in Kenya, Uganda, Tanzania, Zimbabwe and South Africa.

# HIPPOPOTAMIDAE

## *Hippopotamuses*

The only two surviving members of this family are restricted to Africa, although in prehistoric times and at about the time of human settlement in Madagascar (c. 1 500 years before present) at least three species of dwarf hippo were present on the island. Their extinction was probably brought about by hunting. Climatic changes could also have had a negative effect.

## Common hippopotamus
### *Hippopotamus amphibius*

### Description and taxonomy

This hippo is still widespread and considered to be relatively secure in some regions, but it has undergone dramatic reductions in range and numbers in some areas. It is unlikely that any subspecies are valid.

### Distribution and habitat

Present population estimates stand at about 157 000 animals. At first glance this figure looks healthy, but the hippo has suffered major declines in west Africa and has disappeared from the lower Nile River and from all of South Africa except the far eastern areas.

In general, populations in east, central and southern Africa are secure, with substantial numbers in conservation areas. The country with possibly the most hippos is Zambia with an estimated 40 000, of which about half occur in the Luangwa River in the east of the country. The hippo is believed to be extinct in Liberia and Mauritania; it is declining in 18 countries; its status is unknown in eight countries and it is increasing in only two, Congo and Zambia. Declines in Congo (DR) and Uganda are of particular concern as these countries hold some of Africa's

|  | COMMON HIPPO | PYGMY HIPPO |
|---|---|---|
| **Total length** | 2,8-4,2 m | 1,7-1,9 m |
| **Tail length** | 35-50 cm | 15-20 cm |
| **Shoulder height** | 1,5 m | 70-90 cm |
| **Mass** | 1,3-2,0 t or more | 200-275 kg |
| **Social structure** | schools of 10-15 | solitary |
| **Gestation** | 225-257 days | 180-210 days |
| **Birth mass** | 25-55 kg | 5-7 kg |
| **Diet** | selected graze | mixed plant food |
| **Number surviving** | 157 000 | probably below 5 000 |

largest concentrations of hippo. In Uganda the decline had been due to civil unrest, and now that relative peace has returned the hippo population will probably stabilise.

## Conservation

The most serious threat facing hippo populations is undoubtedly destruction of habitat, including grazing grounds and riverine vegetation. This is primarily the result of increasing livestock numbers and conflicts with agricultural interests, both commercial and subsistence. Although illegal hunting

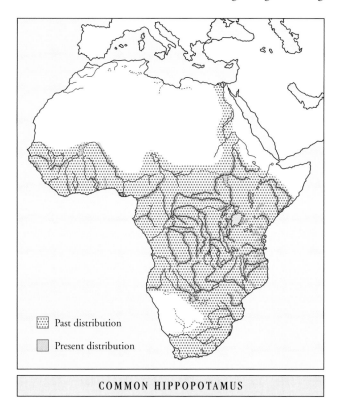

  ☷ Past distribution

  ☐ Present distribution

**COMMON HIPPOPOTAMUS**

takes place for meat, skins and ivory, this seems to be more of a localised than a general threat. However, the species is highly vulnerable to hunting pressure and a population can be wiped out in a short time if there is an increase in demand for meat or ivory, or if animals are perceived as a threat to either people or their activities. Fears had been expressed that the ban on trading in elephant ivory may cause a steep increase in the trading of hippo ivory, but fortunately this does not seem to have happened.

As the elephant is the super keystone species of the savannas and woodlands of Africa, so the common hippo is the super keystone species of freshwater habitats. They improve water flow by keeping channels open; they fertilise the water with their dung and thus stimulate vegetation growth; on their terrestrial grazing grounds they improve conditions for a spectrum of other herbivores.

# Pygmy hippopotamus
## *Hexaprotodon liberiensis* ⓥ

### Description and taxonomy

Two subspecies are recognised: *H.l. liberiensis* from forest patches in Sierra Leone, Liberia and Ivory Coast, and *H.l. heslopi* from the forests of the Niger Delta in Nigeria. Until 1994 this subspecies was generally considered to be extinct but a recent survey indicates it may still be present. Numbers are unknown but can be expected to be very low.

### Distribution and habitat

The bulk of the population is restricted to suitable forest pockets in Liberia, with small outlying pockets in adjacent areas of Guinea, Sierra Leone and Ivory Coast. A specimen shot in Guinea Bissau is generally believed to have been a young common hippo and no other evidence exists from that country. Populations are becoming increasingly fragmented and isolated from each other.

**Below:** *The pygmy hippopotamus* (Hexaprotodon liberiensis) *is restricted to isolated stands of dense forest in western Africa.*

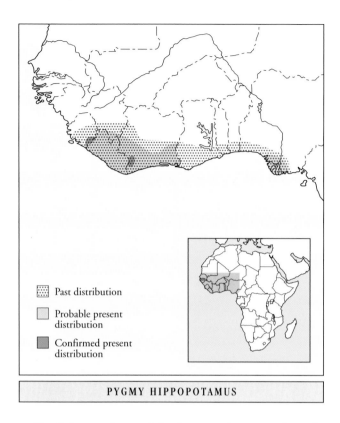

Past distribution

Probable present distribution

Confirmed present distribution

**PYGMY HIPPOPOTAMUS**

The Dahomey Gap is a belt of savanna that runs right to the coast of the Gulf of Guinea, separating the Guinean from the Congolean forest blocks. On the eastern side of the Gap, in the Niger River delta, is believed to be a population of pygmy hippos of the subspecies *heslopi*. This subspecies was described from one shot specimen and two additional skulls, but no further evidence has come to light since 1945. However, an as yet unconfirmed rediscovery, in 1994, of the pygmy hippo in the delta holds out hope for its survival. The delta is an inhospitable environment, unpleasant to survey. Given its vast size (some 500 000 ha of mangrove swamp) it is highly feasible that this and other long dismissed species still occur here.

### Behaviour

Unlike its bulky cousin of the waterways and lakes, the pygmy hippo spends much less time in water, although still being dependent on it. This hippo is restricted to forested areas and does not move onto open grassed areas to feed.

### Conservation

Establishing population sizes for a secretive, nocturnal animal such as the pygmy hippo is difficult at best. In Liberia there may be several thousand but numbers are reported to be declining due to habitat loss and hunting pressure. In Sierra Leone, where these animals are believed to be restricted to only two localities, numbers may be in the low hundreds. The small Guinean population is believed to be stable but information is limited.

Pygmy hippos are present in several conservation areas but

protection is poor to non-existent. Habitat loss and hunting are the main threats throughout much of their range. Being restricted to the forests of west Africa, which are a conservation nightmare, the pygmy hippo is classified as vulnerable.

# PHOCIDAE

*True seals*

## Mediterranean monk seal
*Monachus monachus* Ⓔ

This is one of the world's most seriously endangered seals, with perhaps fewer than 500 but certainly no more than 1 000 animals surviving. Only one other seal, the Cape fur seal (*Arctocephalus pusillus*), occurs as a permanent resident on the South African and Namibian coast, but this species is abundant and under no threat.

| MEDITERRANEAN MONK SEAL | |
|---|---|
| Total length | 2,4 m |
| Mass | 300 kg |
| Birth mass | 16-18 kg |

The Mediterranean monk seal once occurred throughout the Mediterranean Sea, along the north-west African Atlantic Ocean coastline and in the Black Sea. Today it is extinct in the latter. Perhaps 10 to 30 animals live off Algeria, about 10 off Desertas Islands (Madeira), perhaps 20 off Libya (although it may in fact be extinct here), and between 10 and 20 on the Moroccan Mediterranean coast. The largest African population lives at Cap Blanc in extreme northern Mauritania: about 130 individuals. The colonies at Cap Blanc and on the Desertas Islands are protected. It is certain that there is some movement of seals along the Atlantic coastline and that they enter Western Saharan and possibly Moroccan waters.

General threats to these seals' survival include shooting as perceived competitors for declining fish populations, entanglement in fishing nets, disturbance at beaching sites and pollution. Most of the small colonies will probably not survive unless they receive total protection. As is the case with many endangered species, virtually nothing is known about their biology or behaviour. In 1997 perhaps as many as 300 died.

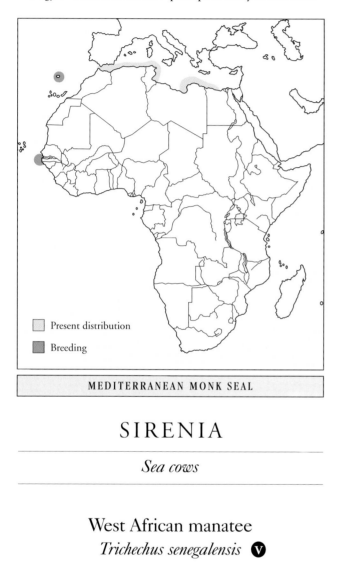

Present distribution

Breeding

MEDITERRANEAN MONK SEAL

# SIRENIA

## Sea cows

## West African manatee
### Trichechus senegalensis Ⓥ

## Dugong
### Dugong dugong Ⓥ

The manatee of west Africa is closely related to species occurring on the eastern seaboard and in rivers of the Americas. This manatee is only found around the coast and in a number of rivers in west Africa, from Senegal to Angola. The dugong occurs along the Indian Ocean and Red Sea coastlines, extensively through the Indian Ocean and in the western Pacific.

Both species are entirely aquatic. They feed on aquatic, shallow-water plants, including sea grasses. The manatee is found in sheltered inshore areas but also penetrates and lives in the

**Above:** *Dugong* (Dugong dugong). PHOTO: *P.K. Anderson.*
**Left:** *Fewer than 600 Mediterranean monk seals* (Monachus monachus) *survive; the most important populations are in Greece and at Cap Blanc in west Africa.* PHOTO: *U. Trotignon, Bruce Coleman Ltd.*

|  | MANATEE | DUGONG |
|---|---|---|
| **Total length** | up to 4,5 m | 2,5-3 m |
| **Mass** | about 360 kg | 360-1 000 kg |

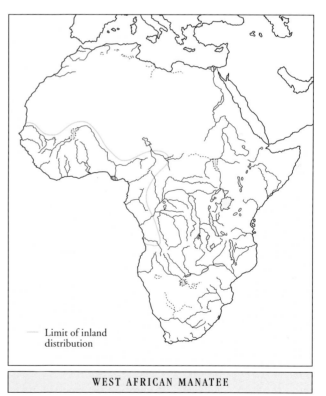

— Limit of inland distribution

WEST AFRICAN MANATEE

major river systems. Hardly anything else is known about this harmless animal. The dugong favours shallow, protected bays and lagoons. It travels close in-shore between these. In the past temporary groupings of up to 500 animals were common but today groups of six to 30 are more usual.

The principal threats facing both species include hunting for meat, siltation of their grazing grounds, which destroys their food supply, and entanglement in nylon fishing nets, which causes them to drown.

Very little is known about the present status of the manatee or dugong, although it is generally accepted that both are in decline and have disappeared from parts of their former ranges. No estimates are available of population sizes.

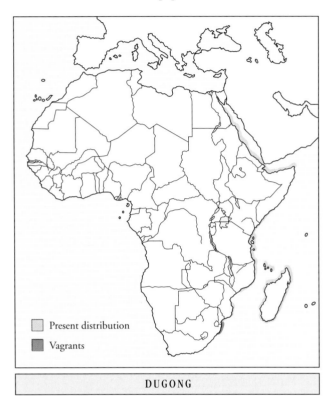

Present distribution
Vagrants

DUGONG

# LAGOMORPHA

*Hares and rabbits*

## Riverine rabbit
### *Bunolagus monticularis* **E**

This rabbit is similar in appearance to the red rock rabbits (*Pronolagus* spp.) but the ears are longer and the hind legs more developed. The fur of the upperparts is grizzled grey and the patch at the base of the ears is deep red-brown. The face is distinctively marked with dark brown and white.

This is one of Africa's most endangered mammal species, occurring only in a limited area of the Karoo plains, in South Africa, where it is restricted to a few patches of riverine scrub.

This attractive rabbit was discovered near the small settlement of Deelfontein in what was then central Cape Province in 1901 by Trooper Grant who was stationed there with the British garrison during the Anglo-Boer War. He sent a specimen to the British Museum in London where it was given the

| RIVERINE RABBIT | |
|---|---|
| Total length | 52 cm |
| Tail length | 9 cm |
| Mass | 1,4-1,9 kg |
| Home range | 12-20 ha |
| Social structure | solitary |
| Gestation | 35-36 days |
| Number of young | 1-2 |
| Birth mass | 40 g |
| Diet | mainly browse |

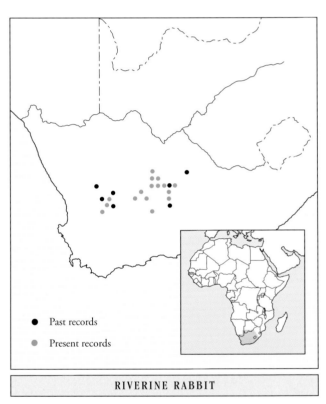

● Past records
● Present records

RIVERINE RABBIT

name *Lepus monticularis* in 1903. The choice of specific name served to mislead future would-be collectors, as this rabbit occupies not mountains but riverine scrub on the fringes of seasonally dry water courses. Only two more specimens were obtained between the original discovery and 1929, but this was enough for taxonomists to realise that the animal was significantly different from all other known hare species. The generic name was therefore changed to *Bunolagus*, which is unique to this animal. One of South Africa's most prolific and diligent zoological collectors, Captain Shortridge, now took up the trail and offered the then princely sum of one pound sterling for the capture of a specimen. To the Karoo farmers and their labourers this rabbit thus became known as the "pondhaas" (pound hare). Even in the late 1970s some of the older resi-

Above: *Riverine rabbit* (Bunolagus monticularis). PHOTO: *Andrew Duthie.*
Below right: *The golden moles (family* Chrysochloridae) *occur only in sub-Saharan Africa. Many have very restricted or vulnerable distribution patterns. Like shrews, they are extremely difficult to trap and their rarity may in many cases be a reflection of this.*

dents still referred to it by this name. It took Shortridge until 1947 – some 20 years – before people living in the Calvinia district, in the west of the species range, informed him that he was searching in the wrong habitat. Armed with this information he caught four specimens in 1947 and more in different locations the following year. But it was only in 1978 that a study of the riverine rabbit's ecology was instituted.

This rabbit is restricted to riverine scrub of 50 cm to 1 m in height. Much of this habitat has been destroyed by clearing for agricultural purposes. Clearing has been most extensive along two river courses, the Fish and Renoster rivers, which had apparently supported the greatest number of these rabbits in the past. The riverine rabbit is known to occur on only 20 farms, all at low densities. Three farms under the same ownership, communally known as *Klipgatsfontein,* have been proclaimed a Natural Heritage Site with the support of the farmer, in order to afford better protection to this rare mammal. A captive breeding programme has been underway for several years but to date no releases have been made.

An estimate of the population size, taking into account available suitable habitat, is a maximum of 1 435 rabbits. The actual figure is probably well below 1 000 animals.

# INSECTIVORA

## *Insectivores*

This is a vast order, with several families and many species, most of which are difficult to catch or study and have therefore not received a great deal of attention from scientists, except on a very localised scale.

In many cases seeming rarity may in fact just be a measure of adverse working conditions for the collector, difficulty in trapping animals and low population densities. We can attest

to the frustrations of trying to survey such difficult-to-catch beasties as golden moles and some of the shrews. There are of course some species that we know to be rare because of limited suitable habitat, but these are the exception.

There are also many small rodent (Order Rodentia) species that are known from one or several specimens, but of whose biology, behaviour and requirements we know absolutely nothing. Many, if not most, are probably more abundant than is generally thought. Several are almost certainly not separate species but if more specimens become available will be shown to belong to other more abundant and widespread species. Conversely, recent developments in genetic fingerprinting are showing that species hitherto regarded as single are in fact complexes of species. This is all quite confusing, particularly on a continent where we know little about most of our rodent and insectivore species, not to mention the bat fauna.

We have selected a few animals to discuss as examples but we acknowledge that our choice is far from complete.

## Golden moles
### *Chrysochloridae*

There are seven genera and 18 species of golden mole, all restricted to sub-Saharan Africa. Of these, 15 species occur only in southern Africa. They are notoriously difficult to trap and in many cases only detailed examination can determine their identification.

Some species are certainly vulnerable, such as the giant golden mole *(Chrysospalax trevelyani)*, which is restricted to a few forest pockets in a limited area of Eastern Cape province,

| GOLDEN MOLES | |
| --- | --- |
| Total length | 7-23 cm |
| Mass | 16-538 g |
| Number of young | 1-2 |
| Diet | invertebrates |

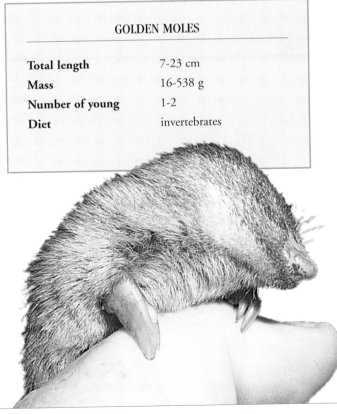

South Africa. Visagie's golden mole *(Chrysochloris visagiei)* is only known from a single specimen but is probably not valid as a separate species. The Somali golden mole *(Chlorotalpa tytonis)* is known from a single locality in the south of Somalia. As this is far from any other golden mole distribution, this mole is probably a distinct species. It is almost certainly far more widespread, given the nature of its environment. Some species that have been classified as rare, such as Grant's (or the Namib) golden mole *(Eremitalpa granti)*, are in fact quite common within their chosen habitat.

It seems likely that in most cases golden mole species, even where localised, are probably safe if not abundant, as long as no major changes are made to their habitat. For example, in the wheatlands of South Africa golden moles (two species) continue to be active despite ploughing, tilling and harvesting of the fields. Of some concern are activities such as open-cast mining, but this is limited in Africa at this stage. Habitat degradation, which includes forest clearance and erosion, is the major threat to golden moles.

# Shrews (all categories)
## *Soricidae*

To date, some 138 species of shrew, in seven genera, have been recognised as occurring in Africa, but it is almost certain that additional species will be collected and described. By far the majority, over 104, belong to the genus *Crocidura*, and of these 102 are African endemics. In most cases no one really knows the true conservation status of these shrews, mainly because of scanty research. Some species are believed to be restricted to very limited areas. Examples are *Crocidura baileyi*, which is endemic to the Simien National Park in the Ethiopian Highlands. *C. eisentrauti* occurs on Mount Cameroon between

| SHREWS | |
|---|---|
| **Total length** | 46-140 mm |
| **Tail length** | 24-87 mm |
| **Mass** | 3-113 g |
| **Number of young** | 2-8 |
| **Breeding** | several times a year |
| **Diet** | invertebrates |

2 000 m and 3 000 m. *C. longipes* is only known from two swamps in western Nigeria. *C. ludia* has been recorded only in Medje in Congo (DR). *C. monax* is believed to be restricted to Mount Kilimanjaro and the Uluguru Mountains in northern Tanzania. *C. nimbae* lives on threatened Mount Nimba on the border between Guinea, Liberia and Ivory Coast. *C. thomensis* is only known to occur on the island Bioko in the Gulf of Guinea.

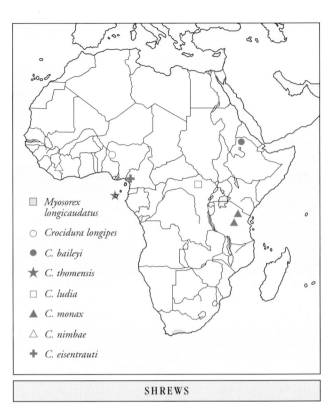

□ *Myosorex longicaudatus*

○ *Crocidura longipes*

● *C. baileyi*

★ *C. thomensis*

□ *C. ludia*

▲ *C. monax*

△ *C. nimbae*

✚ *C. eisentrauti*

SHREWS

**Above:** *Swamp musk shrew* (Crocidura mariquensis). *This small insectivore is known from very few specimens.*

The point is that the shrews, many of which have a mass of no more than a few grams, are under-collected and the limited distribution we know of are probably misleading. Many localities simply indicate where collectors have been active, whereas blank spaces on the distribution maps indicate the lack of collections and surveys rather than the absence of a particular species. For example, South Africa is one of the countries in Africa whose mammals have been best surveyed but in 1978 a new, distinct species of shrew *(Myosorex longicaudatus)* was collected in a forest that lies within one of the country's most popular tourist destinations. If new species are discovered in such locations, what can we expect still to emerge from the tropical lowland forests?

# Otter shrews
## *Potamogalidae*

Three species of otter shrew, in two genera, occur on the African continent. The giant otter shrew *(Potamogale velox)* has a wide distribution and is not known to be threatened. The Ruwenzori otter shrew *(Micropotamogale ruwenzori)* has a limited distribution in the Kivu and Ruwenzori regions of eastern Congo (DR) and western Uganda. It is known from only a few specimens. It seems to have a fairly wide altitudinal as well as vegetation tolerance, so it is probably fairly secure. Growing human populations in the area could, however, have a negative impact in the long term. The Nimba otter shrew *(M. lamottei)*, first described in 1954, is endangered. It is restricted to an area of some 1 500 sq km on Mount Nimba on the border between Ivory Coast, Liberia and Guinea. In the Liberian sector of its range mining has devastated its habitat; bauxite deposits in adjoining areas of Guinea could be exploited in the future.

|  | RUWENZORI OTTER SHREW | GIANT OTTER SHREW |
|---|---|---|
| **Total length** | 22-35 cm | 53-64 cm |
| **Tail length** | 10-15 cm | 24,5-29 cm |
| **Mass** | 135 g | 359 g-1 kg |
| **Diet** | worms, insect larvae, crabs, fish, frogs | crabs, fish, molluscs |

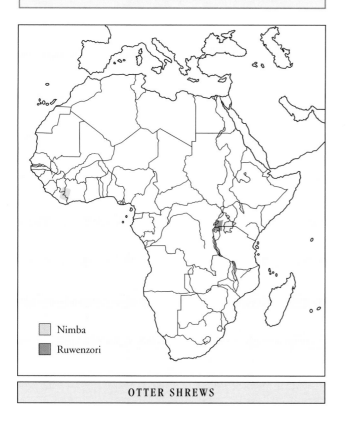

Nimba
Ruwenzori

**OTTER SHREWS**

# Elephant shrews
## *Macroscelididae*

Like the golden moles, elephant shrews are an entirely African group of small mammals, with 15 species recognised. Only the **golden-rumped elephant shrew** *(Rhynchocyon chrysopygus)* is classified as vulnerable. It is restricted to a few forest patches in coastal Kenya, of which the most important is the Arabuko-Sokoke Forest. The major threat to this elephant shrew is habitat destruction. A lesser problem is that the local people trap and eat this species.

| GOLDEN-RUMPED ELEPHANT SHREW | |
|---|---|
| **Total length** | 42-58 cm |
| **Tail length** | 19-26 cm |
| **Mass** | average 540 g |
| **Home range** | 1,7 ha |
| **Gestation** | 42 days |
| **Number of young** | 1 |
| **Breeding** | several times per year |
| **Life span (wild)** | 4-5 years |
| **Diet** | invertebrates |
| **Number surviving** | probably about 20 000 |

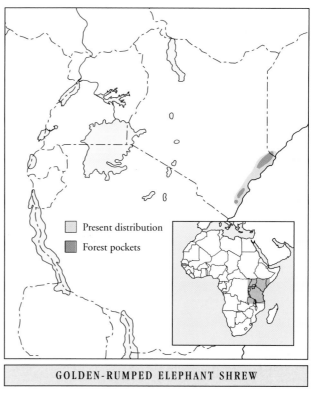

Present distribution
Forest pockets

**GOLDEN-RUMPED ELEPHANT SHREW**

The **chequered elephant shrew** (*R. cirnei*), of which there are at least six subspecies, is not threatened as a species, but two of the subspecies could be. These are *R.c. cirnei*, which is known from a single specimen collected at Quelimane to the north of the Zambezi River in Mozambique, and *R.c. hendersoni*, of which only three specimens have been collected from a small forest on the western shore of Lake Malawi. The other races are also poorly known. Isolated populations could be vulnerable in areas where habitat destruction takes place.

The **black-and-rufous elephant shrew** (*R. petersi*) has a mass of over 400 g. Its two recognised races are classified as rare on the basis of their limited distribution. *R.p. petersi* is restricted to coastal forest pockets from Mombasa in Kenya southwards into Tanzania, and to a few isolated patches in the interior of both countries. Their isolation makes them particularly vulnerable to habitat loss. *R.p. adersi* only occurs on the islands of Zanzibar (Unguja) and Mafia, off the coast of Tanzania.

**Above:** *The golden-rumped elephant shrew* (Rhynchocyon chrysopygus) *is restricted to a few forest pockets along the coast of Kenya. It may possibly occur in similar habitat in Tanzania.*
Photo: *Klaus Rudloff.* **Below:** *Lesser dwarf shrew* (Suncus varilla). *Although many shrew species are known from few specimens, this may not always be an indication of rarity but simply of the fact that they are difficult to trap.*

# Bats
## *Chiroptera*

The bat fauna of Africa is vast and diverse: 10 families, 46 genera and at least 218 species are represented, many of which are endemic to the continent. Our gaps in knowledge of even the commonest bat species are huge. Only a handful of bats have been studied in any depth, mainly in South Africa. Distribution maps usually merely give an indication of where biologists have been active, not necessarily a reflection of actual occurrence.

Bats have successfully occupied most niches available to them. Virtually no area of Africa is without its cohorts of these flying mammals. Some bats are presumed to range throughout the continent, whereas others appear to be restricted to a particular forest or mountain range.

Bats are divided into two major groupings, the fruit-eating bats (Megachiroptera) and the insect-eating bats (Microchiroptera). Both groups play a critical role in the well-being of the environment. The fruit bats, which are larger than most of the insectivorous bats, act as pollinators and seed dispersal agents for hundreds of plants, mainly trees, many of which are commercially important to humans. The relationship between plants and bats are of long standing, perhaps more than 35 million years.

Most fruit bats are tree-roosters and are therefore easier to observe and collect than most insectivorous bats, which hide away during the daylight hours in caves, mine shafts, hollow trees and under bark. A determined effort has to be made to find them. At night they can be caught in fine nets, but surveying has been undertaken in only a limited number of areas in Africa. Many of the insect-eating bat species are known from small numbers of specimens. These bats are of great eco-

forests is high. But is this bat really restricted to the forests, or does it occur further afield?

Although not present on the African continent, there are a number of very large bats of the genus *Pteropus* living on Indian Ocean islands that fall within the Afro-tropical Realm. Most are classified as endangered. These include the Comoros black fruit bat *(P. livingstonii)*, the Rodriguez fruit bat *(P. rodricensis)* and the Pemba fruit bat *(P. voeltzkowi)*, which is the only member of this genus occurring close to the African mainland.

Although declines in fruit bat populations have not been as dramatic in Africa as in other parts of the world, these bats are affected by habitat destruction and conflict with commercial fruit growers. They are also hunted as a source of food.

**Above:** *Seychelles flying foxes at roost.* PHOTO: *Roland Seitre.*

HAYMAN'S EPAULETTED FRUIT BAT

logical importance as harmless aerial pest-control specialists: they consume tons of insects, many of which are potentially harmful to humans.

A few examples will illustrate the difficulties in determining the true conservation status of many bat species. **Hayman's epauletted fruit bat** *(Micropteropus intermedius)*, classified as rare, is only known from four specimens collected in a narrow belt close to the Congolese-Angolan border. However, given the forested nature of the area, the great expanses of seemingly suitable habitat to the north and the lack of collecting it may be more widespread and abundant than it seems at present. On the other hand, perhaps it is so specific in its requirements that it is under threat! We simply do not know.

The **East African collared fruit bat** *(Myonycteris relicta)* is considered to be vulnerable, as it is seemingly restricted to a few forest pockets in south-east Kenya and Tanzania, as far south as the Uzungwa Mountains. Pressure on most of these

EAST AFRICAN COLLARED FRUIT BAT

CHAPTER 8

# BIRDS

## — *As dead as a dodo* —

The Dodo never had a chance. He seems to
have been invented for the sole purpose of becoming
extinct and that was all he was good for.

Will Cuffy – *How to become extinct*

It has been estimated that about one fifth of the birds that
inhabited Planet Earth 2 000 years ago are now extinct.
Some 900 bird species are known only from the worldwide
fossil record, and we do not know why they did not survive to
the present day. The largest number became extinct only in the
last 300 years. Most of these extinctions have taken place on
islands where species had not evolved a means of defence, or
escape, from alien predators.

Today there are an estimated 9 702 bird species worldwide;
some authorities hold that there are a couple of hundred fewer.

Approximately 11% of surviving bird species have been classified as endangered by Birdlife International, a monitoring
body based in England.

There are some 1 400 species in sub-Saharan Africa. Together with island populations and birds in northern Africa,
which falls within the Palaearctic Realm, there are over 2 400
bird species in Africa.

The first birds began to evolve from reptilian stock at least
150 million years ago during the Mesozoic era. The first
known true bird, with feathers, was the celebrated *Archae-*

*opteryx* from Bavaria in Germany. It appeared in the fossil record some 130 million years ago. Bird fossils are rare but become more common from the Eocene era, some 60 million years before present. The largest numbers of bird fossils were preserved in deposits laid down during the Pliocene and Pleistocene eras, starting about 10 million years ago.

Birds have evolved to fill virtually every niche on earth, from the open oceans to the highest mountains, from deserts to rainforests – many species even share our urban sprawl. They feed on everything from fruits to seeds, insects to arachnids, small rodents to monkeys, birds to reptiles, fish to squids. Many species feed in trees, bushes or on the ground, some species dive into the oceans and lakes for their food, others catch it on the wing. This large group of vertebrates is as diverse as it is successful.

When dealing with the birds of Africa, we have to divide them into two distinct groups, those that occur on islands and those that occur on the mainland. It is without doubt the former that have suffered most at the hands of humans and their unwitting agents.

# ISLAND BIRDS

The islands within the Afro-tropical Realm have the dubious distinction of having lost a disproportionate number of bird and other species to extinction. What is worse, this trend is continuing: several taxa are barely hanging on to survival.

Let us first chronicle some celebrated extinctions.

There can be very few people in the English-speaking world who have not heard the expression, "as dead as a dodo". The **dodo** *(Raphus cucullatus)* has become the flagship of bird extinction. This large, ungainly, ground-dwelling bird was in fact a flightless pigeon that occurred only on the western Indian Ocean island of Mauritius. The rapid slide of this large bird (estimated mass: 22 kg) into extinction probably ended in 1681. Some old accounts indicate that it may have survived until 1693 but records are sketchy. Its demise was the direct result of human interference. European sailors killed large numbers of these giant ground-dwelling pigeons, salting them to be eaten at sea. Records indicate that the flesh was tough and not particularly tasty, but with little other meat available, the dodo was not spared the cooking pots of the sailing ships. Pigs and goats, introduced to the island in 1602, competed with the dodo for food, and the pigs preyed directly on its large eggs and on the chicks. By 1644 the Dutch began to settle on Mauritius. They cleared much of the forest, the habitat of the dodo, and planted crops. The dodo was unable to withstand this multi-faceted onslaught, and its fate was sealed.

The extinction of the **solitaire** *(Pezophaps solitaria)* is less well known. This bird occurred only on Rodriguez and Réunion. It was about the size of the dodo but taller and somewhat more slender. Related to the dodo, it clung to life a little longer than its cousin. The birds living on Réunion were probably a different species, *Raphus solitarius*, but little material evidence is available. The solitaire survived into the early years of the 18th century although it suffered the same assaults as its relative on Mauritius.

The little we know about the solitaire was documented by François Leguat, a French Huguenot leader who had fled religious persecution in his home country. The solitaire walked in an elegant fashion and with sleek plumage, in contrast to the apparently clumsy and unkempt dodo. Unlike the dodo, it made excellent eating, particularly from March to September, when it was at its fattest. The solitaire was not as easy a hunting target as the dodo: it was very agile and speedy in its forest home. These strange birds were territorial. Both male and female defended their nesting area with dramatic displays and on occasion physical combat. Males attacked intruding males and combative females took on members of their own sex. They built a large nest, about 50 cm high, of palm leaves.

The solitaires of Réunion were first described as "huge turkey-like" birds by a British naval officer in 1613. A member of a French colony, established on the island in 1669, described two different species of solitaire. As no bones have ever been discovered of these extinct birds, some doubt has been cast on the validity of the separate species, but the birds' existence cannot be discounted.

The largest birds that ever existed in the Afro-tropical Realm, the **elephant birds** (Aepyornithidae) of Madagascar, also became extinct in historical times. Some species are believed to have topped 450 kg; consider that the largest bird living today, the ostrich, averages 60 kg to 80 kg. The largest of all was *Aepyornis maximus*, an appropriate name for a bird that produced an egg six times larger than an ostrich egg, the latter being equivalent to 24 domestic fowl eggs. Such eggs must have provided quite a feast for the Madagascans.

**Top left:** *Breeding colonies of the Damara tern* (Sterna balaenarum) *are highly vulnerable to disturbance by humans and vehicles.* PHOTO: *J.J. Brooks, Aquila.*

**Above:** *The Mauritius kestrel* (Falco punctatus) *has been the subject of an intensive captive breeding programme in a effort to prevent its slide into extinction.* PHOTO: *Olivier Langrand, Bruce Coleman Ltd.*

The first written account of these giant, flightless ratites was included in a book on Madagascar by Sieur Etienne de Flacourt, published in 1658:

*The vouron patra is a giant bird that lives in the country of the Ampatres people* [in the south of Madagascar] *and lays eggs like the ostrich; it is a species of ostrich; so that the people of these places may not catch it, it seeks the loneliest places.*

It is certain, however, that these birds had been extinct for many years by the time he wrote this account. He would have been relying on oral history passed from generation to generation by local inhabitants.

Victor Sganzin, on a visit to Madagascar in 1832, saw one of the eggs of the *vouron patra* being used by villagers as a water container. In 1850 three complete eggs and some bone fragments were taken to France. Since then vast quantities of eggshell fragments and bones of these truly huge birds have come to light.

The different species are believed to have died out between 500 and 700 years ago, as a result of two factors: climatic changes in Madagascar that were apparently unfavourable to these birds, and the human settlement of the island, which probably started about 1 500 years before present. The elephant birds would have been hunted by humans as a source of meat and for their body parts, as the Maoris hunted the 22 species of the closely related moas which once roamed New Zealand.

It is generally believed that the legendary "roc", which according to Sinbad the Sailor in *Arabian Nights* caught elephants and flew with them to feed its young at the nest, derives from the Madagascan elephant birds – considerable literary licence as these birds could not fly! There is no verified record that any non-Madagascan ever sighted an elephant bird.

Many smaller and generally less spectacular bird species have also disappeared from the islands off Africa. They include the **snail-eating coua** *(Coua delalandei)* of Madagascar, a large, ground-living cuckoo. This bird has not been recorded since 1834. It has been suggested that small populations may survive in remote and undisturbed forest patches in the extreme northeast of the island, but this seems highly improbable. The **Canarian black oystercatcher** *(Haematopus meadewaldai)*, which occurred in the Canary Islands off north-western Africa,

**Below:** *This small owl, the Seychelles scops* (Otus insularis) *was pronounced extinct in 1958 but was rediscovered in 1960. It is restricted to the island of Mahé, where it is believed that more than 80 pairs survive.* Photo: *Eric & David Hosking, FPLA.*

is also extinct. The **Mascarene black petrel** *(Pterodroma aterrima)*, last recorded in 1973, occurred on the western Indian Ocean islands of Réunion and Rodriguez, but may now be extinct.

The Mascarene Islands can lay claim to the depressing record of having the highest bird extinction rate in the world, with 25 species having teetered over the brink. They include four parrots, two owls, the Mauritian flightless rail, two starlings and three weak-flying herons.

Of all African and oceanic island bird species threatened at present, 44% are restricted to the islands off Africa; they include 28 species on Madagascar, 11 on the Mascarenes, nine on the Seychelles and Aldabra, and seven on São Tomé.

To illustrate how serious the plight of some of these island featherfolk is, we have selected a few examples.

The **Mauritius parakeet** *(Psittacula eques)* declined from an estimated 50 pairs in 1970 (although it must be said that this was later felt to have been an overestimate) to between 50 and 60 individuals by 1974. By the mid-1980s no more than 11 parakeets survived, but by 1996 it was estimated there were about 50 of these parrots. Destruction of favoured habitat has been the single most important factor causing the Mauritius parakeet's decline. The insensitive actions of the World Bank made a major contribution to its demise: the bank paid for the clearing of 50% of its principal forest home. Competition for tree holes for nesting, particularly with the exotic Indian mynahs *(Acridotheres tristis)*, and competition for food with abundant ring-necked parakeets *(Psittacula krameri)* and crab-eating macaques *(Macaca fascicularis)*, have also had a detrimental impact. Although its remaining habitat has been protected in the Macabe-Bel Ombre Nature Reserve, its chances of long-term survival are slim indeed.

Another endangered Mauritian bird is the **pink pigeon** *(Nesoenas mayeri)*, but unlike the parrot it has been established in several captive colonies. In 1984 the highest count of wild birds was 18, and breeding activity was restricted to one tiny grove of trees. However, the prospects for reintroducing captive-bred pigeons to the wild, if adequate protection is exercised over the habitat and the birds, are good.

The **Mauritius kestrel** *(Falco punctatus)* has been reduced to a few pairs in the wild but captive breeding has proved to be successful. It is unlikely to become extinct in the near future.

We now take a brief glimpse at a few Madagascan birds that are seriously endangered or may already be extinct. The majority of endangered species on this vast island (594 180 sq km) are forest-related, a habitat that is disappearing at an accelerating rate: about 35 000 ha per year at present.

The **Madagascar serpent eagle** *(Eutriorchis astur)* was seen, once, by an ornithologist some 50 years ago. It was believed by some to survive in eastern and north-eastern forests; this was borne out in 1989 when a single eagle was observed by a group of scientists. If indeed a viable population does survive, its numbers would be extremely small.

Another raptor, the **Madagascar fish eagle** *(Haliaeetus vociferoides)*, is considered to be highly endangered. Fewer than 30 breeding pairs occupy suitable habitat on the island.

Among waterbirds, the **Madagascar pochard** *(Aythya innotata)* is almost certainly on the brink of extinction. The threat facing the endangered **Alaotra grebe** *(Tachybaptus rufolavatus)* within its very limited distributional range on Lake Alaotra and its associated marshes, is hybridisation with the abundant and widespread little grebe *(Tachybaptus ruficollis)*.

The **Madagascar red owl** *(Tyto soumagnei)* is only known from the humid forest remnants in the east-central area of the island and there has only been one positive record since 1934.

The **slender-billed flufftail** *(Sarothrura watersi)* is known from four widely scattered localities, and the last positive record dates from 60 years ago. However, all of the flufftails, including those on the African mainland, are extremely difficult to locate and observe and they are easily overlooked.

The **Sakalava rail** *(Amaurornis olivieri)* belongs to another group notoriously difficult to observe, but given its very restricted distribution in a part of western Madagascar it must be considered to be endangered.

On other islands the tale of woe continues. The **Madeira laurel pigeon** *(Columba trocaz)* has a total population of about 500 birds. The **freira** *(Pterodroma madeira)*, a small petrel that breeds at only a few localities on the mountain slopes of Madeira, numbers no more than 50 pairs. Another petrel, the **gon-gon** *(Pterodroma feae)*, breeds on the Cape Verde Islands of São Nicolau, Fogo, Santo Antão and São Tiago, as well as Bugio, which lies off Madeira, but only a few hundred survive. Island-breeding petrels are threatened by habitat destruction, introduced predators such as domestic cats and non-native rats, and direct hunting by humans for food.

Several species of scops owl endemic to islands are also endangered. These tiny owls are elusive and difficult to observe, and like most owls are best located by their calls. The **Grand Comoro scops owl** *(Otus pauliani)* is known from only one specimen and two observations in the forests high on the slopes of Mount Karthala. The call of this scops owl was recorded in 1958, 1981 and a number of times since, but its restricted range and obviously low numbers leave it highly vulnerable to any habitat disturbance. Still in the western Indian Ocean, the **Seychelles scops owl** *(Otus insularis)* was discovered in 1880 but never recorded again until about 1960. There are estimated to be at least 80 pairs, and much of their favoured habitat is being protected in the Morne Seychellois National Park. That this may in fact be a subspecies of the Moluccan scops owl *(Otus magicus)* does not lessen the importance of protecting this dwarf owl, which is behaviourally interesting in that much of its time is spent on, or close to, the ground. In the Gulf of Guinea, the **São Tomé scops owl** *(Otus hartlaubi)* occurs on the island from which it takes its name and possibly on Principe. It has a fairly wide distribution but apparently occurs at very low densities. It is probably not seriously threatened at this stage.

Many other island species could be mentioned here but we feel the point has been made that birds and all other biota on islands are particularly vulnerable. There is little doubt that within the next 50 years many more species will become extinct unless conservation measures are immediately instituted.

# MAINLAND BIRDS

In mainland Africa the greatest percentage of threatened and endangered bird species, some 65%, are associated with forests, principally in the tropics. More than 90% of these birds are found in five areas: the forests in eastern Kenya and forested mountains in eastern Tanzania; the Albertine Rift; the western Angolan escarpment; the forests of Cameroon and the Guinean forests of west Africa.

Forest species that are considered to be endangered, primarily because of very limited habitat, include the Bannerman's turaco *(Tauraco bannermani)*, thyolo alethe *(Alethe choloensis)*, taita thrush *(Turdus helleri)*, banded wattle-eye *(Platysteira laticincta)*, marungu sunbird *(Nectarinia prigoginei)* and the Ibadan malimbe *(Malimbus ibadanensis)*. All these species are

**Above:** *Male Congo peacock* (Afropavo congensis).

restricted to various forest habitats and are under considerable threat from logging (legal and illegal) and other human disturbance. This illustrates the threat to many of Africa's montane, lowland and riparian forests. It is unlikely that the conservation standing of any of these areas will improve; on the contrary, the damage is likely to worsen.

The Sokoke Forest in eastern Kenya is home to several threatened bird species: they include the Sokoke scops owl *(Otus ireneae)*, Sokoke pipit *(Anthus sokokensis)*, east coast akalat *(Sheppardia gunningi)*, spotted ground thrush *(Turdus fischeri)*, amani sunbird *(Anthreptes pallidigaster)* and Clarke's weaver *(Ploceus golandi)*.

The white-breasted guineafowl *(Agelastes meleagrides)* is one of several species suffering because of a decline in the extent of the generally moist forests of west Africa. All other guineafowl species occur in considerably greater numbers, although some concern has been expressed for the plumed guineafowl *(A. plumifera)*, a resident of primary forest in the northern Congolean region. These forests are, however, not under the same measure of threat as those west of the Dahomey Gap.

Other birds of considerable concern in the Guinean forest block are the yellow-throated olive greenbul *(Criniger olivaceus)*, the western wattled cuckoo-shrike *(Campephaga lobata)* and the white-necked picathartes *(Picathartes gymnocephalus)*. The importance of these forests can be judged from the fact that they hold three bird species new to science, which were described only in the last three decades (Nimba flycatcher, yellow-footed honeyguide, Gola malimbe). At least two more, a

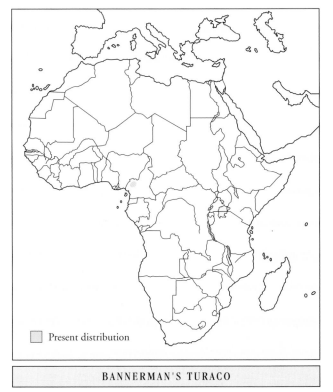

Present distribution

**BANNERMAN'S TURACO**

forest oxpecker and a sunbird, have been reliably reported but still need to be described.

When one considers that less than one third of Afro-tropical bird species occupy forested and dense woodland habitats, it is clear that all is not well within this green-bowered world. Collar and Stuart sum up the situation in the *ICBP/IUCN red data book,* 1985:

> The rate of forest destruction in Africa west of the Dahomey Gap is so severe that any bird species endemic to primary forest in this region must now be considered gravely at risk.

Nevertheless, there are no recently documented cases of bird

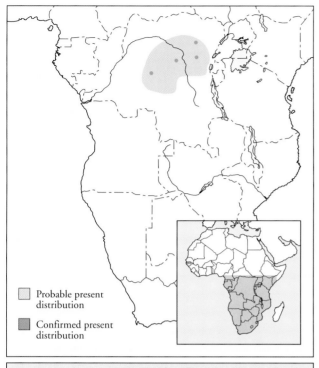

Probable present
distribution

Confirmed present
distribution

CONGO PEACOCK

Above: *Female Congo peacock* (Afropavo congensis).

specimens were collected in 1910, and in 1921 a further specimen was obtained, with the last record in 1926. In 1986 it was rediscovered by scientists studying the okapi. They recorded several sightings, including of a flock of 22 birds.

A mainland species that has eluded scientists for more than a century is the **yellow-throated serin** *(Serinus flavigula)*, known from three specimens collected in a limited area of the Ethiopian Shoa province. Given its small size and forested habitat it seems almost certain that it still survives, but it occupies a zoologically poorly known region. If it is rediscovered, like the golden-naped weaver, then no known bird has become extinct on the African mainland this century.

Although this is a positive sign, diminishing and destroyed habitats are, sadly, putting more and more bird species under pressure, particularly those with specific habitat requirements. There is also the problem of regional extinction, or drastic numerical declines in limited areas, while elsewhere ranges and numbers remain little changed. Added complications arise with the conservation status of certain subspecies, where one race may be abundant, whereas another is about to plunge into the abyss of extinction.

An African bird only discovered this century is the **Ethiopian bush crow** *(Zavattariornis stresemanni)*, which occupies an area of 6 000 sq km in southern Ethiopia. This is one of the few bird species that is a cooperative breeder. Although it has been listed as rare, it is in fact fairly abundant within its rather limited range, but destruction of its habitat poses a medium-term threat to its survival.

An amazing saga is the discovery in Congo (DR) of the **Congo peacock** (peafowl) *(Afropavo congensis)*, a species with a limited range that has been classified as being of special conservation concern. In 1913 the ornithologist James P. Chapman was exploring the Ituri Forest near Avakubi and noted the feather of an unfamiliar bird stuck in the hat of one of the locals. He took the feather back to the United States of America. Despite his best efforts it was only in 1936 that the mystery bird was identified. While visiting the Congo Museum at Tervuren in Belgium, Chapman found two mounted specimens of peacock-like birds. They were labelled as juvenile Indian peacocks but it was immediately obvious to him that this was incorrect. Examining the wings of the female, he recognised the same brown, black-tipped feather that he had obtained in the Ituri Forest. Chapman wrote the first description of this peacock-like bird, giving it the name it still carries. A Belgian, De Mathelin de Papigny, who had resided for many years in the then Congo, described a large, unfamiliar bird that he had eaten in 1930, probably the newly identified peacock. A government employee, T. Herrlig, based at Ikela, Tshuapa, was the first person known to have kept this bird in captivity: not one but three, in 1938. Several zoos, mainly in Europe and North America, now have captive breeding populations. The main population is in Antwerp Zoo.

The Congo peacock is an inhabitant of primary forest. Its distribution is not uniform and it occurs at very low densities, as indicated by the few skins in museum collections and the small number of live birds that have come out of the Congolean

extinction on the African continent, although several species have not been recorded for a decade or more.

Some species, believed to have disappeared forever, are even sometimes rediscovered. The **golden-naped weaver** *(Ploceus aureonucha)* was first recorded in a relatively small area within the Ituri Forest of north-eastern Congo (DR). The first

forests. The species is of special conservation concern because of seemingly low numbers, limited range and the fact that it is the only true member of the pheasant group occurring in Africa, and the closest relative of the two Asian peacock species.

An insect-eating avian migrant from Eurasia to Africa, the **lesser kestrel** *(Falco naumanni)*, once abundant and arriving in large flocks, has seen dramatic declines both within its northern breeding range and in Africa. Agricultural poisons, throughout its entire range, have primarily been blamed for its decline. Other migrant populations have also declined in recent decades, including the western red-footed kestrel *(F. vespertinus)* and the eastern red-footed kestrel *(F. amurensis).* There are several species, such as the jackass or black-footed penguin, that still occur in substantial numbers but have undergone catastrophic declines in recent times.

Although no African mainland bird is known to have become extinct in recent times, 12 are considered to be endangered, a further nine are vulnerable and many are classified as rare, with a substantial number being so poorly known that their true conservation standing is uncertain. The selection we have made, we feel, gives an indication of the range of problems faced by African birds, but the limitations of space prevent us from covering all species falling within the different categories of threat.

The following accounts do not follow any conventional taxonomic order but are roughly in order of measure of threat.

# PLATALEIDAE

*Ibises and spoonbills*

## Northern bald ibis
### *Geronticus eremita* **Ⓔ**

This endangered bird is also known as the waldrapp, hermit ibis and red-faced ibis.

### Distribution and habitat

The northern bald ibis was once found widely in central Europe, probably throughout the coastal plain of north Africa and extending into the Middle East and northwards to Turkey. It had disappeared from the present Hungary, Austria, Switzerland, Germany and the former Yugoslavia by the end of the 17th century. The last non-African breeding colony, at Birecik in Turkey, numbered an estimated 3 000 pairs in 1890 but it was extinct as a breeding species by 1989. Sightings during the 1990s in south-western Saudi Arabia strongly indicate that as yet unrecorded colonies survive in isolated and undisturbed regions of the Arabian Peninsula. There is also a recent sighting from Yemen that supports this possibility.

The only known breeding colonies today are located in Morocco, with about 90 pairs. One small group in Algeria of

| | NORTHERN BALD IBIS | SOUTHERN BALD IBIS |
|---|---|---|
| **Total length** | 70-80 cm | 79 cm |
| **Wingspan** | up to 1,35 m | about 1 m |
| **Social structure** | flocks up to 100 | flocks up to 100 |
| **Breeding** | colonially on cliffs | colonially on cliffs |
| **Number of eggs** | 2-4 | 1-3 |
| **Incubation** | 24-28 days | 27-31 days |
| **Diet** | invertebrates, occasionally small vertebrates, some plant food | invertebrates, small vertebrates |
| **Habitat** | arid, semi-arid plains, plateaux, high grassland | high grassland |
| **Number surviving** | about 400 | below 8 000 |

**Above:** *Northern bald ibis (waldrapp)* (Geronticus eremita).
**Right:** *Southern bald ibises* (Geronticus calvus) *are restricted to South Africa and Lesotho.*

fewer than 10 pairs, which was still present in the mid-1980s, is no longer active. Outside the breeding season northern bald ibises have been sighted as far afield as Mali, Mauritania and Western Sahara, but these observations are increasingly rare as the population declines. The eastern populations probably moved southwards along the Red Sea when not breeding, as there are numerous records from Ethiopia, Eritrea and Sudan from the 19th and the first half of the 20th century, where most observers recorded substantial flocks.

## Conservation

It has been estimated that there may be no more than 400 birds surviving in the wild, but several release programmes involving captive-bred birds in central Europe and north Africa have been, or are to be, implemented.

What is particularly worrying is the rapid decline in populations, particularly in their north-west African and Turkish range, in just 30 years. Even as recently as the 1930s there were at least 1 000 breeding pairs in Morocco. Throughout its range this ibis has lost at least 96% of its 20th century population; a sobering thought indeed!

The dramatic decline in the north-west African population has been largely attributed to direct hunting, poaching and changes in land-use practices. Although not identified as a major cause of ibis mortality in Morocco, agricultural poisoning, which caused the extinction of the Turkish breeding population, must be seen as an ever-present threat. Just one poisoning incident could reduce ibis numbers to such low levels that they could not recover.

A little understood but probably critical factor playing a role in the survival of the northern bald ibis is changing weather patterns. It has been surmised that direct hunting and climatic changes caused them to disappear in central Europe more than three centuries ago. Extended dry periods have also impacted heavily on populations in other parts of their range. Another factor that has to be considered is the opportunity presented to predators of ibis eggs and chicks when the adults are frightened away from the breeding colony by human intruders.

Today, there are more northern bald ibises in captive colonies (over 700) than there are in the wild. There is a need to ensure that suitable areas, particularly in Morocco, are set aside as formal national parks before major release programmes are undertaken. However, some reintroductions have already taken place. No reserve will be large enough to contain these ibises but breeding colony protection, at least, would be useful if not the complete solution.

Although it is feasible to reintroduce captive-bred birds to suitable areas in their former range, the goal should be to protect existing colonies. According to some authorities reintroductions require at least some wild birds to lead the migration to overwintering areas. Migration is believed not to be instinctive, but behaviour learned from the previous generation. If this is true, it could have serious implications for the long-term survival of reintroduced colonies.

# Southern bald ibis
## *Geronticus calvus* Ⓥ

This relative of the northern bald ibis lives at the other end of the continent. Its population has stabilised and probably numbers about 8 000 birds, with more than 1 250 breeding pairs. Nevertheless, until about 1970 this ibis underwent massive declines in both numbers and range, having previously occurred widely in the eastern half of South Africa, extending westwards on the coastal plain to the vicinity of Cape Town.

Reasons for its decline up to 1970 are not clearly understood but can be partly attributed to habitat changes resulting from excessive grazing pressure by domestic stock. Harvesting of eggs and chicks for food, wherever the cliff-nesting colonies were accessible to humans, probably also played an important role.

The southern bald ibis generally favours short grassland, particularly burnt areas with new grass growth. It is now resident only in KwaZulu-Natal province and the south-eastern Free State, with a few outlying colonies scattered through parts of the old Transvaal; there are also recent records from Lesotho.

Although there has been discussion for several years of reintroducing this bald ibis to the former western limits of its range, no such release is contemplated in the near future as far as we could ascertain. Given the increased public conservation awareness in South Africa, reintroduction could prove successful, particularly as these ibises breed readily in captivity.

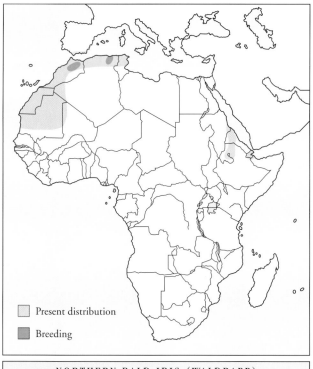

Present distribution

Breeding

**NORTHERN BALD IBIS (WALDRAPP)**

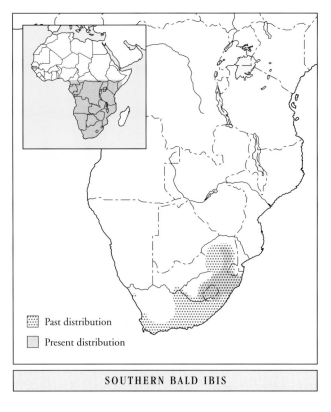

Past distribution

Present distribution

**SOUTHERN BALD IBIS**

# PHASIANIDAE

*Guineafowls, francolins and others*

## White-breasted guineafowl
### *Agelastes meleagrides* **E**

### Description and taxonomy

The genus *Agelastes* may represent the most primitive of living guineafowls (the other species it contains is the black guineafowl *A. niger*). For this reason it is important to conserve the genus.

### Distribution and habitat

This highly endangered species is restricted to a few areas in the rapidly dwindling Guinean forest block of west Africa. Although widespread in the past, its present range is very limited. It previously occurred almost contiguously in suitable habitat from Sierra Leone in the west to Ghana in the east. Recent records indicate that it survives in south-western Ghana within Nini-Suhien National Park, Tano-Anwai and the Boin-Tano Forest Reserve and adjacent forest patches, but in extremely low numbers. In Ivory Coast it is known to survive only in the south-west, in the Tai National Park. In Liberia it occurs in Grebo National Forest, Sapo National Park, Mount Nimba and suitable forests in Grand Gedeh

County. Surveys undertaken in the last five years have confirmed its presence in Gola in extreme south-eastern Sierra Leone. It is believed to occur on the Guinean side of Mount Nimba but this has never been confirmed. The only viable populations now seem to be those in extreme south-eastern Liberia and adjacent areas of Ivory Coast.

Recent limited findings indicate that the white-breasted guineafowl is largely restricted to primary forest, with only a few records from secondary and disturbed forests. There is an urgent need to undertake intensive surveys of west Africa's remaining forests.

| WHITE-BREASTED GUINEAFOWL | |
|---|---|
| **Length of wing** | 20,7-22,7 cm |
| **Social structure** | flocks of 15-30 |
| **Breeding** | nesting habits and clutch size not known but probably as for other guineafowls |
| **Habitat** | primary forest; rarely secondary forest |
| **Diet** | invertebrates, fruits, other plant parts |
| **Number surviving** | perhaps over 20 000 |
| *Nothing else is known* | |

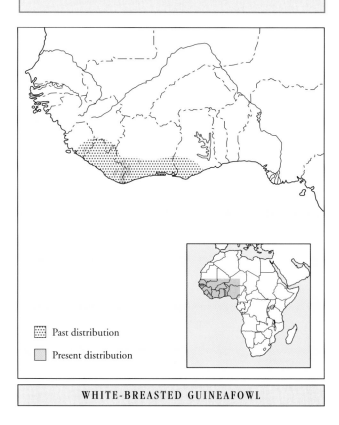

Past distribution

Present distribution

**WHITE-BREASTED GUINEAFOWL**

**Above:** *Apart from a few old museum specimens and occasional sightings, little is known about the rarest of all guineafowl, the white-breasted* (Agelastes meleagrides). Painting: *Used with permission from the World Pheasant Association and the artist Wulf Gatter.*

## Behaviour

A behavioural aspect of interest, noted in Tai, is that white-breasted guineafowl flocks may to an extent rely on plant parts dropped by troops of monkeys feeding in the trees. One author has suggested that heavy hunting pressure on monkeys may therefore have had a negative impact on the guineafowl. Evidence is minimal at this stage but this link certainly warrants further research.

## Conservation

Surviving numbers of white-breasted guineafowl are not known but in an area of approximately 12 sq km around the forest station in Tai National Park, and in the Gola forest reserves, densities of these guineafowl were estimated at 10 to 12 birds per square kilometre. This results in an estimate for the whole of Tai of several thousand birds, and for Gola as high as 7 000. However, density estimates made in limited areas and then extrapolated for whole reserves need to be treated with caution. The population is known to be very fragmented.

Although one estimate puts the total population size at almost 60 000, this seems exceedingly optimistic. The white-breasted guineafowl is threatened not only by habitat loss, but it is also sought after by human hunters. Destruction and dis-

turbance of favoured forest habitats, as well as shooting and trapping, continue. There are only minimal controls in conservation areas where this guineafowl occurs and even within these areas, disturbance by humans is considerable.

The situation in Liberia has been worsened by the protracted civil war, and in the Tai National Park by an influx of refugees from Liberia. Settlement, logging and poaching are the main problems affecting the white-breasted guineafowl.

## Djibouti francolin
### *Francolinus achropectus* Ⓔ

The Djibouti francolin occurs only in the 1 400 ha Forêt du Day, a primary forest that has experienced massive destruction in the past two decades. It has been estimated that just 2 000 years ago the Day Forest extended over 400 000 ha! Unconfirmed reports indicate that a few francolins may be present in a small secondary forest some 60 km to the east of Day. The total population size is estimated at some 5 000 birds.

Like most francolin species the Djibouti francolin feeds on seeds, wild fruits and probably some invertebrates such as termites. It is a ground-nester but little is known of its breeding biology, except that chicks have been observed between December and February.

This species is endangered because of its very restricted distribution within the country whose name it carries. Given the level of destruction of its habitat it could well be extinct within only five years. Habitat loss as a result of human activities is being aggravated by an extended natural period of increased aridity.

If this francolin can survive in secondary and disturbed forest – which is uncertain – this could extend its survival chances by a few years. However, its long-term prospects remain gloomy.

## Other francolins

Other members of the family Phasianidae that are of conservation concern are the Mount Cameroon francolin, Swierstra's francolin and Nahan's francolin.

The **Mount Cameroon francolin** *(F. camerunensis)* is rare. It only occurs in montane forests on the slopes of Mount Cameroon, as do several other unrelated bird species. Although numbers are believed to be relatively high, its limited range could pose long-term problems, particularly if large-scale logging and human settlement take place. It also faces the unusual threat of habitat destruction by volcanic eruption, as happened in 1982.

**Swierstra's francolin** *(F. swierstrai)* is probably rare. It occurs in the mountains of western Angola, in montane forest and high altitude grasslands. As most records come from montane forest, a habitat that has been largely destroyed in Angola, its long-term survival is doubtful. If it is able successfully to occupy other habitats – which is uncertain – it may have some chance of survival. Given the protracted war in Angola, little

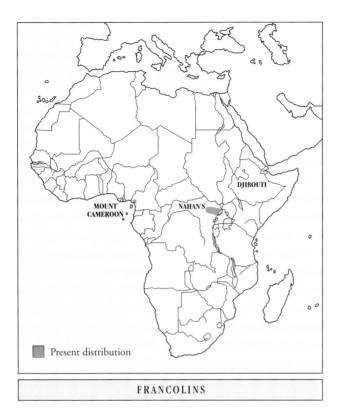

Present distribution

FRANCOLINS

recent information is available on the conservation of this or any other bird species.

**Nahan's francolin** *(F. nahani)* is a lowland forest dweller. It is considered to be rare because very few specimens have been collected or observed. The last specimen was collected in 1970, as far as we have been able to ascertain. Its forest habitat makes the bird particularly difficult to observe in the dense undergrowth, but it certainly occurs only at low densities. Nahan's francolin is only known from a few scattered localities in eastern Congo (DR) (Ituri Forest and Semuliki Valley) and forest pockets in western Uganda (Bugomo and Budongo). Part of the Semliki Valley population lies within the Virunga National Park.

Although a number of other francolin species are hunted, or are losing favoured habitat, none can be considered to be under any major threat. Some species, particularly in inten-

**Below**: *Direct and indirect poisoning is a major threat to the survival of the blue crane* (Anthropoides paradiseus). PHOTO: *Ann Scott.*

sively cultivated areas of South Africa and Zimbabwe, have increased in numbers, whereas others have declined but not to the level where they can be considered to be rare or particularly vulnerable.

The effect of agricultural poisons, such as herbicides and insecticides, on the health of francolins, and of course other species, is cause for concern. In some areas poisons are deliberately laid out to control such species as helmeted guineafowl, which feed in similar habitats to a number of francolin species.

# GRUIDAE

## *Cranes*

Six of the world's 15 species of crane occur in Africa. Four are found only in sub-Saharan Africa, and the other two are predominantly migratory visitors to northern Africa, although one has a remnant breeding population. They are the grey crowned crane, demoiselle crane, Eurasian (or common) crane, wattled crane, blue (or Stanley's) crane and black crowned crane. All species have experienced declines in numbers and range as a result of direct persecution, construction of artificial impoundments, draining and overutilisation of wetlands, floodplains and adjacent grasslands, and in some cases capture for the live-animal trade.

The **grey crowned crane** *(Balearica regulorum)* is the most abundant sub-Saharan resident. Perhaps 100 000 of these elegant birds survive.

The **demoiselle crane** *(Anthropoides virgo)* is a close relative of the blue crane. It was once a common breeding resident in

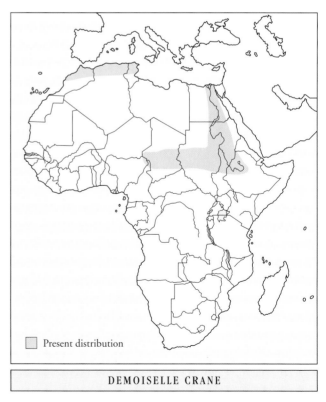

Present distribution

DEMOISELLE CRANE

north Africa but now only nests in tiny numbers in Morocco. The last nesting in Algeria and Tunisia was recorded more than 50 years ago. This resident crane is therefore endangered in north-western Africa. However, the migratory population is abundant in its non-breeding range in the east. These cranes arrive from Eurasia to overwinter as far south as north-eastern Nigeria, in a belt across to west-central Ethiopia and north-wards in a broad swathe on either side of the Nile River. The greatest concentration is centred on Sudan. The number of seasonal migrant birds is not known but it could be some 35 000 individuals.

The **Eurasian crane** *(Grus grus)*, a non-breeding migrant to Africa, enters the continent along three migration routes to overwinter: down the Iberian Peninsula to north-western Africa, over Italy to Algeria, and along the Nile River valley to Sudan and Ethiopia.

We now look at the three cranes of greatest conservation concern and the causes of their decline. The flock sizes of all three these species are now generally much smaller than they used to be. The two species with the lowest populations are the wattled crane, with possibly fewer than 12 000 individuals, and the blue crane, numbering an estimated 13 000.

# Wattled crane
## *Grus carunculatus* Ⓥ

This species occurs patchily and at low densities from Ethiopia to eastern South Africa, and in Angola, Botswana, Malawi, Mozambique, Namibia, Tanzania, Congo (DR), Zambia and Zimbabwe. It is restricted to wetlands, notably floodplains

|  | WATTLED CRANE | BLUE CRANE | BLACK CROWNED CRANE |
|---|---|---|---|
| **Standing height** | 1,2 m | 1,05 m | 1,05 m |
| **Length of wing** | 61-71 cm | 51-59 cm | 52-64 cm |
| **Social structure** | pairs; flocks to 400 | pairs; flocks to 300 | pairs; flocks 100-1 000 or more |
| **Number of eggs** | 1-2, usually 1 | 1-3, usually 2 | 2-3 |
| **Incubation** | 39-40 days | 30 days | 30 days |
| **Diet** | opportu-nistic: seeds, insects, small vertebrates | opportu-nistic: seeds, insects, small vertebrates | opportu-nistic: seeds, insects, small vertebrates |
| **Habitat** | floodplains, highland marsh, high grassland | grasslands, cultivated areas | floodplains, grassland |
| **Number surviving** | below 12 000 | above 13 000 | below 50 000 |

**Below:** *Wattled cranes* (Grus carunculatus)*, Moremi Game Reserve.*
PHOTO: *Daryl Balfour, ABPL.*

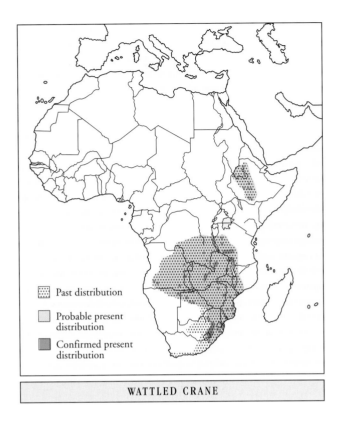

WATTLED CRANE

and marshes throughout its range.

Estimates of the total population size range from a low of 6 000 to a high of 12 000; the true figure probably lies somewhere in between. Populations in the very limited area of suitable habitat in Namibia (East Caprivi) probably number below 50 birds; in South Africa there are only about 100 breeding pairs; there are fewer than 40 pairs in Malawi. The largest population is in Zambia, but even here there have been considerable declines. Flocks of several hundred birds take part in some areas in short migrations, but very little is known about this aspect of their ecology.

Several factors have caused the decline in the number and range of wattled cranes, principally habitat loss and direct disturbance by humans, particularly at the nest. Habitat loss results from the building of dams that disrupt seasonal flooding, which is essential to wattled cranes. The gradual disappearance of large grazing herds of wild ungulates has also changed the vegetation and created

**Left:** *Grey crowned crane* (Balearica regulorum). *The more common of the two crowned cranes , this species is nevertheless in decline, with only about 100 000 of these elegant birds surviving.*

unfavourable conditions for these birds. Draining of wetlands and afforestation have been important causes of this crane's decline in South Africa. Although wattled cranes occur in a number of conservation areas throughout their range, protected populations only form a small part of the total.

# Blue crane
## *Anthropoides paradiseus* ⓥ

This crane, South Africa's national bird, was considered to be safe and not threatened until very recently, when it was realised that it had suffered a drastic reduction in numbers throughout much of its range, with only one stable population. The total population has decreased by more than half in just 20 years, to about 13 000, although one recent estimate puts the population figure at about 20 000.

This bird has the most limited range of all the African cranes, being restricted to South Africa, with marginal populations in Lesotho and Swaziland, and an apparently isolated group in Etosha National Park, Namibia (about 80 individuals). Populations in South Africa's KwaZulu-Natal and Eastern Cape provinces have experienced declines of as much as 95%, with some 1 000 birds surviving in the eastern parts of the range. An estimated 6 000 blue cranes still occur in the dry grasslands of the Northern Cape interior, with the largest and most stable population occupying the grainlands and pastures, known as the Overberg, of the southern coastal plain of Western Cape province. Unlike many other species, blue cranes do well in these agricultural lands and are only rarely seen in areas of natural vegetation. This population, although

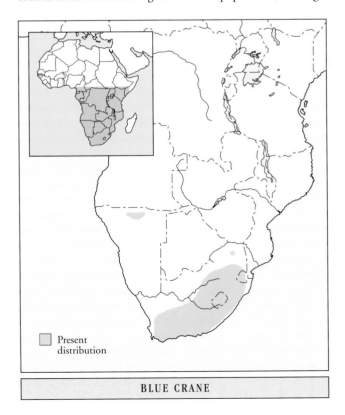

Present distribution

BLUE CRANE

completely protected, faces a number of threats, the most serious being direct and indirect poisoning. In this area Egyptian geese and helmeted guineafowl, both abundant, are deliberately poisoned in an attempt to reduce losses of grain, on which they feed. The poisoned grain, however, is eaten by many other bird species, including blue cranes, and mortalities frequently include several blue cranes.

Particularly during dry periods, blue cranes compete directly for food put out by farmers for their sheep. Direct persecution of cranes therefore occasionally takes place, although high penalties have almost eliminated this. The Overberg Crane Group was formed in 1991, with the express goal of ensuring that this crane population is adequately conserved.

## Black crowned crane
### *Balearica pavonina*

This crane occurs in considerably lower numbers than its cousin the grey crowned crane and is seriously threatened in the western sector of its range. It occurs across the Sahelian belt and other savannas of west Africa, from Senegal to as far east as western Ethiopia. The bulk of the surviving population is probably centred on southern and central Sudan but the west African flocks have now become highly fragmented. Like the blue crane, this crowned crane has seen a massive decline in numbers in the past two decades. In the early 1970s there were an estimated 10 000 black crowned cranes in the Waza National Park of Cameroon. Today the largest west African population, perhaps some 3 000, are concentrated in Senegal, Gambia and south-western Mauritania, with only a few thou-

**Above:** *Blue cranes* (Anthropoides paradisea).

sand elsewhere in the west. In Nigeria, where this crane is the national bird, it is now virtually extinct, yet only a few years ago it was considered to be abundant in the north of that country. This crane undertakes local seasonal movements outside the breeding season.

# OTIDAE

### *Bustards and korhaans*

These large to medium-sized, long-legged birds show a strong preference for open country in arid, semi-arid and savanna regions. Of the 22 species, 18 occur in Africa and of these 15 are endemics: they are not found outside the continent. Some

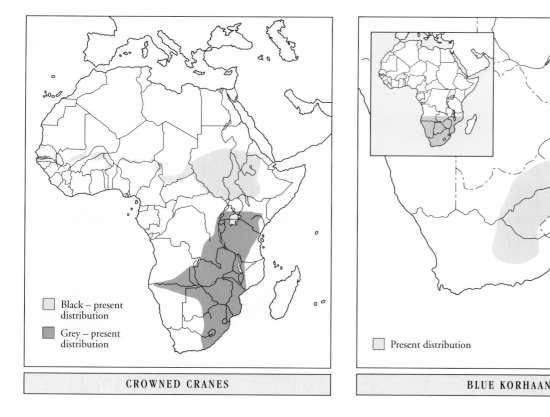

Black – present distribution

Grey – present distribution

**CROWNED CRANES**

Present distribution

**BLUE KORHAAN**

species have extensive distributional ranges but others occur in limited areas or are restricted to a particular habitat. For example, the kori bustard *(Ardeotis kori)*, Stanley's bustard *(Neotis denhami)* and the black-bellied korhaan *(Eupodotis melanogaster)* have extensive sub-Saharan ranges, but the blue korhaan *(E. caerulescens)* is restricted to the eastern interior of South Africa and Rüppell's korhaan *(E. rueppellii)* occurs only in the Namib Desert. Some species, most notably the kori bustard in South Africa, have seriously declined in numbers. The most threatened species occur in northern Africa. Two species, neither of which is an African endemic, are likely to become extinct in Africa in the near future unless drastic measures are taken to protect them. They are the little bustard *(Tetrax tetrax)* and the great bustard *(Otis tarda)*. The houbara bustard *(Chlamydotis undulata)* has undergone drastic population declines in its north African range, although it still occurs widely as a resident.

Bustards and korhaans are threatened by detrimental agricultural practices. They are also targets for poachers, and are eagerly hunted by oil-rich individuals from the Arabian Peninsula states. As these people have largely denuded their own countries of wildlife, they frequently make hunting forays into such countries as Sudan and Egypt. Their equipment often includes refrigerated lorries to transport the meat of their kills.

# Little bustard
## *Tetrax tetrax* Ⓔ

# Great bustard
## *Otis tarda* Ⓔ

Both these species are endangered in their African range. They are still widespread in Eurasia in spite of having undergone declines in many areas there.

The **little bustard** is now virtually extinct as a viable breeding resident in Africa: only a few survive in Morocco and extreme northern Algeria. There is also a non-breeding migrant population, presumed to come from south-western Europe, but its numbers have also been greatly reduced. Small numbers of these migrant birds enter Morocco, Algeria and occasionally Tunisia and northern Libya, but they no longer visit the Nile Delta area of Egypt. The little bustard was previously widespread and abundant in north-western Africa, where

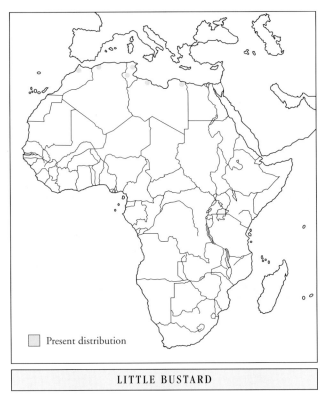

Present distribution

LITTLE BUSTARD

|  | LITTLE BUSTARD | GREAT BUSTARD |
|---|---|---|
| **Total length** | 43 cm | ♂ 100 cm; ♀ 80 cm |
| **Wingspan** | 90 cm | ♂ 2,3 m; ♀ 1,8 m |
| **Mass** | below 1 kg | ♂ 8-16 kg; ♀ 3,5-5 kg |

Left: *The little bustard* (Tetrax tetrax) *is almost extinct as a breeding species in north Africa, but several decades ago it was much more abundant as both a resident and a seasonal migrant.* PHOTO: *Kevin Carlson, Aquila.* **Below left:** *On the Arabian Peninsula and in north Africa the houbara bustard* (Chamydotis undulata) *has been greatly reduced in numbers, this being in large part attributable to falconry, as well as habitat changes.* PHOTO: *Mark N. Boulton, Bruce Coleman Ltd.*

it occurred both as a resident and as a seasonal visitor.

The **great bustard** has been reduced to fewer than 100 resident individuals in Africa, virtually all in a limited area of northern Morocco. Vagrants occasionally enter north-west Algeria.

# BALAENICIPITIDAE

## Shoebill
### *Balaeniceps rex* Ⓡ

The prehistoric-looking shoebill or whalebill is of special conservation concern. Although it is sometimes referred to as a stork, it belongs to a separate genus in which it is the only species. The plumage is overall dark grey. The bird has long, dark legs and an enormous bill shaped like a wooden clog. This unusual bird has a wide eastern and central African distribution, largely in association with wetlands in or close to the Great Rift Valley. However, locations where it is known to occur are spottily spread through this area. Most of the population occurs in swamps in Sudan, Uganda, Congo (DR) and Zambia, with much smaller numbers in Tanzania, Rwanda, Central African Republic and Ethiopia. Vagrants occasionally turn up in other countries but soon move on. By far the largest population is found in southern Sudan, but even here numbers have been declining since the beginning of the century. When civil order returns to Sudan, it seems likely that the Jonglei Canal will be completed. The canal lies in prime shoebill habitat and its completion would have serious consequences for these birds. Uganda has many areas of suitable swampland but shoebills almost certainly number well below 800 individuals there. The greatest proportion of the small Zambian population lives in the Bangweulu Swamp in the north-east, but given the high levels of disturbance by fishermen and game poachers in the area, these birds are far from secure.

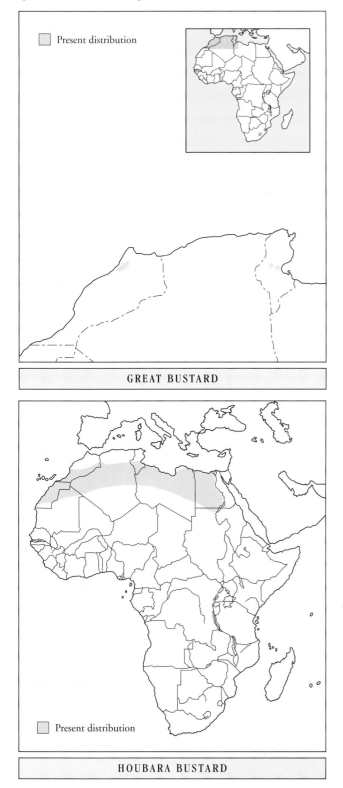

GREAT BUSTARD

HOUBARA BUSTARD

Present distribution

| **SHOEBILL** | |
|---|---|
| **Total length** | over 1,1 m |
| **Standing height** | over 1 m |
| **Breeding** | solitary nest in marsh |
| **Number of eggs** | 1-3, usually 2 |
| **Incubation** | about 30 days |
| **Diet** | fish, reptiles, amphibians, occasionally small mammals |
| **Habitat** | freshwater swamps, vegetated lake fringes, areas with dense beds of floating plants |
| **Number surviving** | 5 000-10 000 |

**Above:** *The shoebill* (Balaeniceps rex) *is also known as the boatbill and whalebill. This species is very sensitive to disturbance.*

# CICONIIDAE

## *Storks*

There are no threatened storks in Africa; all have wide sub-Saharan distributions. However, two species have suffered serious declines and are briefly discussed.

## Saddlebilled stork
### *Ephippiorhynchus senegalensis*

This species has probably always occurred at low densities, but has declined in numbers and range in several areas, particularly in southern and west Africa. No population estimates are available but we personally doubt that as many as 50 000 sur-

| SADDLEBILLED STORK | |
|---|---|
| **Total length** | 145 cm |
| **Wingspan** | up to 2,7 m |
| **Number of eggs** | 1-5, usually 3 |
| **Incubation** | 30-35 days |
| **Diet** | fish, frogs, other small vertebrates, invertebrates |
| **Habitat** | wetlands |

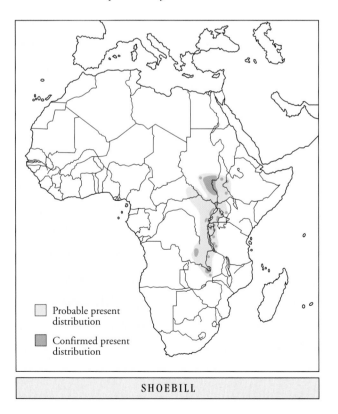

Probable present distribution

Confirmed present distribution

SHOEBILL

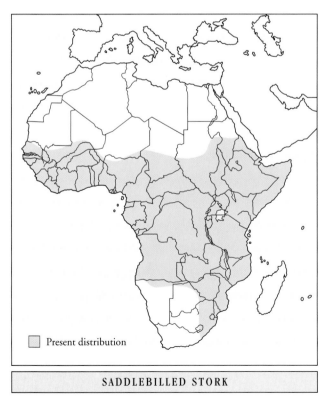

Present distribution

SADDLEBILLED STORK

vive. These storks are particularly vulnerable to changes in wetland regimes caused by dam construction and drainage, and to the impact of agricultural and pastoral factors on floodplains.

The saddlebilled stork is present in many conservation areas where there is suitable habitat.

# White stork
## *Ciconia ciconia*

This stork is not yet threatened but it has declined during the past few decades. There are tiny resident breeding populations in Morocco, Tunisia and the extreme southern tip of South Africa. Substantial numbers of non-breeding migrants from Eurasia occur on the Mediterranean coastal plain, along the

| WHITE STORK | |
|---|---|
| **Total length** | 1,2 m |
| **Wingspan** | 1,55-1,65 m |
| **Mass** | 2,3-4,4 kg |
| **Number of eggs** | 2-4 |
| **Incubation** | 33-34 days |
| **Diet** | insects, other invertebrates, small vertebrates |
| **Habitat** | grasslands, agricultural lands, marshes, Karoo |

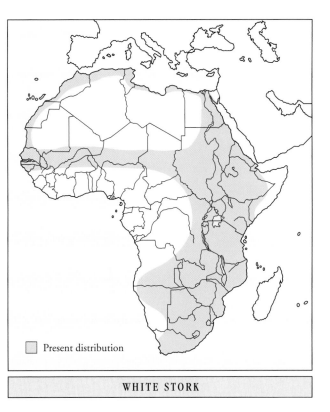

Present distribution

**WHITE STORK**

Atlantic coastline as far as Gambia and Senegal, eastwards through the Sahel to the Red Sea, and southwards to the southern tip of Africa. These storks avoid true deserts and

**Below:** *The white (European) stork* (Ciconia ciconia) *is largely a non-breeding migrant but small numbers breed in the extreme south-west and north-west of Africa.*

DALMATIAN PELICAN

forested areas but may overfly them when on the move. Declines can be largely attributed to the impact of pesticides, herbicides and other agricultural poisons, including those used in locust control programmes in Africa. These poisons can kill the birds themselves, but a more serious problem is that they reduce egg fertility. This threat needs to be closely watched.

# PELECANIDAE

## *Pelicans*

The **Dalmatian pelican** *(Pelecanus crispus)* is a rare winter migrant to north-eastern Egypt, principally in the vicinity of the lower Nile River and its delta. It is the rarest pelican breeding in the Palaearctic, with probably fewer than 600 pairs surviving. This species is as large as the common white pelican *(Pelecanus onocrotalus)* but it has a characteristic straw-coloured curly crest on the top of the head. Within its limited African range there are no known threats to its survival.

**Below:** *The Dalmatian pelican* (Pelecanus crispus) *is a non-breeding migrant to the lower Nile River and its delta.*
PHOTO: *Udo Hirsch, Bruce Coleman Ltd.*

# ARDEIDAE

## Herons, egrets and bitterns

The **slaty egret** *(Egretta vinaceigula)*, a waterbird, was only confirmed as a distinct species in 1971. Most of the population is centred on the Okavango Delta in Botswana and the Linyanti Swamp and river systems in Eastern Caprivi, Namibia. It also occurs in a few swamps and floodplains in Zambia. All these wetlands are potentially under threat and many biota would be adversely affected by human disturbance.

No estimate of slaty egret numbers has been made. In undisturbed areas, such as the central region of the Okavango, this egret is not uncommon and forms flocks of up to 40 birds. This small heron could be a relict species that is naturally sliding into extinction as a result of some factor that we do not understand, perhaps an inability to compete successfully with other small herons.

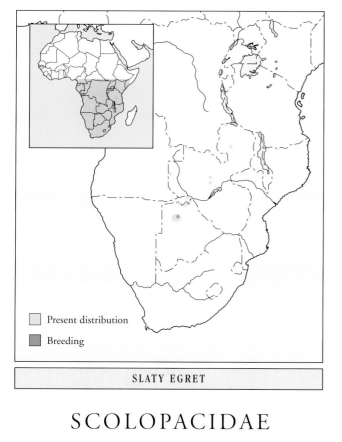

**SLATY EGRET**

# SCOLOPACIDAE

## Waders

Many Palaearctic waders overwinter in Africa as non-breeding migrants. Most species are abundant and not threatened.

One species, the **slender-billed curlew** *(Numenius tenuirostris)* is now rare. This 40 cm long curlew was once a common visitor to the Mediterranean coastline of north Africa and the Atlantic shores of Morocco, but has experienced a massive reduction in numbers. There have been no recent records from Libya and Egypt, and only a scattering of sightings in Tunisia and Algeria. Only Morocco sees reasonable numbers, but probably fewer than 1 500 of these curlews arrive each year.

The **African black oystercatcher** *(Haematopus moquini)*, although not yet rare, is under threat because of its limited dis-

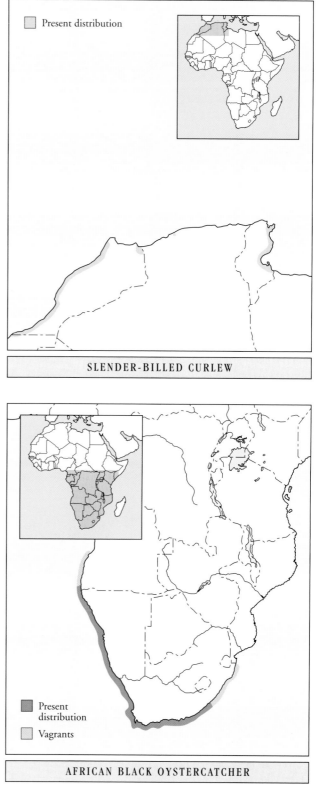

**SLENDER-BILLED CURLEW**

**AFRICAN BLACK OYSTERCATCHER**

tribution, narrow habitat requirements and considerable declines in population size. It is resident along the coast of Namibia and South Africa with the exception of KwaZulu-Natal province; vagrants have been recorded as far north as Lobito Bay in Angola. The total population is probably fewer than 5 000 birds. Its linear distribution on rocky and sandy shorelines means that the increased development and utilisation of this environment by people is going to increase disturbance and other pressures greatly.

# LARIDAE

## *Skuas, gulls and terns*

The **Damara tern** (*Sterna balaenarum),* like the African black oystercatcher, is dependent on a narrow strip of rocky and sandy coastline. It occurs mainly on the Atlantic coast in Namibia and South Africa. It is rare and very vulnerable to disturbance at the few known breeding colonies, which are on the high-water mark. Outside the breeding season it migrates northwards to the shores of the Gulf of Biafra. Population estimates vary widely but from available evidence it would seem that between 5 000 and 10 000 birds survive.

The most important threat it faces is at its breeding sites, because the areas are heavily used by pedestrians and vehicles, which endanger both the eggs and the chicks. Although "off-road" driving bans are in place, they are often ignored.

*Below right: The jackass penguin* (Spheniscus demersus) *is Africa's only resident penguin.*

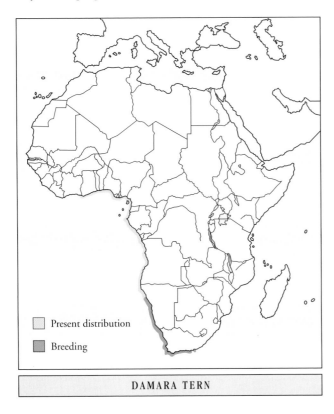

| | |
| --- | --- |
| ☐ | Present distribution |
| ■ | Breeding |

**DAMARA TERN**

**Above:** *African black oystercatcher* (Haematopus moquini).
Photo: *Alan Weaving.*

# SPHENISCIDAE

## *Penguins*

## Jackass penguin
### *Spheniscus demersus*  Ⓡ

The jackass (or black-footed) penguin is a flightless marine species with a southern African coastal distribution. It is Africa's only resident penguin.

| JACKASS PENGUIN | |
| --- | --- |
| **Total length** | average 60 cm |
| **Length of flipper** | 16,5 cm |
| **Mass** | 2,5-3,5 kg |
| **Number of eggs** | 1-2 |
| **Incubation** | 38-41 days |
| **Diet** | fish, squid |
| **Habitat** | coastal |
| **Number surviving** | about 500 000 |

The jackass penguin lost an estimated 75% of its population during the course of the 20th century. Between 1900 and 1930 a staggering 14 million eggs were harvested. If one takes breakages into account, and eggs discarded because of advanced embryo development, the total number of eggs lost is much higher still. Jackass penguin eggs

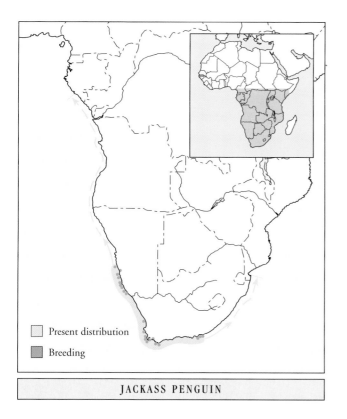

**JACKASS PENGUIN**

Present distribution

Breeding

remained highly sought after until their collection was outlawed in 1969.

No accurate counts, past or present, of the jackass penguin population exist. Estimates for the early 1980s range between 50 000 and more than 170 000 pairs distributed over 20 offshore islands and two mainland breeding sites. Present estimates of the number of breeding pairs range between 500 000 and one million. The higher figure is probably more realistic; the total could be even higher.

Guano, accumulated bird droppings that constitute a superior fertiliser, was and still is collected on the offshore islands where most jackass penguins and other species such as gannets and cormorants live. This has caused disturbance and a loss of nesting habitat, because penguins often nest in burrows excavated in the hardened guano. It has also created a suitable beaching environment for Cape fur seals, which compete with penguins for space. A ban has now been placed on guano collection in areas occupied by penguins. It has been suggested that low walls with gaps to allow the birds free and easy access should be constructed, or repaired where they already exist, to keep fur seals away from penguin breeding colonies.

Direct persecution of penguins by fishermen has been reported but has very little effect on overall penguin numbers. Some fishermen perceive the penguin as a competitor for fish, but the bird is a non-starter compared to humans: the penguins eat about 45 000 tons of pelagic fish per year, whereas fishing operations yield many hundreds of thousands of tons. In the 1950s and 1960s overfishing of pilchards *(Sardinops ocellata)* by commercial trawlers so greatly reduced the numbers of this fish – an important component of the jackass penguin's diet – that penguin populations crashed. However, it has

been shown that in time penguins are able to change their diet: although pilchards were previously a critical component in the diet, their place has now been taken by other species. It has nevertheless been suggested that commercial fishing for pelagic species should be banned within 10 km of any penguin colony.

The impact of media reports about the effect of oil spills on penguins is immediate, emotional and dramatic: after all, who likes to see pictures of penguins, or any bird for that matter, covered in black, sticky goo that will kill the bird unless it gets help? The most serious oil spill along the South African coast took place at the end of June in 1994. An estimated 20 000 to 30 000 adult penguins were oiled, but mortality figures are unknown. In addition, some 9 000 chicks and an unknown number of eggs were affected by being smeared in oil from the plumage of the adults. Chicks would also have starved to death if the parent birds were heavily oiled and had died. However, we believe that penguin mortality from oil spills may be lower than from general disturbance and competition with commercial fishing operations.

# ANATIDAE

## *Ducks, geese and swans*

The rare **white-headed duck** *(Oxyura leucocephala)* is one of six species of stiff-tailed ducks, of which there is only one other in Africa, the more widespread and abundant maccoa duck *(Oxyura maccoa)*. The white-headed duck is both a rare breeding resident and a non-breeding Palaearctic migrant to parts of the Mediterranean coastal plain of north Africa. The resident population has a spotty distribution and numbers have declined. It possibly no longer breeds in Morocco. Small numbers occur on Algeria's Lake Tonga and more substantial numbers in northern Tunisia and the Nile Delta. Declines have probably resulted from excessive hunting and deterioration of many of the white-headed duck's favoured water bodies.

**Below:** *The white-headed duck* (Oxyura leucocephala) *of north Africa.*

**WHITE-HEADED DUCK**

# ACCIPITRIDAE

## *Diurnal raptors*

As these diverse predatory birds are at the top of the food chain they are particularly vulnerable to direct and indirect persecution by humans. In South Africa two large eagles, the **bateleur** *(Terathopius ecaudatus)* and the **martial eagle** *(Polemaetus bellicosus)*, have undergone catastrophic population and range declines, but elsewhere on the continent healthy numbers are maintained.

Africa has the greatest variety of vultures and griffons on any continent, with a total of 11 species. The **Egyptian vulture** *(Neophron percnopterus)*, once widespread in South Africa, is now extinct as a breeding species in that country but elsewhere it is frequently observed and appears to be under no threat.

The **palmnut vulture** *(Gypohierax angolensis)*, also called the vulturine fish eagle, has a patchy sub-Saharan range. It is fairly common, except in South Africa where it has been reduced to a few breeding pairs in KwaZulu-Natal province.

## Bearded vulture
### *Gypaetus barbatus*

This magnificent bird has undergone serious population declines in parts of its range but is holding its own in others. The race *G.b. barbatus* occurs in Eurasia and north Africa, and *G.b. meridionalis* in north-eastern and southern Africa. In two of the three population centres in Africa, namely in the Atlas

Mountains in north-western Africa and in the Drakensberg range of South Africa and Lesotho, numbers have declined during the course of this century.

By far the largest bearded vulture population is centred on the Ethiopian Highlands and along the Great Rift as far south as the volcanic highlands of northern Tanzania. Vagrants are observed from time to time in montane areas between north-eastern and southern Africa, suggesting that there may be some genetic interchange between these regions. To what extent the southern and north-eastern populations were linked in the past is not known. The population associated with the Atlas Mountains appears to be isolated but in the past may have experienced interchange with European birds. Given this vulture's flying abilities it seems likely that movements would have taken place between the Atlas birds and those in the north-east. The Saharan massifs of Haggar and Tibesti seem to be suitable for occupation by this magnificent bird. In the past when great herds of addax, scimitar-horned oryx, gazelles and Barbary sheep roamed these desert areas there would certainly have been no shortage of carrion; sadly these great herds are but a vague memory.

The total African population of the bearded vulture may number 12 500 individuals, with perhaps 120 breeding pairs in South Africa and Lesotho, and the same or an even smaller number occupying the Atlas and environs. The southern population previously extended much further to the west, and breeding was reported in the coastal mountain chain of Western Cape province. In Ethiopia the bearded vulture is common to locally abundant, with records of up to 20 birds occurring together.

| **BEARDED VULTURE** | |
|---|---|
| **Total length** | 1,1 m |
| **Wingspan** | 2,6-2,8 m |
| **Mass** | 5 kg or more |
| **Social structure** | solitary but up to 25 when soaring or at feeding sites; large numbers only in north-east Africa |
| **Breeding** | solitary nests on high cliffs |
| **Number of eggs** | 1-2 |
| **Incubation** | 55-58 days |
| **Diet** | carrion, especially bones |
| **Habitat** | rugged mountains, gorges, cliffs |
| **Number surviving** *meridionalis:* *barbatus:* | about 12 000 maybe below 500 |

Legend: Past distribution / Present distribution

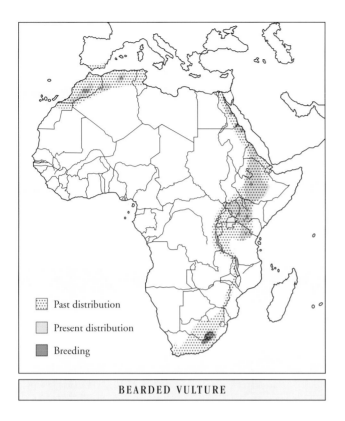

Past distribution

Present distribution

Breeding

**BEARDED VULTURE**

**Above:** *The bearded vulture* (Gypaetus barbatus).

Reasons for the decline of this species in South Africa and Lesotho are not clearly understood but are probably associated with reduced game numbers, changing animal husbandry practices and direct persecution. Unfortunately, this giant of the thermals also has the common name lammergeier, which implies that it is a lamb-catcher, a totally erroneous label that reflects the prejudices of stock farmers, who sometimes still kill it. In Lesotho this vulture is reported to be persecuted for its plumage which is used in certain traditional ceremonies. By contrast, in Ethiopia there is no conflict with the bearded vulture. It is a frequent visitor to village rubbish dumps, particularly immature birds which find it difficult to compete for food because of the high density of territorial adults. What is interesting is that many Ethiopian villagers also encourage the presence of spotted hyaenas, as a valuable means of refuse disposal, whereas elsewhere in Africa they are heavily persecuted.

Although there have been declines in bearded vulture numbers in north-western Africa, little evidence is available that indicates any drastic decline in recent years.

## Cape vulture (griffon)
### *Gyps coprotheres* Ⓡ

The Cape vulture (also called the Cape griffon) is the most intensively studied of any African vulture, in part because most of Africa's ornithologists live within its range, but also because of its scarcity. This raptor is now rare, with an estimated 10 000 birds surviving, including about 2 000 breeding pairs. However, it was once a common sight soaring on the thermals over much of its southern African range. Although no accurate

estimates exist of previous population levels, there may well have been over 100 000 birds.

The Cape vulture is classified as rare on the basis of its precipitous population decline and continuing threats to its long-term survival. In 1982 there were estimated to be between 1 900 and 2 500 breeding pairs, but since that date some small breeding colonies have not been in use and in a few cases there has been a decline at larger colonies. It seems unlikely that many more than 2 500 breeding pairs survive today, with by far the majority – perhaps 75% – occurring in what used to be the Transvaal province of South Africa. Many of this vulture's traditional breeding and roosting cliffs have been abandoned over the last 50 years or so. Today, fewer than 30 breeding sites are in regular use. These include 11 in the former Transvaal, several in Western and Eastern Cape provinces, three in Lesotho and two in the Free State; the remainder are in KwaZulu-Natal. In Botswana, where there are at least two breeding colonies, the Cape vulture has undergone numerous

| CAPE VULTURE (GRIFFON) | |
|---|---|
| **Total length** | up to 1,2 m |
| **Length of wing** | 65-76 cm |
| **Mass** | 7-11 kg |
| **Social structure** | colonial, gregarious |
| **Breeding** | colonial nests on cliffs |
| **Number of eggs** | 1, rarely 2 |
| **Incubation** | 55-58 days |
| **Diet** | carrion, mainly soft tissues |
| **Habitat** | mountains, open plains with hills, gorges |
| **Number surviving** | below 10 000 |

ups and downs. The last estimate for Botswana was about 300 pairs. The largest known colony in that country, and probably the most stable, is in the Tswapong Hills. Lesotho, with an estimated 250 breeding pairs in the mid-1980s, is an important country for this large vulture. There was also a substantial breeding colony of perhaps 200 pairs in southern Mozambique, but because of the recently ended war in that country no up-to-date information is available. The only known breeding colony in Namibia, located in the Waterberg National Park, has declined dramatically since the 1960s. The Cape vulture is believed to be extinct as a breeding species in Zimbabwe.

The dramatic decline in Cape vulture numbers has been ascribed to a number of factors. During a major rinderpest outbreak in 1896 huge numbers of domestic cattle died and it is believed that over the following few years food availability was greatly reduced, causing the vulture population to crash. Numbers picked up again until the early 1960s, but then many vulture colonies started to disappear or decline. Another early problem was the disappearance of the great herds of game that once roamed the plains, and their attendant large predators. In recent decades the tightening of animal husbandry procedures has considerably reduced the number of carcasses available to carrion-eating birds such as the griffons. Direct persecution by means of poisoning carcasses, shooting the birds and disturbance at nesting and roosting colonies has been a long-standing threat.

Chick mortality has increased dramatically, with only an estimated 11% of fledglings reaching the age of four years. One reason is the lower levels of bone fragments being available for the parent birds to feed the chicks, resulting in a calcium shortage and dramatic increase in the incidence of osteodystrophy in the chicks. This causes wing and leg deformities which leave the young birds with no hope of survival.

In several areas vulture restaurants (feeding sites where carcasses are put out) have been established to give the birds regular access to carrion and bone fragments. These restaurants not only serve an important dietary function, they have also proved to be valuable conservation education tools, drawing many members of the public. Being able to observe these birds at close quarters frequently changes attitudes and helps people to recognise the value of these useful "garbage disposers".

Direct and indirect mortality of birds as a result of poison is a persistent problem. Poisoned carcasses are laid out to control predatory species such as the black-backed jackal, but the vultures also eat the poisoned carrion and are killed. Some farmers even deliberately poison these vultures. Although this is decreasing, such incidents, occasionally involving dozens of birds, still occur.

Cape vultures are killed for their body parts, which are used in traditional medicine. They are also vulnerable to electrocution on power lines, although in South Africa mortality from this cause has been greatly reduced by the modification of electricity pylons.

Despite their bad reputation, vultures play an important part in keeping the savanna clear of carcasses.

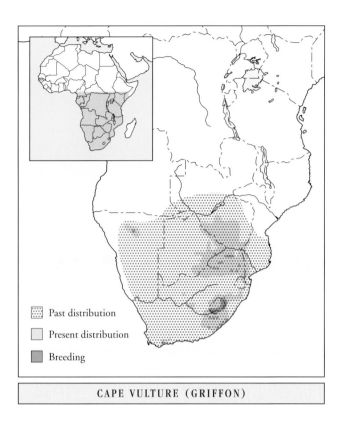

Past distribution
Present distribution
Breeding

**CAPE VULTURE (GRIFFON)**

**Below:** *Cape vulture (griffon)* (Gyps coprotheres).

## Cinereous (black) vulture
### *Aegypius monachus* Ⓔ

This vulture has declined even more precipitously than the Cape vulture. It is endangered in its African range and under serious threat in its European range, but is probably secure in Asia, where it extends as far east as China. It no longer breeds in Africa. Although records are sketchy, it probably did nest in Morocco in the past.

Today the cinereous vulture is a rare winter migrant to north Africa, particularly the north-east.

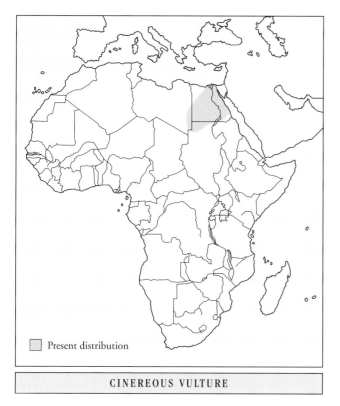

☐ Present distribution

**CINEREOUS VULTURE**

## Imperial eagle
### *Aquila heliaca* Ⓡ

Another species that may have once bred in Morocco and is now only a rare winter migrant, the imperial eagle has seen declines throughout its Palaearctic range. The migrants roughly follow a broad belt along the Nile River, south-eastwards into Ethiopia and as far south as Kenya. The race that follows this migration route is *heliaca* and the bulk of these raptors head no further south than Egypt and the savannas of Sudan. Very few birds enter Morocco today but the few that do are probably of the western race, *adalberti*.

Declines in imperial eagle populations can be ascribed to direct persecution and probably the use of agricultural poisons. Apart from the catastrophic declines undergone within its African range, elsewhere the imperial eagle has also faced shrinkage in numbers and distribution.

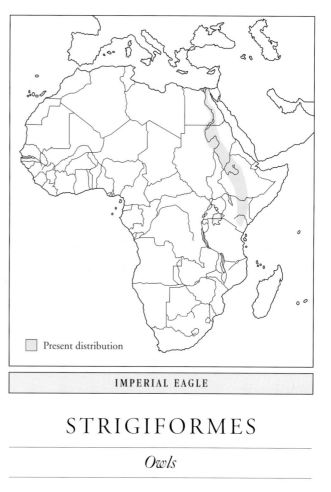

☐ Present distribution

**IMPERIAL EAGLE**

# STRIGIFORMES
## *Owls*

If it is difficult to establish population sizes of diurnal raptors, it is at least doubly difficult to determine numbers of nocturnal birds of prey. Owls, like many diurnal raptors, are vulner-

**Below**: *Although this magnificent raptor, the imperial eagle* (Aquila heliaca) *probably once bred in Morocco, today it only occurs as a non-breeding migrant.* PHOTO: *Jose Luis Gonzalez Grande, Bruce Coleman Ltd.*

able to habitat loss and indirect poisoning. In much of Africa, habitat loss probably has the greatest impact on owl numbers, although it is possible that agricultural poisoning in some areas, such as South Africa, may be reducing breeding success and killing adult birds.

The **Itombwe owl** *(Phodilus prigoginei)* is known from a sin-

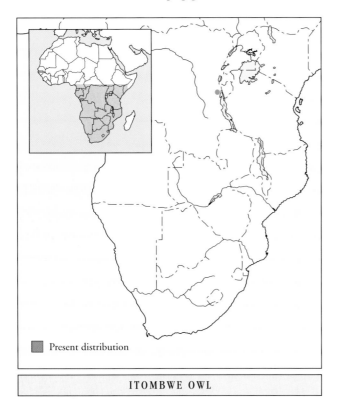

Present distribution

**ITOMBWE OWL**

Present distribution

**SOKOKE SCOPS OWL**

**Above:** *The rufous fishing owl* (Scotopelia ussheri) *is one of three species of fish-hunting owls on the continent and the one with the most restricted distribution.* PHOTO: *Eric & David Hosking, FLPA.*

gle specimen collected in 1951 in montane forest in the Itombwe Mountains of eastern Congo (DR). In the mid-1970s an owl that is believed to have been this species was observed on the Rwegura Tea Estate in Burundi, where it was disturbed from among grass in a forest clearing. How does one categorise a species that is known from a single museum specimen and a probable sighting, and occupies a habitat that precludes easy observation? We have no idea whether it is endangered, rare or merely overlooked.

The **Sokoke scops owl** *(Otus ireneae)* is considered to be endangered on the basis of massive pressure on its forest habitat, despite the fact that an estimated 1 000 breeding pairs occupy the Sokoke Forest close to the Kenyan coast. The first of these scops owls was collected in 1965 and by 1979 a further seven specimens had been obtained. Since then the Sokoke scops has been observed and heard regularly. Of critical importance is the full protection of the 111 sq km core of the forest reserve to which this owl is believed to be restricted, as surrounding areas are being rapidly cleared of trees. What complicates their conservation is that these owls are largely restricted to *Cynometra/Manilkara* forest, where they occur at densities of up to eight pairs per square kilometre.

The **Usambara eagle owl** *(Bubo vosseleri)* also has a very limited distribution. It inhabits probably less than 240 sq km of montane forest at altitudes between 900 m and 1 500 m in the Usambara Mountains in north-eastern Tanzania. Up to 1977 it had been recorded only nine times; a further 10 sightings were made between that year and 1985. Given the difficulties of accurate counting in this owl's chosen habitat, census figures range widely from 200 to 1 000 birds. Although a number of sightings of a similar owl were made in the 1950s in the Nguru Mountains, some 200 km south-west of the Usambaras, there has been no confirmation that this was the same species, nor any sightings since. Destruction of the Usambara forests was

**USAMBARA EAGLE OWL**

**Below:** *Grey-necked picathartes* (Picathartes oreas) *of western Africa.* PHOTO: *Roland Wirth.*

already well underway between 1880 and 1935, and the pace of clearing has increased in recent years, for both timber and space for subsistence agriculture. The already heavy utilisation of most east African forests by people is likely to continue intensifying.

The beautiful **albertine owlet** *(Glaucidium albertinum)* is only known from five specimens collected in lowland and montane forests in eastern Congo (DR) and Rwanda. The first specimen was obtained in 1950. Although forest clearance could pose a risk to this owl, its occurrence in both forest types could indicate that it has a wider distribution than present records show.

The rare **rufous fishing owl** *(Scotopelia ussheri)* occurs in the lowland forest zone to the west of the Dahomey Gap in west Africa. Specimens and sightings are few, and there has been a decrease in records over the past three decades. Fishing owls, of which three species occur in sub-Saharan Africa, are, however, elusive and easily overlooked. Forest destruction in the region has nevertheless almost certainly impacted heavily on this owl.

# MUSCICAPIDAE: TIMALIINAE

*Picathartes*

## White-necked picathartes
*Picathartes gymnocephalus* **V**

## Grey-necked picathartes
*Picathartes oreas* **R**

These two species are closely related. The grey-necked picathartes is also known as the bare-headed rock fowl and bald crow. These birds are something of a taxonomic mystery, having initially being placed with the crows, then with the starlings. At present they are believed to be aberrant babblers but some taxonomists are still baffled and are unhappy with this classification. Whichever group they belong to, they are fascinating birds with several characteristics which separate them from other species.

Both species seem to be restricted to rocky ground and caves below a rainforest canopy, a habitat that is under considerable pressure. However, the white-necked picathartes, at least, may be able to survive where there is a certain level of disturbance and forest modification by humans.

Both species build half-cup mud nests on rock faces, in much the same manner as some swallows and martins; what is particularly interesting is that they construct them within caves or under deep overhangs.

The **white-necked picathartes** occurs patchily in suitable habitat in the Upper Guinea forests from Sierra Leone to Togo. It numbers in the low thousands, principally because of its specialised habitat requirements, but also because of habitat

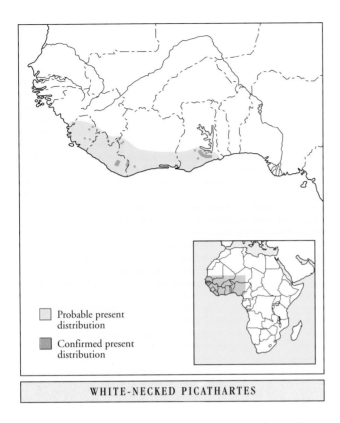

**WHITE-NECKED PICATHARTES**

destruction, hunting for meat in some areas and, to a lesser degree, capture for the illegal trade. It has been suggested that numbers may be higher than thought because its chosen nesting sites are very isolated and easily overlooked.

The **grey-necked picathartes** only occurs in the forests of southern Cameroon, north-eastern Gabon and possibly Rio Muni (Equatorial Guinea). It may be more secure than its western relative. Although it faces similar threats, deforestation is not as severe in this region.

# ALAUDIDAE

## *Larks*

Many African larks have a wide distributional range and are abundant. They are secure in the long term because their habitats are widespread. However, a few species are very restricted and concern has been expressed for their survival. Their apparent rarity may however merely reflect the difficulty of identifying them or of tracing them in the inhospitable environment they inhabit.

The **Degodi lark** *(Mirafra degodiensis)* is only known from two specimens collected in 1971 in the Degodi region of

**Above:** *Botha's lark* (Spizocorys fringillaris) *is a rare South African endemic, restricted to the high altitude grasslands in the east of the country.* PHOTO: *Warwick Tarboton.*

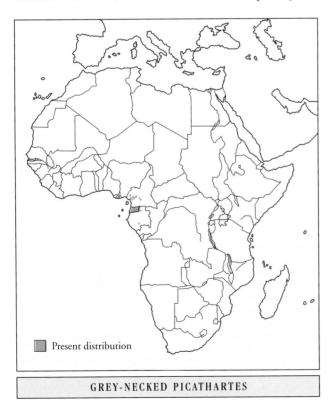

**GREY-NECKED PICATHARTES**

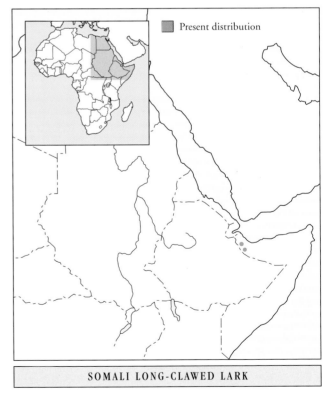

☐ Present distribution

**SOMALI LONG-CLAWED LARK**

southern Ethiopia. We have no knowledge of its total range or requirements.

Ash's lark *(Mirafra ashi)* is known from a single site some 80 km north of the Somali capital Mogadishu, where six specimens were collected. The species may be threatened by habitat changes but its range may be more extensive than is currently believed.

The **Somali long-clawed lark** *(Heteromirafra archeri)* is only known from an area of approximately 200 sq km in north-

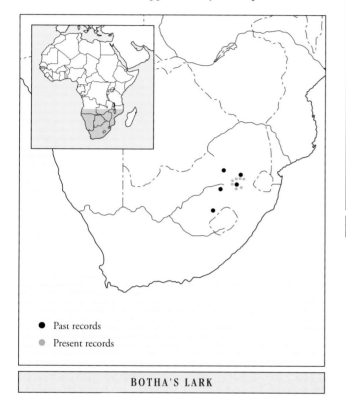

● Past records
● Present records

**BOTHA'S LARK**

western Somalia. The last confirmed record dates from 1955.

The **Sidamo long-clawed lark** *(Heteromirafra sidamoensis)* is only known from two specimens, one collected in 1968 and the other in 1974, in the Sidamo province of Ethiopia.

**Botha's lark** *(Spizocorys fringillaris)* occurs only in high altitude grasslands in central South Africa. Population numbers may be in the low thousands.

# PSITTACIDAE

## *Parrots and others*

The two races of the **African grey parrot** *(Psittacus erithacus)* are entering the pet trade in large numbers. The west African population is of particular concern because of the rapid loss of its favoured habitats.

The **black-cheeked lovebird** *(Agapornis nigrigenis)* is restricted to an area of less than 6 000 sq km in southern Zambia. This small parrot is considered to be rare on the basis of its limited range and infrequent sightings. However, this may merely

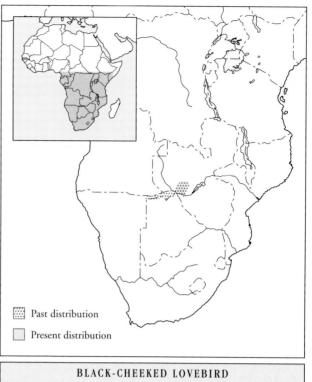

▦ Past distribution
▨ Present distribution

**BLACK-CHEEKED LOVEBIRD**

reflect that its range is extremely difficult of access (we tried!). Human population density is very low in the area, which could account for the few sightings. Certainly the black-cheeked lovebird was more abundant in the past, and in the early decades of this century it was caught in large numbers for the cage-bird trade: some 16 000 in 1929. This lovebird has very specific habitat needs and this seems to be its principal limiting factor.

The other species of African lovebird also enter the pet trade. Although most of them are common to abundant at this stage, it is important that the authorities watch for any dramatic increase in the number of parrots and lovebirds entering the international market, so that appropriate action can be taken in time.

# OTHER GENERA

Rare and deserving of mention are Prince Ruspoli's turaco *(Tauraco ruspolii)*, Schoutedenapus swift *(Schoutedenapus schoutedeni)*, African green broadbill *(Pseudocalyptomena graueri)*, white-tailed swallow *(Hirundo megaensis)* and Monteiro's bush shrike *(Malaconotus monteiri)*. Many other bird species have seen declines in both numbers and range, even though they cannot be considered rare, threatened or endangered in Africa at this stage. There is general concern for those that are restricted to rapidly shrinking forest habitats, pressured wetlands and developing coastlines. Little information is available on a high percentage of the continent's bird species: the question is whether we will have the chance to study them before they fall into the bottomless pit of extinction.

# CHAPTER 9

# REPTILES, AMPHIBIANS & FISH

## *Uncharted waters*

There are such plenty of land tortoises in this isle that
sometimes you can see two or three thousand in one flock, ...

Leguat, 1708

We have considerable gaps in our knowledge of many
African mammals and birds, but our ignorance about
the many hundreds of species of reptiles, amphibians and fish
in Africa is profound. Not only do we know very little about
the biology and behaviour of the vast majority of species, but
even their distribution and conservation status are largely
unknown. There are of course a few exceptions.

One of the most thoroughly surveyed regions of the continent is southern Africa, where most of Africa's herpetologists
and ichthyologists work, but even here new species are constantly being discovered. Seventeen new species of amphibian

**Below:** *Nile crocodile* (Crocodylus niloticus)*, St Lucia, South Africa.*
PHOTO: *Shaen Adey, ABPL.* **Right:** *Nile crocodiles basking.*

were added to the region's inventory in only about 20 years: 12 since 1975, and five which are in the process of being described – and this in a region that has been thoroughly studied! Just think what species remain undiscovered in the tropical lowland forests, the mountain ranges and isolated peaks and the largely unexplored marshes and swamps scattered across the continent.

The fish fauna of some freshwater systems are well known, others less so. In the Congo system more than 700 species are known, but it is estimated that there may be as many as 1 000 species present; they have just not been collected yet!

Some reptile species, such as the marine turtles, are wide

ranging and not restricted to the coastlines of Africa. Others, such as the African rock python *(Python seabae)*, the Nile crocodile *(Crocodylus niloticus)* and a number of small reptiles, have extensive sub-Saharan distributions.

There are also a number of fish species that occur in several drainage systems, for example the sharptooth catfish *(Clarias gariepinus)*, which occurs from the Nile River to the Orange River in South Africa, and the vundu *(Heterobranchus longifilis)*, which has a wide sub-Saharan range, extending from the upper reaches of the Nile in the north-east to the Zambezi in the south.

A number of amphibians occur from southern to east Africa, including the red-backed toad *(Schismaderma carens)* and the banded rubber frog *(Phrynomerus bifasciatus)*. A few amphibians have wide sub-Saharan ranges, for example the bullfrog *(Pyxicephalus adspersus* and *P. edulis)*.

However, it is not the wide-ranging species that are usually of major conservation concern, but those that have limited distributions, particularly animals living in areas most vulnerable to human influences. These influences include land clearing, excessive burning, erosion, cultivation, drainage and direct hunting, either for food or in a few cases for commercial gain. Many areas experience a combination of these factors. The most serious are factors causing habitat degradation and habitat destruction.

Species inventories are available for some African countries, but in most cases they are far from complete. On paper, South Africa has the greatest number of reptiles of any African country, some 301, and more than 100 amphibians, but detailed surveys in other countries would almost certainly result in their

totals exceeding South Africa's. Zimbabwe has been fairly thoroughly surveyed and is known to have 155 reptiles and 120 amphibians. There are at least 191 reptiles and 88 amphibians in Kenya.

Because of the general lack of knowledge about these animals, we discuss only a few species that are, or could be, threatened because of commercial exploitation, or because in their very limited distributional ranges they are suffering habitat destruction or other human influences.

# REPTILES

# CROCODYLIDAE

## *Crocodiles*

Worldwide there are 23 members of the crocodile family. Three occur only in Africa (all belonging to the subfamily Crocodylinae), namely the Nile crocodile *(Crocodylus niloticus)*, the slender-snouted crocodile *(C. cataphractus)* and the dwarf crocodile *(Osteolaemus tetraspis)*.

The name "crocodile" is derived from the Greek *krokodeilos*, which simply means lizard. However, crocodiles are in fact more closely related to birds than to lizards. Crocodiles similar in form and appearance to those of the present first appear in the fossil record some 200 million years ago. From about 65 million years ago, crocodiles have remained virtually unchanged. Their largest known fossil ancestor, *Deinosuchus*, was a massive 11 m in length.

Although crocodiles, particularly the Nile crocodile, have been heavily persecuted, notably over the last 100 years or so, they have been venerated by some peoples. The ancient Egyptians believed the crocodile to be the son of Neith, one of the goddesses, and named it Sobek, also spelled Souchos. During the annual flooding of the Nile River, when great quantities of riverborne silt were deposited on the banks and

|  | NILE | SLENDER-SNOUTED | DWARF |
|---|---|---|---|
| **Total length** | 2,5-3,5 m | 3-4 m | below 2 m |
| **Number of eggs** | 50-60 | 13-27 | over 10 |
| **Incubation** | 80-90 days | unknown | 100 days |
| **Diet** | varies with age: mainly fish | fish, crustaceans, frogs | fish, crabs, frogs |
| **Skin value** | high | quite high | low |
| **Number of countries in which it occurs** | 40 | 24 | 20 |

replenished the soil for the following harvest, large numbers of crocodiles would also appear. The Egyptians associated their appearance with the life-giving silt and by 2 400 BC the crocodile god Sobek had risen to the ranks of the great gods. Murals depicting Sobek with a human body and the head of a crocodile are abundant in the temples and tombs of the region. Crocodiles were kept at several temples venerating Sobek, including the major centre of crocodile worship, Crocodilopolis in the Fayoum. As the ancient Egyptians did with many creatures, they mummified many thousands of crocodiles. Excavations have revealed these mummies stacked like woodpiles at some sites.

Several tribes in sub-Saharan Africa treat crocodiles with great respect, and some worship them, but others see them as messengers of evil.

Crocodiles are keystone species in that their activities help to maintain the health of the aquatic ecosystems in which they occur, for example their selective predation on certain fish species, and their role in the recycling of nutrients. Crocodiles are highly efficient predators and large individuals readily prey on land-based mammals, including humans, when the opportunity presents itself. Between 10 and 15 people are killed by crocodiles each year in Malawi, for example.

It is unlikely that any of the three crocodiles will become threatened with extinction over their entire ranges within the next 100 years, but local extinctions and reductions in numbers can be expected to escalate, particularly in those regions with high human population densities.

# Nile crocodile
## *Crocodylus niloticus* Ⓥ

This is the largest, most widespread and abundant of Africa's three crocodile species, yet numbers have decreased greatly over much of its range. Nile crocodiles occupy a wide variety of aquatic habitats, including rivers, lakes, swamps, estuaries and mangrove swamps. In some areas they cross short stretches of sea to reefs and offshore islands. This is the only African species that has been studied in any detail, particularly as regards diet and reproduction.

Although the building of large dams across major river systems has proved harmful to many creatures, this has frequently been of benefit to crocodiles. In historical times the crocodile occurred along the entire length of the Nile River, including the delta, but the last animals in the Egyptian Nile had been wiped out at the beginning of this century. After the building of the Aswan Dam in southern Egypt, however, crocodiles returned to the area. In January 1989 a 2,4 m specimen died in fishing nets in Lake Nasser. Reports from Ghana indicate that populations of all three crocodile species have increased since the building of a dam wall across the Volta River. Natural mortality of crocodile eggs and hatchlings in their first year can be as high as 90%. They are eaten by monitor lizards, several mongoose species, baboons, marabou storks, large terrapins, fish and some other predators.

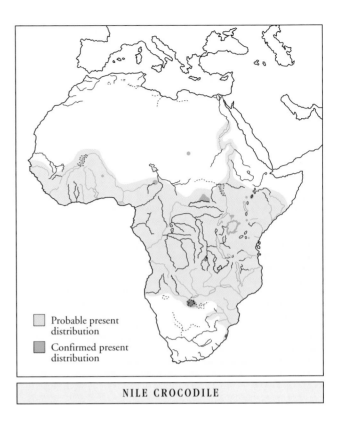

| | |
|---|---|
| ▢ | Probable present distribution |
| ▨ | Confirmed present distribution |

**NILE CROCODILE**

Although crocodiles had been hunted for many centuries, either as a source of food and medicines or in defence, this probably had little impact on their numbers until the 19th and 20th centuries. With the advent of modern firearms, large-scale slaughter of crocodiles began. Initially crocodiles were mainly shot in eradication programmes, but by the 1930s there was some commercial hunting for their belly skins, which produce fine leather. This hunting swung into top gear after the Second World War and by the mid-1950s almost 60 000 skins per year were exported from east Africa. Between 1956 and 1977 a South African tannery purchased about 40 000 skins from Botswana. The actual number of skins exported from Africa is unknown but the figure is certainly in the hundreds of thousands. Limited hunting under licence is still permitted in a few countries that hold viable crocodile populations, but there is some illegal hunting throughout the crocodile's range.

In some regions, such as Ethiopia, loss of nesting sites along the banks of rivers and other water bodies as a result of high human densities is even more significant than direct persecution in reducing crocodile numbers.

The Nile crocodile has become extinct in four countries and in a further 19 its numbers are known to have declined. Its status is unknown in a further 19 countries; in some of these, at least, it is certain that numbers have decreased. We have little or no information on the present distribution and status of this reptile in some 25 of the 40 countries within its range.

Counting crocodiles is a difficult task and estimates are available for only a few countries. The total population in northern Botswana, the only part of the country with crocodile habitat, is believed to be between 9 000 and 10 000.

Estimates for other countries vary considerably: for eastern Central African Republic from 5 500 to 16 500, for Congo from 4 000 to 13 000, and for Malawi from 8 000 to 15 000. Most of these figures are pure guesswork. In Sudan there were reported to be as many as one million crocodiles in 1975, but even though there are many suitable areas in southern Sudan, this figure seems unrealistic, as the total for the whole of Africa is probably well below a million. One of the most accurate estimates – some 8 500 – is for South Africa, where the majority of crocodiles are restricted to conservation areas in the far east of the country. The large population in Zimbabwe, concentrated along the Zambezi River in the north, is believed to total some 50 000 individuals. One of the largest populations live in Tanzania. Total figures are not known but some 5 000 crocodiles are believed to inhabit Lake Rukwa in the south-west of the country.

The establishment of crocodile farms, particularly in Zimbabwe and South Africa, has resulted in decreased pressure on wild populations but depressed skin prices may affect the commercial viability of some farms.

## Slender-snouted crocodile
### *Crocodylus cataphractus* **V**

This large crocodile occurs widely through west and central Africa, where it is mostly associated with well-vegetated water courses in lowland forest. Small populations are recorded in coastal lagoons. It occurs as far south as north-eastern Zambia, where it is very rare. It is present in Lake Tanganyika. The largest known population lives along the Ogoue River in Gabon. Its estimated size is 90 000 crocodiles but the true figure is probably much lower. Congo has a fairly substantial

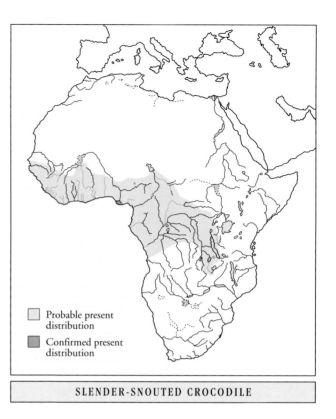

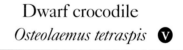

SLENDER-SNOUTED CROCODILE

Probable present distribution

Confirmed present distribution

population of between 15 000 and 45 000. This country is an important refuge for many species because of its still relatively undisturbed forests and very low human population.

Although the slender-snouted crocodile is known to have declined in numbers and range in at least nine countries, its status in much of its range is unknown. Although it is hunted for its belly skin, this has not been as intense as hunting of the Nile crocodile. It is also hunted for meat for local consumption. Destruction of riverside vegetation reduces cover and could be detrimental to this crocodile's nesting success.

## Dwarf crocodile
### *Osteolaemus tetraspis* **V**

This is the smallest and least known of the three African crocodiles. Two subspecies have been recognised but their validity is doubtful. The dwarf crocodile has a similar range to the slender-snouted crocodile but does not extend as far south-east. It shows a marked preference for slow-moving rivers and static water bodies in lowland forest and swamp forest. It is also known to occur in some coastal lagoons. It has been recorded in pools in savanna areas but this appears to be exceptional. This crocodile moves around extensively on land at night in forested areas, particularly after rain.

No population estimates have been made for any of the 20 countries in which it is known to occur but numbers are believed to have declined in most. In some areas the dwarf crocodile is hunted for its meat. The destruction of habitats, particularly in west Africa, is the most significant factor causing population declines.

**Top:** *African slender-snouted crocodile* (Crocodylus cataphractus).
**Above:** *Dwarf crocodile* (Osteolaemus tetraspis).

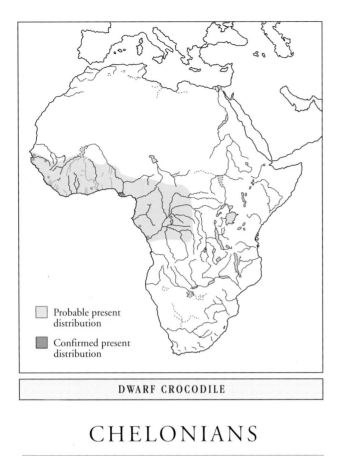

Probable present distribution

Confirmed present distribution

**DWARF CROCODILE**

# CHELONIANS

*Turtles, terrapins and tortoises*

Five species of marine turtle, at least 25 species of freshwater terrapins and turtles, and 23 species of land tortoise occur on the African continent and associated islands within the Afrotropical Realm. They range in size from the leatherback turtle (*Dermochelys coriacea*), which tips the scales at more than 600 kg and is 1,7 m long, to the diminutive Egyptian tortoise (*Testudo kleinmanni*), which is no more than 200 g and 10 cm.

Marine turtles, as their name implies, occupy the oceans and seas around the African continent. Some live close to shore while others frequent more open waters, but all females must come ashore to lay their eggs. Freshwater turtles occupy rivers, lakes, swamps, temporary pools and inundated floodplains, as well as estuaries. Land tortoises range from desert to savanna, dry forest to rocky hills.

Although a number of the freshwater turtles or terrapins have apparently limited distribution ranges, none is known to be generally threatened, although in some areas they form part of people's diet.

At least seven species of giant tortoise once roamed the islands of the western Indian Ocean. Some had carapace lengths exceeding 1 m and a mass of several hundred kilograms. The largest specimens today are below 130 kg in mass. In earlier centuries giant tortoises were heavily utilised as a source of meat, particularly by ships passing the small islands on which they lived. Even though they occurred in vast numbers, their populations were rapidly depleted.

After the arrival of the first human colonisers on the island of Madagascar, two species of giant tortoise became extinct there, even before their cousins on the smaller Indian Ocean islands. The sole surviving species, the **Aldabran giant tortoise** (*Geochelone gigantea*), is still abundant: about 150 000 individuals. Several thousand have been translocated from their

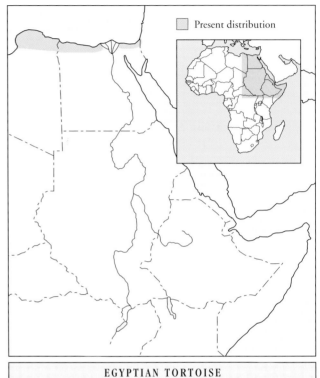

Present distribution

**EGYPTIAN TORTOISE**

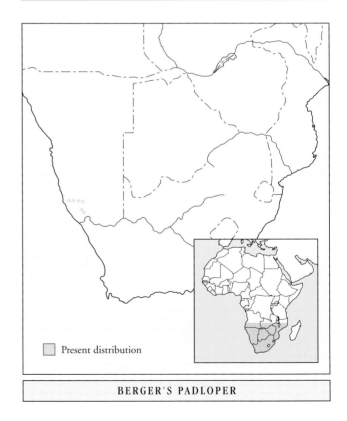

Present distribution

**BERGER'S PADLOPER**

native Aldabra to a number of other islands in the Seychelles, including Moyenne, Frégate, Curieuse and Cousin. This is the largest of all land tortoises in the Afro-tropical Realm.

The **Réunion Island giant tortoise** *(G. indica)* was first discovered in 1611 but by 1773 it was extinct. One farmer, at the beginning of the 1700s, used the meat from about 40 000 of these tortoises to feed his pigs!

In 1691 the **Rodriguez tortoise** *(G. peltastes)* was described by Leguat (written in 1708) as follows:

> *There are such plenty of land tortoises in this isle that sometimes you see two or three thousand in one flock, so that you may go above a hundred paces on their back.*

**Vosmaer's giant tortoise** *(G. vosmaeri)*, which also lived on Rodriguez Island, had more than 30 000 of its number exported to Mauritius over an 18-month period in the late 1750s.

The **Mauritius tortoise** *(G. inepta)* was extinct by 1894.

Although people were directly responsible for the demise of many giant tortoises, the pigs, dogs, cats and rats people transported with them to the islands contributed greatly to the tortoises' extinction by destroying countless eggs and hatchlings. At present there is little threat to the giant tortoise, although some are entering the pet trade both legally and illegally.

Four species of other tortoise occur on the island of

**Above:** *Spurred tortoise* (Geochelone sulcata) *of the Sahel.*
**Below:** *The rare Egyptian tortoise* (Testudo kleinmanni).

Madagascar. One, the **ploughshare tortoise** *(G. yniphora)*, is classified as endangered. No more than 400 survive in a total area of suitable habitat measuring less than 100 sq km.

The **spurred tortoise** *(G. sulcata)* is Africa's largest mainland tortoise, with a maximum carapace length of 83 cm and a mass exceeding 60 kg: the record is 105 kg. It occurs in the Sahelian belt, sandwiched between the Sahara in the north and the higher rainfall savannas to the south, from the Atlantic coast of Mauritania to the Red Sea in Eritrea. Despite its extensive range it apparently occurs at very low densities. It is not known whether the spurred tortoise has been adversely affected by the extended droughts and the increasing levels of habitat modification in its range in recent decades.

Two species of tortoise occur along the Mediterranean seaboard of north Africa. The **Egyptian tortoise** *(Testudo kleinmanni)* is tiny: average length is 10 cm and mass 200 g. It is limited to a 60 km wide belt in Egypt and occurs marginally in Libya and Israel. Because of its limited range this tortoise is considered to be vulnerable. The **spur-thighed tortoise** *(T. graeca graeca)* occurs from Morocco to Libya. A number of other spur-thighed tortoise subspecies occur on the Eurasian continent. This tortoise was heavily exploited up to the 1970s for the European pet trade, but numbers traded have now dropped considerably.

Several tortoise species, notably the **Natal hinged tortoise** *(Kinixys natalensis)* of southern Africa and **Home's hinged tortoise** *(K. homeana)* of the lowland forests of west Africa, are threatened by habitat destruction. In west Africa tortoises are also eaten by local people.

In southern Africa there are a number of small tortoise species occurring in arid and semi-arid habitats with ranges limited to a few thousand square kilometres, but indications are that they are not under any particular threat. A number of

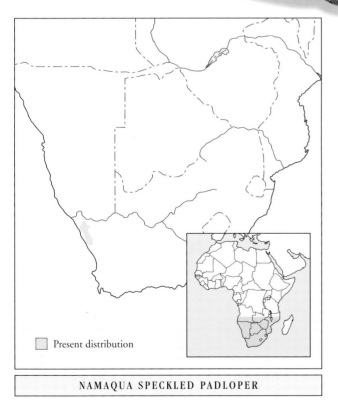

NAMAQUA SPECKLED PADLOPER

Present distribution

species, including **Berger's padloper** *(Homopus bergeri)* of south-western Namibia, and the **Namaqua speckled padloper** *(H. signatus)* of extreme north-western South Africa, have somewhat flattened carapaces and occupy rocky habitats where they seek shelter in crevices and cracks.

# Geometric tortoise
## *Psammobates geometricus* Ⓔ

This is the one endangered tortoise species on the African mainland. The beautifully marked geometric tortoise is only found in the extreme south-west of Western Cape province (South Africa) in a few remnant patches of low-lying "renosterveld" (low scrub vegetation).

Although the geometric tortoise is protected in several provincial government reserves, by far the majority of these tortoises occur on one privately owned nature reserve. This could present long-term conservation problems.

Its favoured habitat was once much more extensive but most areas have been put to the plough or modified in other ways. Habitat destruction remains by far the greatest threat throughout its very limited range. Factors such as the frequent burning of the vegetation in tortoise areas could also be detrimental, as well as infestation of its habitat by aggressive exotic plants that displace indigenous species, particularly after fire.

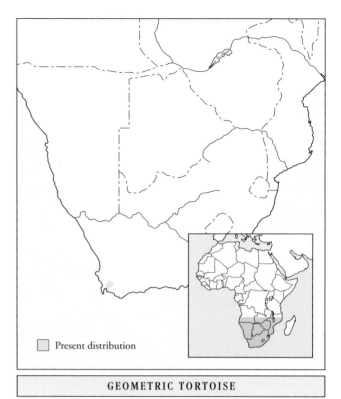

☐ Present distribution

**GEOMETRIC TORTOISE**

### GEOMETRIC TORTOISE

| | |
|---|---|
| **Total length** | ♂ 100 mm; ♀ 125 mm |
| **Mass** | ♂ 200 g; ♀ 430 g |
| **Sexual maturity** | 7-8 years |
| **Breeding** | September-November |
| **Number of eggs** | 2-8 |
| **Hatchling mass** | 6-8 g |
| **Life span (wild)** | over 30 years |
| **Number surviving** | maybe below 7 000 |

# Pancake tortoise
## *Malacochersus tornieri* Ⓥ

The small pancake tortoise, sometimes called the soft-shell tortoise, has a flattened carapace, which enables it to enter the shelter of rock crevices. This unusual tortoise is sparsely distributed from the northern edge of the Samburu District in central Kenya southwards into central Tanzania, with a few isolated populations in the south of the country. It is restricted to hill country with rocky outcrops, in low rainfall areas at altitudes ranging from 30 m to 1 800 m. In the past, large numbers of these tortoises were exported from Kenya for the international pet trade, and such exports still continue today from Tanzania.

### PANCAKE TORTOISE

| | |
|---|---|
| **Total length** | 15-17 cm |
| **Total height** | 4 cm |
| **Breeding** | July-August |
| **Number of eggs** | 2 |
| **Incubation** | 113-221 days |
| **Diet** | variety of plants |

*Below:* The pancake tortoise (Malacochersus tornieri) *is highly adapted for retreating into crevices, with its dorso-ventrally flattened carapace. Unfortunately its unusual form makes it popular in the illegal pet-trade.*

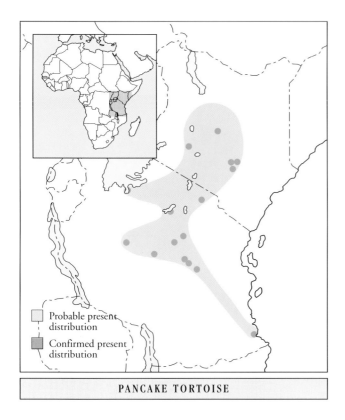

**PANCAKE TORTOISE**

# Marine turtles

Of the eight species of marine turtle occurring worldwide, six have been recorded on African shores. One is a very rare vagrant to the north-west. The remaining five species all breed on African mainland beaches or on islands in the Afro-tropical Realm, principally in the Indian Ocean. These five species also nest widely in other tropical and subtropical areas. They are the **leatherback turtle** *(Dermochelys coriacea)*, which is the largest, with a length of 1,3 m to 1,7 m; the **loggerhead turtle** *(Caretta caretta)* at 70 cm to 1 m; the **olive ridley turtle** *(Lepidochelys olivacea)* reaching some 65 cm; the **hawksbill turtle** *(Eretmochelys imbricata)* at 60 cm to 90 cm, and the **green turtle** *(Chelonia mydas)* reaching 1,4 m.

Rookeries (as turtle breeding sites are called) of most species in Africa are known to involve relatively small numbers of turtles. Although a few of these nesting sites fall within protected areas, most are on unprotected beaches. Here many of the eggs are harvested by people and some females are killed as a source of meat. Turtles are also accidentally and deliberately caught in fishing nets.

Rookeries in KwaZulu-Natal province (South Africa) are the most southerly for leatherback and loggerhead turtles. This stretch of coast is one of the best protected for marine turtles in Africa and numbers of nesting females have increased steadily since the area was protected. The most southerly rookery of the olive ridley turtle is on the northern Mozambique coast.

Important rookeries for the hawksbill turtle are in north-eastern Madagascar and on the Mascarene Islands. Apart from being hunted as a source of food, the hawksbill was heavily

**Above:** *Although marine turtles spend virtually their entire lives in the ocean, adult females beach to dig nests and lay their eggs, as this loggerhead turtle* (Caretta caretta) *is doing.* PHOTO: *George Hughes.*

persecuted for its particularly beautiful scutes. The Japanese market absorbed an average of 31 000 turtle shells each year, at prices of about US $375 per shell, until this trade was banned in the late 1980s. The shells were used primarily for the manufacture of combs and jewellery.

One of the biggest green turtle rookeries, with between 4 000 and 9 000 females coming ashore to lay their eggs every year, is on Europa Island in the Mozambique Channel. Other important sites are on the Comoros Islands. It has been estimated that there may be as many as 100 000 adult green turtles in the south-western Indian Ocean, but this is difficult to verify. Although all species are hunted for food, in the past the green turtle was particularly sought after. An expensive soup was made from its green-coloured fat.

# LIZARDS & SNAKES

There are hundreds of species of lizard and snake on the African continent and associated islands. Although some are threatened by loss of habitat, or caught for the pet trade, or affected by agricultural poisons and other factors, very few can be described as endangered.

Some of the most threatened lizards and snakes occur on islands in the Afro-tropical Realm. Most species known to have become extinct within this realm inhabited islands. These include the **giant day gecko** *(Phelsuma gigas)*, which was said to reach a total length of almost 38 cm. It occurred on Rodriguez Island and Frégate in the Mascarenes. It was first discovered in 1691, when it was said to be common, but it is believed to have become extinct by 1874. Introduced rats were probably responsible for its demise.

The **Réunion skink** *(Gongylomorphus bojeri borbonica)* is believed to be now extinct, as is the **Cape Verde giant skink** *(Macroscincus coctei)*, which has not been seen since 1913.

**Above:** *One of several recently described species, Smith's dwarf chameleon* (Bradypodion taeniabronchum) *has a very limited distribution.* PHOTO: *Duncan Butchart, African Images.*

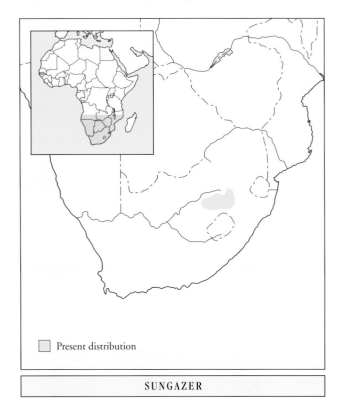

Present distribution

**SUNGAZER**

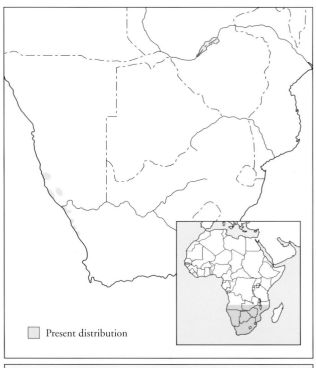

Present distribution

**NAMAQUA DWARF ADDER**

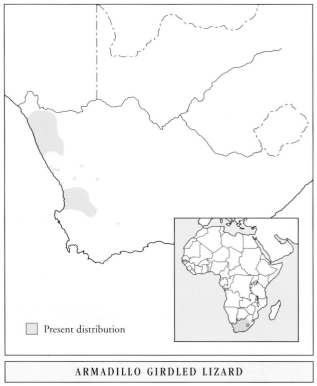

Present distribution

**ARMADILLO GIRDLED LIZARD**

One mainland species, **Eastwood's longtailed seps** *(Tetradactylus eastwoodae)*, which is known from just two specimens collected in northern South Africa more than 80 years ago, is believed to be extinct. A number of other species have also not been encountered since their initial discovery. Although this may indicate extinction, it could merely mean that further collecting has not been undertaken in the area, that later collectors visited the area in a different season or when other conditions prevailed, and so forth.

The only South African lizard known to be endangered, **Smith's dwarf chameleon** *(Bradypodion taeniabronchum)*, is restricted to part of one mountain. Only two specimens were collected from before 1831 to 1980, but further specimens have since been collected. In other regions of Africa there are

numerous lizard species restricted to a single area on one mountain, to isolated outcrops or to tiny forest patches.

Not all is gloom and doom, however, as the conservation effort to save the **sungazer** or giant girdled lizard *(Cordylus giganteus)* indicates. This is the largest of the cordylid species, reaching 40 cm. It is restricted to the interior grassland plateau of South Africa, usually referred to as the Highveld. Much of this area has been put to the plough and in place of natural vegetation one sees great swathes of maize, sorghum and sunflowers, which are drenched in millions of litres of agricultural poisons every year. The sungazer, living in self-excavated burrows, had been unable to withstand this onslaught of habitat loss and the poisoning of its insect prey. Several efforts were made to translocate isolated and scattered populations to suitable protected areas. The most successful translocation was to an unlikely site, a 400 ha nature reserve surrounding the Majuba power station. This now houses one of the largest known populations of this magnificent lizard, with more than 1 500 burrows. To implement similar programmes for other species whose behaviour allows for it, is a partial solution to species conservation. However, there is no substitute for conserving entire systems together with their species.

Areas of concern are those where extensive surface mining is taking place. This has a negative impact on not only reptiles and amphibians but on all other biota as well. Continuing mining activities on Mount Nimba in west Africa, a location with a number of endemic species, have resulted in

**Below:** *The true giant of the amphibian world, the goliath frog* (Conrana goliath). *Because of its large size it is readily sought after for the "bush meat" trade.* PHOTO: *Daniel Heuclin, NHPA.*

massive habitat loss. The activities of alluvial diamond mining companies in the coastal sands of south-western Namibia and north-western South Africa are of considerable concern as there are several species of reptile and one amphibian restricted to this belt. Habitat destruction is massive in some parts and will undoubtedly worsen in the future.

One of the species restricted to this habitat is the smallest known viperine snake, the **Namaqua dwarf adder** *(Bitis schneideri)*, which reaches an average length of 20 cm and a maximum of 30 cm. The adder is classified as vulnerable, but a classification of endangered would probably be more correct, as its situation is likely to deteriorate further. An additional cause for concern is the number of these tiny snakes entering the illegal pet trade, even though the chances of successfully breeding this snake in captivity are small because of the difficulty of feeding the minute youngsters. Another species restricted to this habitat is the **desert rain frog** *(Breviceps macrops)*.

It is difficult to obtain accurate information on the illegal pet trade, but other attractive species, apart from the Namaqua dwarf adder, are known to be traded. They include several of the larger geckos and other lizards, and the vulnerable **armadillo girdled lizard** *(Cordylus cataphractus)*. This attractive, heavily armoured lizard is restricted to the far western areas of South Africa. It is popular in the illegal pet trade, although numbers collected and exported are unknown. This species is not threatened to any great extent by habitat changes.

## AMPHIBIANS

African amphibians range in size from the truly giant goliath frog *(Conrana goliath)*, with a mass of several kilograms, to the minute micro frog *(Microbatrachella capensis)*, which reaches a maximum of a few grams. Many species have wide distributional ranges but many more are restricted to tiny areas, which may consist of just a few pools or a tiny patch of rainforest on a mountain slope. Some are fully aquatic, some only enter water to breed, others never enter water. Many species live in the continent's highest rainfall zones, and a few have overcome the problems of surviving in regions that receive nothing but scant seasonal rains.

Many amphibians, like many reptiles, are known from only one, or just a few, specimens. The following are examples of species, each of which is only known from a single locality: four species of caecilians (legless, burrowing amphibians) endemic to Cameroon; 10 of the 30 amphibian species en-

Present distribution

**DESERT RAIN FROG**

demic to Ethiopia; the remarkable viviparous toad *(Necto-phrynoides occidentalis)* from forests on the slopes of Mount Nimba in Ivory Coast and Guinea; the toad *Schoutedenella milletihorsini,* which is restricted to Bata Pool, Sahel de Nioro, in Mali; 11 of the 40 endemic amphibian species in Tanzania, of which most are associated with vulnerable forest pockets; and 16 of the 51 endemic amphibians in Congo (DR). The list goes on and on and many other species could be cited.

Beyond the boundaries of South Africa little has been documented on the decline of any amphibian species. Certain taxa, particularly those occurring in areas undergoing drastic habitat modification, are however known or presumed to be declining.

The examples we discuss below are from the south-western tip of Africa, an area that has been greatly influenced by agricultural and urban development, infestation by exotic vegetation, and pollution.

Within a radius of just a few kilometres from the city of Cape Town, South Africa, there are three species of endangered frog, and several more that are considered to be vulnerable or rare as a direct result of the actions of humans. The decline in these frog populations is fairly well documented but there are still many unanswered questions.

By contrast, the situation in many other parts of Africa is poorly documented, if at all. There are probably many species still to be discovered, and some of those may well disappear before they are documented. In Africa it is virtually impossible to establish the true status of all, or even most, amphibian populations. We lack even the most basic knowledge about them. What we do know, is that frogs are sensitive environmental indicators, and the sharp downward trend in frog numbers worldwide is cause for alarm.

## Table Mountain ghost frog
### *Heleophryne rosei* Ⓔ

This frog inhabits steep, forested mountain streams at only nine known locations on Table Mountain, above the urban sprawl of Cape Town. The adult frog has large friction pads on the broad tips of its fingers and toes as an aid to holding onto rocks in the fast-flowing streams. The tadpoles have large,

**Above:** *Table Mountain ghost frog* (Heleophryne rosei).
Photo: *Atherton de Villiers.*

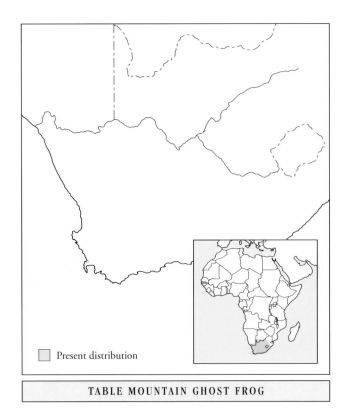

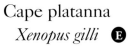

TABLE MOUNTAIN GHOST FROG

☐ Present distribution

sucker-like mouths which allow them to grip firmly onto the rocks while feeding on algae. The building, in the early part of this century, of five reservoirs in streams presumed to be suitable ghost frog habitat could have reduced populations. Invasions of alien plants probably constitute the greatest threat to these frogs. These exotics, including established plantation species, make the habitat less suitable for the frogs, primarily by reducing water flow. Although no population decline is obvious at present, the very restricted area occupied by this species makes it highly vulnerable to even minor influences.

## Cape platanna
### *Xenopus gilli* Ⓔ

This small (below 6 cm), aquatic frog has been assaulted on several fronts. It has lost extensive areas of its former, already limited range in the vicinity of Cape Town to urban sprawl. It has also suffered the draining of wetlands, the alteration of natural drainage systems and the spread of aggressive alien vegetation which disrupts the water balance. Apart from these man-made influences it is seriously threatened by hybridisation with the abundant common platanna *(X. laevis).*

Viable Cape platanna populations are only known from a few locations between Cape Town and Africa's most southerly point, Cape Agulhas. A population of some 1 000 adults lives in a few acidic ponds in the Cape Point Nature Reserve, but only two ponds are free of the common platanna. Common platanna adults and tadpoles are regularly removed from the reserve, and this is probably the only area where the Cape platanna could survive in the long term.

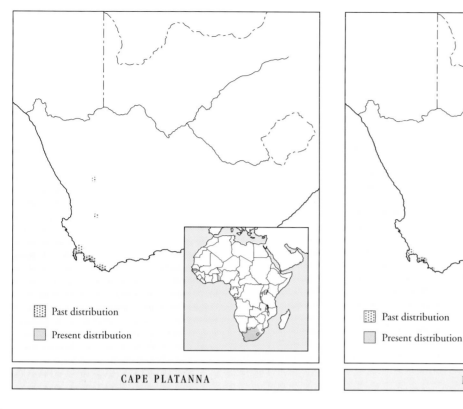

CAPE PLATANNA

MICRO FROG

## Micro frog
### *Microbatrachella capensis* Ⓔ

This tiny frog (below 1,8 cm) had a similar distribution to the Cape platanna. It has also disappeared from the immediate vicinity of Cape Town and is now only found at a few isolated sites along the coast, south-eastwards from Cape Town.

Loss and modification of habitat have been the major causes of its decline. Another reason is the regular burning of vegetation around the shallow, seasonal pans in which the micro frog breeds. Its original collection site on the Cape Flats now forms part of suburban Cape Town and the micro frog no longer occurs here. At present it is known from some 20 locations, but a number of these are threatened by coastal development and dense stands of alien tree species, which lower the water table. At a few locations micro frogs are nevertheless abundant. There has been at least one record of micro frogs calling in their thousands! Their very localised distribution however means that entire populations can easily be wiped out by habitat loss or habitat alteration.

## FRESHWATER FISH

Threats to fish include the effects of dam construction, the introduction of exotic fish species into waters with endemics, pollution and the perennial problem of habitat degradation and habitat loss.

Only a minute proportion of all African fish species has been studied in any detail. Some freshwater fish populations have received attention from scientists because of their commercial value, primarily as a source of protein, or because of their value for angling or the aquarium trade. A few species (mainly in South Africa) have been studied because of their threatened status or general interest. The fish fauna inhabiting some river systems have been fairly well surveyed, but the species in others, such as the Congo, are still poorly Congo: the number of species present is uncertain. In the Congo River catchment we know of at least 700 species, but scientists expect that a further 300 species, as yet undescribed, also occur in these waters. This total excludes the vast cichlid species complex that occurs in the waters of Lake Tanganyika, which falls within the area drained by the Congo.

We have virtually no knowledge of the conservation status of African fishes, with a few exceptions. All we can do in this section is to cover a few of those exceptions in order to illustrate the problems faced by fish on the African continent. We look below at the endangered species in the Olifants River in Western Cape province (South Africa) and the cichlid fishes of the Great Rift Valley lakes, particularly Lake Victoria, and give an overview of what is happening in some of the west African river systems.

Some fish are threatened simply by their very restricted distribution, for example the **cave catfish** *(Clarias cavernicola)*, which is classified as endangered. This small catfish (up to 16 cm) is only known from a small lake in the Aigamas Cave in northern Namibia, where it feeds on bat droppings and items falling into the water. Because of its troglodytic existence it has lost the use of its eyes and it lacks pigmentation. A major depletion of ground water poses a serious threat to its long-term survival.

Barombi Mbo, a crater lake situated within the rainforest of south-west Cameroon, has a diameter of 2,5 km and a maximum depth of 110 m. Such small water bodies are particularly vulnerable to changes that can threaten not only the fish populations but also all other organisms. Twelve of the 17 species of fish living in the lake are endemic to it, and most are threatened by overfishing, dam construction hampering water flow, deforestation leading to increased siltation, agrochemicals and increases in the human population using the lake: the common threats affecting most African fish populations. One endemic species, the cichlid *Stomatepia mongo*, is possibly extinct, although it may live in deep water and has therefore not recently been caught by fishermen. Another species in the lake, the **pungu** *(Pungu maclareni)*, is believed to number only a few thousand individuals.

Dangers to fish populations are not restricted to small water bodies, however. Africa's largest lake, Victoria, as well as major and smaller river systems and floodplains are all threatened to a greater or lesser extent. Traditional fishing techniques are still in use in many areas but gill nets, usually with small mesh, are increasingly used and have had a devastating impact in many rivers and lakes.

Dam construction may benefit certain fish species but others decline as a result of it, not only in the impoundment itself but also downstream of the wall, where water flow usually decreases. Dam building can also have serious consequences for floodplains, which are of prime importance as feeding and spawning grounds for a great number of fish species. Changes in river flow due to dam construction cause fish species that rely heavily on seasonal floodplains to be largely replaced by other fish that are not so relient on them, such as barbel *(Clarias* spp.). Studies undertaken on the Benue River in Nigeria have shown that the combination of dam construction, prolonged drought and overfishing resulted in drastic changes in the composition of the river's fish fauna. One species, *Hepsetus adoe*, is now considered to be commercially extinct (meaning there are no longer enough to catch commercially), and other once abundant species have declined.

## The greatest mass extinction in modern times

The African great lakes, Victoria, Tanganyika and Malawi, are treasure troves of fish diversity and evolution, particularly fish of the cichlid group.

Sadly, this statement today is only true of Lakes Tanganyika and Malawi, as Victoria has experienced the greatest and most catastrophic mass extinction of vertebrates ever observed by scientists. There were more than 300 fish species in Lake Victoria in the early 1970s, more than half of which were described for the first time during that decade. Today more than 90% of those species are known, or believed, to be extinct. An evolutionary miracle has been wiped out in just a few years. The continuing devastation is starkly obvious in the *Red data book of endangered species* (1988), which lists scores of

the remaining endemic fish species occurring in Lake Victoria under one ominous heading: endangered.

Apart from its great evolutionary value, Lake Victoria was, and still is, home to major subsistence and commercial fishing operations. But whereas fishing once yielded hundreds of species, the bulk is now made up of three species. How could such a diverse fauna have been brought to this appalling state, and 14 000 years of amazing speciation have been wiped out in only a few decades?

The cause was a combination of factors, not least of which being that more than 30 million people are wholly or partly dependent on the lake for food. The first negative impact on the lake's fishes was therefore overexploitation. However, the introduction of species exotic to the system has been the most damaging. A number of tilapia species were introduced into the lake in the late 1950s to take the place of the heavily exploited endemics. Only one, *Oreochromis esculentus*, soon established itself successfully. Apart from competing with the endemic fish, it also interbred with a number of species. The real problem, however, was the release of Nile perch *(Lates niloticus)* into Victoria in 1954. For almost 30 years this species survived at low densities and had little effect on the fauna of the lake. Then, in the early 1980s, the Nile perch populations began to grow at an explosive rate. They devastated indigenous fish species by preying on them and outcompeting them for the available food. Today some 200 000 tons of Nile perch are caught each year: a valuable commercial harvest mostly sold far away from the lake.

The recent civil war in Rwanda caused thousands of human bodies to be washed into the lake. This has greatly reduced perch sales – people refuse to buy fish that they believe had fed

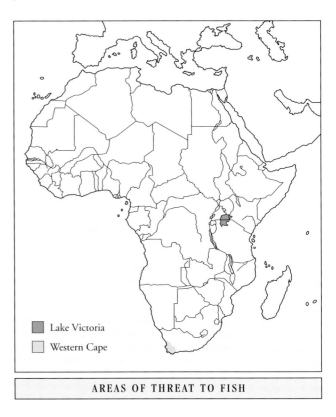

Lake Victoria

Western Cape

**AREAS OF THREAT TO FISH**

on human flesh – and it could take considerable time before sales pick up again.

Many endemic fish species in Victoria were specialist feeders on phytoplankton, zooplankton, detritus and a wide range of organisms. The loss of this great diversity of species has resulted in huge quantities of dead and rotting organic material settling on the lake bottom, as well as massive increases in algal growth. This has served to reduce the oxygen content of the water in the shallows. The massive spread of the exotic water hyacinth *(Eichhornia crassipes)* has further complicated the issue. Such is the complex of problems that has destroyed one of the most diverse freshwater fish populations in the world. Vanishing wildlife indeed!

## The Olifants River system

In the far south-west of Africa, another fish tragedy is in the making, in the Olifants River system in Western Cape province, South Africa.

The Olifants River only contributes 2% of the total mean annual water run-off of South African rivers and draws on a catchment area of slightly more than 46 000 sq km. Threats to the endemic fish include the extraction of water for irrigation purposes, dams which block spawning migrations, and agricultural pollutants, but the most serious threat is the presence of aggressive alien piscivorous fish species.

**Eight endemic fishes are at risk:**

| | | |
|---|---|---|
| Barnard's rock catfish | *Austroglanis barnardi* | **E** |
| Fiery redfin | *Pseudobarbus phlegethon* | **E** |
| Twee River redfin | *Barbus erubescens* | **V** |
| Sawfin | *Barbus serra* | **V** |
| Clanwilliam rock catfish | *Austroglanis gilli* | **R** |
| Clanwilliam yellowfish | *Barbus capensis* | **R** |
| Clanwilliam redfin | *Barbus calidus* | **R** |
| Clanwilliam sandfish | *Labeo seeberi* | **R** |

Although many different factors have contributed to this sorry state of affairs, the principal threat is the presence of voracious alien predatory fish, particularly the largemouth bass *(Micropterus salmoides)* and the smallmouth bass *(M. dolomieu)*. These predators feed not only on the smaller endemic fish species, they also eat large numbers of the young of the larger species, such as the Clanwilliam yellowfish.

Because of South Africa's relatively high level of agricultural and industrial development, many of its rivers and other freshwater systems have been affected by pollution, drainage and depletion of water bodies and dam building. Infestations of exotic plants and the introduction of exotic predatory fish species also cause concern.

When these introductions were made, they were primarily aimed at providing angling opportunities.

## West Africa

Two large impoundments have been developed in the Senegal River valley: the Manantali Dam, which lies upstream in Mali, and the Diama Dam near St Louis in Senegal. These dams have effectively destroyed one of the great riverine ecosystems in the world. Flooding in the rainy season once replenished the rich silts for subsistence agriculture, which supported many people and a diverse fauna including fish. Since the building of the dams, there has been no seasonal flooding and the once rich floodplains are barren.

Salt water used to intrude up to 200 km from the coast. This is now prevented by the Diama Dam, which has caused the upstream sectors of the river to become choked with aquatic vegetation. This in turn has a negative impact on fish populations. These dams were built with aid money in order to produce vast quantities of rice, but the local people cannot afford the costs involved in producing this grain. So, one has two large dams, a network of irrigation canals, many people who can no longer produce their staple crops in sufficient quantity and one of the worst bilharzia epidemics in the world. In addition the fish, birds and other organisms are threatened.

**Top:** *Sawfin* (Barbus serra) *are classified as vulnerable.*
**Above:** *The introduction of largemouth and smallmouth bass, both exotic predatory fish, has caused the decline of many indigenous fish species in southern Africa.*

# CHAPTER 10

# THE FUTURE

### *And now where?*

Yol Bolsun – "May there be a road ..."

*Battle cry of the Petchenegs*

The threats facing African ecosystems and their associated wildlife are many and diverse, and with very few exceptions they are caused by humans. Apart from the common threats to biodiversity that Africa shares with many other parts of the world, it faces the typical Third World problem of human population growth rapidly outstripping available natural resources. This causes massive habitat degradation and destruction.

No one knows exactly how many species there are on earth. Estimates range from five million to more than 30 million. To date only some 1,4 million species have been described and named by scientists. How many will be lost before we even know of their existence?

Not only is it essential to maintain healthy ecosystems in order to maintain species diversity, but some species are essential to the survival of a specific ecosystem. Examples are elephants in the forests and savannas of Africa, and hippos in its lakes, waterways and wetlands.

Africa has an awe-inspiring wealth of ecosystems and organisms, but almost without exception they have undergone impoverishment and degradation. The highest levels of species diversity exist in the lowland rainforests, with their moist, lush and warm conditions that are highly condusive to prolific growth. The greatest diversity is usually associated with areas receiving the highest rainfall.

It is interesting to compare the biodiversity of the different countries in Africa, even though their borders were artificially drawn by people who did not take ecosystems into account. The greatest botanical wealth is found at the southernmost tip of the continent. South Africa has a staggering 20 300 identified plant species. Its closest rivals are Madagascar, Tanzania and Congo (DR) with about 11 000 each. Congo (DR) has by far the richest animal fauna, with 409 mammal species and 1 086 bird species recorded.

However, our knowledge of lower vertebrates and particularly the invertebrates is virtually nonexistent.

Long before any Western influences were felt in Africa, the indigenous peoples had begun utilising and harvesting the continent's natural resources, including the soil, plants, animals and water. This was done in accordance with tribal laws and traditions. Even today, the African rural poor remain the greatest users of natural resources for food, building materials, fuel and medicines. Consider that 90% of domestic energy needs in Malawi and Tanzania are provided by wood and dried animal droppings. About 75% of the human population in Ghana is reliant on wild sources of protein, ranging from duikers to terrestrial snails.

However, the foremost cause of the reduction in Africa's biodiversity is **human overpopulation.** On 11 July 1987 the human baby was born who took the world population over the five billion mark. Today there are more than 5,4 billion people on earth, and it is estimated that by 2050 there will be well over 10 billion people. Looking at it in another way, three human babies are born every second – some 250 000 every single day. The continent of Africa has the fastest mean population growth rate on earth: 2,9%. In 1989 there were an estimated 600 million people in Africa; by 2014 the figure is expected to have doubled to 1 200 million. Unless the growth rate is brought within reasonable limits very soon the prospects for Africa's ecosystems and biodiversity are grim, because the natural resources are simply not adequate to sustain so many "naked apes".

Africa has extremely low levels of literacy, and poverty and disease are rampant. Its population is predominantly rural but unrealistic expectations draw ever-increasing numbers of people to the towns and cities. The populations of some of the larger urban complexes are growing at an average of 3,6% per year. It seems logical that by reducing population growth, poverty can be alleviated, basic human needs can be met and pressures on the environment and its full biodiversity can be alleviated, but in reality there are massive and seemingly insurmountable problems associated with a lowering of the population growth rate. Many experts believe that to have any meaningful impact, average family size must have been reduced by the turn of the century or shortly thereafter. If this fails – and many people fear it will – then any efforts to bring an end to warfare, intertribal and ideological conflicts, political instability and continuing environmental deterioration and destruction are bound to fail.

Some people believe that only a compulsory population control system, such as is enforced in China, could be successful at lowering the birth rate, but apart from being contrary to all notions of human rights and free choice, such a system causes a range of other problems and dislocations, as has become evident in China.

Although repeated calls are made for curbs on population growth in Africa, many proposals are impractical and do not take into account such considerations as traditions, norms and different moral standards. The only way is to develop a complete change in the perception of fertility, so that people will choose small families over large ones. Very little success has been achieved in bringing about such a change to date. One problem is the multitude of traditions, cultures, backgrounds, tribes and clans in Africa, each with its own beliefs and customs regarding families and children.

**Top left:** *Can the great African rainforests survive more than 100 years? With their loss will go one of the earth's greatest collections of biota.* PHOTO: *Jason Laure, ABPL.*

**Below:** *The Arabian Peninsula, once part of the African continent, has a tragic conservation record, with several species having been wiped out or greatly reduced in numbers. Arabian oryx (Oryx leucoryx) once roamed widely and in vast numbers but became extinct as a wild species in the early 1970s. However, captive breeding programmes and successful reintroductions at several locations could result in large enough herds to allow for harvesting of skins, meat and trophies. It is possible that the addax and scimitar-horned oryx of Africa could hold similar potential if proper reintroduction and management methods could be put in place.*

One group of experts proposes that the solution is to introduce guidance services on family planning and pregnancy into school syllabuses, in order to reach a large percentage of the population. Apart from resistance among many Africans to discussing such matters with children, however, most African children receive minimal or no formal schooling.

In the Third World, peasant farmers, slum dwellers and most citizens have no welfare state, government help or pensions that they can rely on. Therefore, the larger one's family, the greater is one's labour force and the better one's chances of being looked after in one's old age.

It is easy to mouth truisms such as, "people will have to change their perceptions of family size; economic development will have to be accelerated at all costs; education will have to receive priority; contraceptives must be readily available". What is lacking, however, is a realistic solution or set of solutions that will effectively address the core issues. There is grow-ing consensus that such solutions have to involve the economic development and empowerment of people. This applies especially to women, who are in the best position to limit population growth if they have the motivation and means to do so.

**Deforestation** in Africa has accelerated to alarming proportions. It is worst in the tropics, notably in the Guinean forest block of west Africa and the montane forests within a few degrees north and south of the equator. African tropical lowland rainforests have been subject to change for centuries, but human pressures have increased dramatically during the course of this century. More than 60% of all endangered, threatened and rare species are forest-associated.

Most of the forests on the African continent are geological-

**Below:** *The human population explosion poses the greatest threat to Africa's environment. Unless this can be halted, all conservation efforts will be in vain.* PHOTO: *Guy Stubbs, ABPL.*

ly extremely young. Rainforests retreated into numerous small patches during the last major ice age some 18 000 years ago. As the glaciers started their retreat once temperatures rose, the forests were able to expand, particularly during the past 10 000 years, which experienced fairly stable climatic conditions. The comparative severity of the glacial period in Africa had a negative impact on biodiversity, whereas the great rainforest areas of South America and Southeast Asia were less touched by the cold. This allowed these forests to maintain a greater extent and a wider variety of organisms. Nevertheless, it must be emphasised that African forest fauna and flora are extremely rich and diverse.

Apart from natural factors, humans have been influencing the environment for more than 10 000 years. Hunter-gatherer peoples used fire to turn vast areas of dry woodland into savanna grassland. The advent of domesticated animals, such as goats, sheep and cattle, in the drier areas also played a major role in creating many of the vegetation patterns we see today.

Until the advent of the Portuguese in the 16th century, the tropical rainforests in Africa were largely untouched. But the Portuguese brought crop species such as maize, plantains and yams, which grew well in these areas. The clearing of these moist, warm forests was underway.

When other Europeans entered Africa in the middle of the 19th century, they started to exploit the timber resources of west Africa. During the early years of this century some of the world's greatest trading companies cleared fairly large tracts of rainforest in order to establish extensive plantations to produce coffee, rubber, palm oil and cacao, but these agricultural enterprises did not have as severe an effect on the forests as is generally believed. There was, however, an ever-increasing demand for the fine forest timbers, for buildings and furniture.

With the colonial administrations and the big companies came medical services, improved agricultural methods and rigid controls over intertribal warfare, which heralded a massive increase in the human population. At about the time when most African countries were gaining their independence in the late 1950s and early 1960s, great strides were being made in medical care, further increasing human survival levels.

Timber exploitation and forest clearing to meet the expanding need for subsistence farming and living space have led, it has been said, to more rainforest destruction in the past 30 or so years than in the previous 10 000 years.

Increasing aridity in the Sahel belt has caused vast movements of people southwards into the west African forests. The human population of Ivory Coast jumped from some three million in the early 1960s to more than 12 million by 1990, primarily because of immigration from Burkina Faso and Mali.

Another major and growing threat to forests is the production of charcoal for the cities and towns with their burgeoning populations and insatiable demand for fuel.

How do the African forests look today? The central Congolean forest block is the least damaged. The advantage that these forests have over those in west and east Africa is that many areas are inaccessible except on foot. The west African, or Guinean, forests have become seriously fragmented and

many of the smaller blocks will disappear within the next decade. Only an estimated 36% of the original closed-canopy broadleaf forests of Africa remained in 1980. By now the percentage will be much lower. Various estimates have been made by different authorities and although they vary considerably, all indicate dramatic losses. Only an estimated 9% of the original closed-canopy forest remains in Nigeria, 12% in Ivory Coast and 7,4% in Senegal. In east Africa the situation is also bleak. Less than 10% of the original forests remain and they are under growing pressure. Only three countries in Africa retain more than 50% of their original closed-canopy forest, of which Gabon is the highest with over 80%. However, the tempo of destruction in all countries is increasing each year.

When forest habitats are degraded or destroyed, the species that depend on them have to move to constantly shrinking suitable patches, or they become extinct. Although formal conservation areas are located in most of the major forest types occurring in Africa, a great number, especially in west Africa, are poorly managed and often have large resident as well as transitory human populations. Between 10% and 15% of African forests are protected on paper, but in practice only a few are really protected. If all were properly managed and controls were optimised, this would go a long way towards maintaining biodiversity. However, the rate of species extinctions could not be stopped, even if it could be slowed down, unless large buffer areas were created that are only lightly utilised but largely left intact. The sad fact is that human population levels and demands have reached such a peak that no forest reserve is likely to retain its integrity in the long term, and there is absolutely no hope of rehabilitating already damaged forests.

**Desertification**, often caused by overgrazing, is a growing problem in many parts of Africa. It is particularly acute in the Sahel zone to the south of the Sahara Desert, the central interior of southern Africa and some areas of east Africa. The Sahara is said to be expanding southwards by as much as 50 km each year. Quantifying desertification is extremely difficult, but this would appear to be a gross overestimate. What is certain is that natural desertification – a continuous process – is aggravated by overgrazing. This happens when too many domestic animals graze in already arid to semi-arid areas, when

**Above:** *The planting of fast growing, exotic plantation timber introduces a range of complex problems for conservationists.*

ill-conceived agricultural projects are undertaken in marginal areas and when previously nomadic people increasingly establish permanent settlements. All of this causes adverse conditions, which lead to the extinction of species and the loss of biodiversity.

Although climatic changes, particularly decreasing rainfall in some areas, complicate the issues, man-made pressures on the environment may in fact be partly responsible for these very climatic changes. Some evidence is coming to light that reduction of plant cover, whether it be high forest or semi-arid grassland, increases the incidence of dry spells.

The growth in arid areas is not a recent phenomenon. Certain times during the Pleistocene era were even drier than today. Recent deteriorations can however be directly linked to the activities of people. One of these has been the eradication of the tsetse fly in many regions, allowing people and their cattle to enter areas previously closed to them.

**Overharvesting** of natural resources is illustrated most dramatically by animals that have been hunted virtually to extinction, but almost every organism of practical use to people has been plundered to some extent. Elephants have been slaughtered by the tens of thousands for their "white gold", the two ivory tusks. The once abundant black and white rhinoceroses have been reduced to barely 2 000 and 5 000 animals respectively – just because of their two horns! It will be a sad day indeed when the only rhinos in Africa survive in small, electrically fenced pens, patrolled around the clock by heavily armed guards. Larger numbers may live on ranches in North America and Australia; in our view this is the only way viable populations can survive, with constant exchanges required to ensure genetic diversity.

Extensive poaching, both at the subsistence and commercial level, has set numerous ungulates on the road to certain extinction unless serious and urgent steps are taken to halt the reasons for their harassment.

There is nothing good to say about commercial poachers, traders or buyers of illegally killed or collected wildlife.

**Below:** *Subsistence poaching is not as serious a problem as commercial poaching, which employs modern firearms and supplies large markets.*

William Shakespeare unwittingly said it all:

*Here's the smell of the blood still: all the perfumes of Arabia will not sweeten this little hand. Oh! oh! oh!*

*Macbeth* Act V Scene 1

In west Africa and parts of central Africa thousands of tons of "bush meat" are harvested every year to feed the rapidly growing human population. Most frequently killed are small forest antelope, particularly duikers. Primates, large rodents and birds are also hunted for their meat. The combination of heavy, and increasing, harvesting and the destruction of available habitat is pushing a number of biota dangerously close to the brink of extinction. Worst is that, given present circumstances, there appears to be nothing we can do about it.

Marine organisms have not escaped unscathed either. Pelagic fish resources have been massively reduced in the cold ocean currents of the Atlantic. The Indian Ocean coral reefs have been exploited and sometimes irreparably damaged, and serious inroads have been made into the mangrove forests along both mainland and island coastlines.

Another factor in overutilisation is the movements of millions of refugees fleeing wars, civil strife and natural disasters. More than 200 000 refugees have crossed the border from Liberia into Ivory Coast. Most settled in the area of the Cavalla River, which is where Ivory Coast's best rainforests are located. A further 30 000 or more mostly Kran refugees live around the Tai National Park in Ivory Coast. It seems unlikely that many will be returning to Liberia soon. In their flight and at the localities chosen for their temporary settlement, refugees in their plight are forced to exploit anything that is edible or suitable for fuel. Around long-term refugee camps such as those in Sudan, clearing of land and undertaking of subsistence planting have a devastating effect on vegetation and animals. Biodiversity suffers seriously as a result.

**The introduction of alien species** by people, either wittingly or unwittingly, often has disastrous results. Domestic cats, dogs, goats, pigs and donkeys, which often become feral, cause untold damage by feeding on indigenous wildlife and plants, creating erosion problems and outcompeting endemics that have developed no means of defending themselves. On continental Africa the impact of exotic animals and plants has not been as severe as in some other parts of the world (such as Australia), but the same cannot be said for the oceanic islands in the Afro-tropical Realm. Several species on these islands became extinct as a direct consequence of introduced species. On the mainland one of the most serious consequences of introduced species is felt in freshwater systems, where aggressive, predatory exotic fish literally eat many endemics into extinction. They also alter the water quality and compete directly with indigenous fish for living space.

Vegetation imports can also have serious consequences, with aggressive species invading and strangling indigenous species and even entire ecosystems. Once again, the result is a loss of habitat and biodiversity.

**Sustainable use** has become something of a political and

environmental catch phrase, but it is the only viable option. The concept of inviolate sanctuaries where there is absolutely no resource utilisation is naive and unworkable, especially in Africa with its dire human needs. The argument that it is our duty to protect and conserve biodiversity, to the exclusion of people and their requirements, may sound fine in theory. But how can one explain or justify such a position to peasants who live a largely hand-to-mouth existence on the outskirts of reserves teeming with natural resources they desperately need?

The concepts of conservation and utilisation have to be brought into balance. But in the field of conservation, long dominated by Western or First World thinking, mental barriers are a major obstacle. There are those who idealise wildlife and claim that it is immoral to put a price tag on any wild creature. However, the truth is: no price tag, no game! Sustainable use and development are said very rarely to work in practice; conservation and development are believed to be mutually exclusive. Not so: sustainable harvesting and utilisation have worked in a number of instances, even though this approach has only recently been seriously implemented.

In 1995 the Zimbabwean authorities intended to cull about 5 000 elephants because of gross overpopulation of this species in the north-west, particularly in Hwange National Park. Such overpopulation has serious consequences for many biota within that particular system, by changing the composition of the vegetation and consequently the animal life reliant on it. The idealists advocate a non-lethal solution: capture the animals to be culled and translocate them to Zambia, which has suffered losses to its elephant population as a result of poaching and, sad to say, a total lack of commitment by the authorities. But where will the vast amount of money come from to translocate these animals? Even if such an amount could be raised – which is unlikely – surely it would be better used for a truly worthy conservation cause, such as a project to involve a local community in conserving and managing a valuable ecosystem to their own advantage and to that of the fauna and flora.

Game ranching has served the cause of conservation well, particularly in marginal agricultural areas in Namibia, South Africa and Zimbabwe. It offers meat for harvest, skins and curios, as well as sport hunting and photographic safaris, which are becoming ever more popular. Many rare and potentially threatened species have had their salvation in this form of land use, which at the same time generates far greater income than could have been achieved by conventional farming practices. The one obstacle to many potential game ranchers is that start-up costs are very high. Some people may find hunting for trophies or meat morally repugnant, but farmers are there to make a profit like any businessman, and in this case game numbers are greatly boosted. Africa's native ungulates hold many advantages over cattle, including their immunity to sleeping sickness, which is carried by the tsetse fly. In general they require much less water, they make far better use of the natural vegetation and cause less damage to it, their numbers grow more rapidly, and the carrying capacity and diversity of the habitat are much greater. Apart from providing meat for consumption, they also have trophy value and attract tourists.

There are numerous other, interlinked problems facing Africa's vanishing wildlife not covered here. They include pollution, siltation of coral reefs as a result of serious abuses in land use in the interior, too frequent burning and eco-tourism spinning out of control in some areas where organisations, companies and individuals exploit wildlife tourism but pay only lip service to conservation. Cynics have labelled this "economic tourism" rather than ecological tourism. It must be stressed, however, that wildlife tourism is an essential component of African conservation, and that conservation would fall by the wayside with no economic incentive.

On a map of Africa quite an impressive extent is shown as conservation areas. But this is misleading: many declared conservation areas are in no way managed or controlled, and protection of fauna and flora in them exists only on paper. Some countries do indeed have impressive coverage but others have little or nothing, not even on paper. Even more important is the lack of adequate protection of Africa's many different ecosystems. The savanna areas with spectacularly large herds of ungulates are best protected: some of Africa's largest national parks and game reserves are here. However, most species occurring in these areas are widespread and not endangered or threatened with extinction. By contrast, areas with very limited protection, especially montane forests in the tropics, hold many endemics. Pressures on these systems are great. Many of the vanishing wildlife species covered in this book do not occur in protected areas, and if they do only part of the population often receives protection.

The truth about conservation in Africa is that in some cases there is hope, but other ecosystems and their biota are doomed to be totally destroyed or modified to such an extent that biodiversity is bound to dwindle. Changes will result from escalating population growth and the urban and agricultural development necessary to sustain this growth.

Vanishing wildlife should be seen as an early-warning signal of a sick and troubled ecosystem. Each year the list of endangered and threatened species grows. Some people may be satisfied with fencing off national parks and nature reserves and creating islands in a sea of destruction and modification; others entertain utopic thoughts of convincing all humanity that our fate is inextricably linked to that of the environment at large. But we have to face the fact that elaborate conservation plans, proposals and programmes are futile unless the growth of the human population can be slowed.

People who must use every natural resource available to them merely to survive have no energy left – nor can it be expected of them – to consider the long-term implications of the loss of biodiversity to which they are contributing. The only real solution is to increase economic wealth and stability, which will lead to a drop in the birth rate. Only in this way can a complete change of values in the Third World be accomplished.

Let us end on a positive note:

*Nothing in life is hopelessly tragic; even a tear tickles as it rolls down the cheek.*

Fabio Gustavo Sandoval

# • U S E F U L   R E A D I N G •

ANDERSON, D. and GROVE, R. 1987. *Conservation in Africa: people, policies and practice.* Cambridge University Press, Cambridge.

BROOKE, R.K. *South African red data book: birds.* SANSP Report. FRD, CSIR, Pretoria.

COLLAR, N.J. and STUART, S.N. 1985. *Threatened birds of Africa and related islands: the ICBP/IUCN red data book.* ICBP/IUCN, Cambridge.

COLLAR, N.J. and STUART, S.N. 1988. *Key forests for threatened birds in Africa.* ICBP/IUCN, Cambridge.

CORBET, G.B. and HILL, J.E. 1980. *A world list of mammalian species.* British Museum and Cornell University Press, London and New York.

DE VOS, A. 1975. *Africa, the devastated continent?* Junk, The Hague.

DORST, J. and DANDELOT, P. 1983. *A field guide to the larger mammals of Africa.* Collins, London.

DOUGLAS-HAMILTON, I., MICHEL-MORE, F. and INAMDAR, A. 1992. *African elephant database.* United Nations Environment Programme (European Commission African Elephant Survey and Conservation Programme).

DUNCAN, P. 1992. *Zebras, asses and horses: an action plan for conservation of wild equids.* IUCN, Gland, Switzerland.

EAST, R. 1988. *Antelopes: global survey and regional action plans. Part 1. East and northeast Africa.* IUCN, Gland, Switzerland.

EAST, R. 1989. *Antelopes: global survey and regional action plans. Part 2. Southern and south-central Africa.* IUCN, Gland, Switzerland.

EAST, R. 1989. *Antelopes: global survey and regional action plans. Part 3. West and central Africa.* IUCN, Gland, Switzerland.

EHRLICH, P.R. and EHRLICH, A.H. 1981. *Extinction: the causes and consequences of the disappearance of species.* Random House, New York.

FOSTER-TURLEY, P., MACDONALD, S. and MASON, C. 1990. *Otters: an action plan for their conservation.* IUCN, Gland, Switzerland.

GINSERG, J.R. and MACDONALD, D.W. 1990. *Foxes, wolves, jackals and dogs: an action plan for the conservation of canids.* IUCN, Gland, Switzerland.

HALL-MARTIN, A. and BOSMAN, P. 1986. *Elephants of Africa.* Struik, Cape Town.

HALTENORTH, T. and DILLER, H. 1984. *A field guide to the mammals of Africa including Madagascar.* Collins, London.

HUNTLEY, B.J. (ed.) 1989. *Biotic diversity in southern Africa: concepts and conservation.* Oxford University Press, Cape Town.

IUCN. 1986. *African wildlife laws: environmental policy and law.* Occasional Paper 3. IUCN, Gland, Switzerland.

IUCN. 1986. *The IUCN Sahel report.* IUCN, Gland, Switzerland.

IUCN. 1988. *The IUCN red list of threatened animals.* IUCN, Gland, Switzerland.

IUCN. 1989. *La conservation des ecosystèmes forestiers d'Afrique centrale.* IUCN, Gland, Switzerland.

IUCN. 1989. *Tortoises and freshwater turtles: an action plan for their conservation.* IUCN, Gland, Switzerland.

IUCN. 1990. *IUCN red list of threatened animals.* IUCN, Gland, Switzerland, and Cambridge.

IUCN/UNEP. 1987. *The IUCN directory of Afrotropical protected areas.* IUCN, Gland, Switzerland, and Cambridge.

KINGDON, J. 1971-82. *East African mammals: an atlas of evolution in Africa.* Academic Press, London.

LEE, P.C., THORNBACK, J. and BENNETT, E.L. 1988. *Threatened primates of Africa: the IUCN red data book.* IUCN, Gland, Switzerland.

LEUTHOLD, W. 1977. *African ungulates: a comparative review of their ethology and behavioural ecology.* Springer-Verlag, Berlin.

MACKINNON, J. and MACKINNON, K. 1986. *Review of the protected areas system in the Afrotropical Realm.* IUCN Commission on National Parks and Protected Areas, Gland, Switzerland.

MARTIN, C. 1991. *The rainforests of west Africa: ecology, threats and conservation.* Birkhauser, Basel.

NICOLL, M.E. and RATHBUN, G.B. 1990. *African insectivora and elephant shrews: an action plan for their conservation.* IUCN, Gland, Switzerland.

NIEVERGELT, B. 1981. *Ibexes in an African environment: ecology and social system of the Walia Ibex in the Simien Mountains, Ethiopia.* Springer-Verlag, Berlin.

NOWAK, R.M. and PARADISO, J.L. (eds) 1983. *Walkers' mammals of the world.* 2 vols. Johns Hopkins University Press, Baltimore.

OATES, J.F. 1986. *Action plan for African primates: 1986-90.* IUCN, Gland, Switzerland.

PATTERSON, J.H. 1907, 1973. *The man-eaters of Tsavo.* Fontana/Collins, London.

SAYER, J.A., HARCOURT, C.S. and COLLINS, N.M. (eds) 1992. *The conservation atlas of tropical forests: Africa.* World Conservation Monitoring Centre, Cambridge.

SCHREIBER, A., WIRTH, R., RIFFEL, M. and VAN ROMPAEY, H. 1989. *Weasels, civets, mongooses and their relatives: an action plan for the conservation of mustelids and viverrids.* IUCN, Gland, Switzerland.

SIDNEY, J. 1965. *The past and present distribution of some African ungulates.* Transactions of the Zoological Society of London. Volume 30.

SMITHERS, R.H.N. 1986. *South African red data book: terrestrial mammals.* South African National Scientific Programmes Report No. 125. FRD, CSIR, Pretoria.

STUART, C. and STUART, T. 1994. *Field guide to the mammals of southern Africa.* New Holland, London.

STUART, C. and STUART, T. 1995. *Africa: a natural history.* Southern, Halfway House.

STUART, S.N. and ADAMS, R.J. 1990. *Biodiversity in sub-Saharan Africa and its islands: conservation, management, and sustainable use.* IUCN, Gland, Switzerland.

THORBJARNARSON, J., MESSEL, H., KING, F.W. and ROSS, J.P. 1992. *Crocodiles: an action plan for their conservation.* IUCN, Gland, Switzerland.

# • I N D E X •

# • I N D E X •